Gender, Race and National Identity

Routledge Research in Gender and Society

Gender, Race and National Identity

Nations of Flesh and Blood

Jackie Hogan

Routledge
Taylor & Francis Group
New York   London

First published 2009
by Routledge
711 Third Avenue, New York, NY 10017

Simultaneously published in the UK
by Routledge
2 Park Square, Milton Park, Abingdon, Oxfordshire OX14 4RN

Routledge is an imprint of the Taylor & Francis Group, an informa business

First issued in paperback 2011

© 2009 Jackie Hogan

Typeset in Sabon by IBT Global.

Library of Congress Cataloging in Publication Data
Hogan, Jackie, 1967–
Gender, race and national identity : nations of flesh and blood / by Jackie Hogan.
p. cm. -- (Routledge research in gender and society ; 17)
Includes bibliographical references and index.
ISBN 978-0-415-38476-6
1. Gender identity. 2. Race. 3. Ethnicity. I. Title.

HQ1075.H64 2008
305.3089--dc22   2008010547

ISBN13: 978-0-415-38476-6 (hbk)
ISBN13: 978-0-415-89798-3 (pbk)
ISBN13: 978-0-203-89124-7 (ebk)

For Leo, Michael, and Zoe
And
Marilyn and David Hogan

Contents

Abbreviations

ABC	Australian Broadcasting Corporation
ABS	Australian Bureau of Statistics
BBC	British Broadcasting Corporation
IOC	International Olympic Committee
NMA	National Museum of Australia
NMJH	National Museum of Japanese History
NPG	National Portrait Gallery
SNMAH	Smithsonian National Museum of American History

Tables and Figures

FIGURES

Preface

My experiences as a global wayfarer have profoundly shaped my perspective on national identity. Although born an American, I was living in Sheffield, England, in 1989 when ninety-six people were crushed to death in a melee at the Hillsborough football ground. Newspaper headlines and editorial pages lamented the state of the national culture, contrasting the famed English civility and restraint with the equally infamous English hooliganism.

I was living in Japan in 1995 when the *Aum Shinrikyō* sect released deadly sarin gas in the Tokyo subway system, killing twelve commuters and injuring thousands. The saturation news coverage in the days and weeks after the attack not only demonized Aum leader Asahara Shōkō and his followers, but also deeply disturbed my Japanese friends' cherished assumptions about Japan as a harmonious, homogenous, and collectivist society.

I became a naturalized Australian citizen just as three momentous events were sparking heated debates on Australian national identity. In November 1999 the nation voted in a referendum on cutting Constitutional ties with the British monarchy, a proposition that was rejected by the electorate. At the same time, the nation was both preparing to present itself to the world at the 2000 Sydney Olympics, and preparing to celebrate the 2001 centenary of its Federation. Just as I was negotiating my own identity as a New Australian, the nation itself was engaging in what Prime Minister John Howard called "endless and agonised navel-gazing" about Australian national identity.

I had just moved back to the US after roughly a decade abroad when I found myself glued to my television watching the devastating events of September 11, 2001, unfold. Like millions of Americans I was overwhelmed by sorrow and fear that day. It didn't matter that none of my family or friends were victims of the 9/11 attacks. I was part of a national family that day, and I grieved along with the nation.

Monumental events, whether tragic or joyous, invariably provoke national introspection, and exploration of the nation's history, its character, its challenges, its destiny, its identity. Whether we do this for consolation, for validation, for diversion, or for other more complex material or psychological reasons, what is clear is that national identity is a powerful force in contemporary nation-states. We all feel it, in some ineffable way. But in more concrete ways we also actively construct it—endorsing certain visions of the nation, rejecting others, and constantly tinkering with the meanings and images of national belonging.

And yet, for the most part, discourses of national identity are generated quietly, without much fanfare and without considerable critical analysis. The primary aim of this volume is to examine in detail the ways national identities are constructed and the ways they reflect, reinforce, or challenge hierarchies of power, particularly hierarchies based on gender, race, and ethnicity. To this end, I compare discourses of national identity in four nations, Australia, Japan, the United Kingdom, and the United States—all the nations I myself have called home. This cross-national approach makes it possible to draw certain generalizations about the ways national identities "work," that is, how they are constructed, sustained, and revised in relation to the exercise of power.

The first chapter of the book develops a theoretical framework for the analysis of gendered and racialized national identities. Then, the chapters of Part I provide brief overviews of the themes, archetypes, and events that have dominated discourses of national identity in each of the four nations.

Part II of the book consists of six case studies, each cross-national in scope and each focusing on a different cultural form. Chapter 6 examines Olympic opening ceremonies in Japan, Australia, and the US. Chapter 7 analyzes television advertisements in Japan and Australia. Chapter 8 considers post-9/11 letters to the editor in the US, UK, and Australia. Chapter 9 examines press coverage of US Army Private Jessica Lynch in the US, UK, and Australia. Chapter 10 focuses on travel brochures in all four nations, and Chapter 11 analyzes national museums and living history tourism sites in all four nations. Each of these case studies unequivocally demonstrates that discourses of national identity in these four nations are both gendered and racialized in ways that mirror and potentially maintain or modify power relations.

Acknowledgments

In the twelve years of research for this book, I have accumulated many debts of gratitude. Although I fear I will never be able to fully repay these debts, I take a moment here to thank, in roughly chronological order, all those who have contributed their time, knowledge, and perspectives to this project.

First, I thank the faculty and my fellow graduate students at the University of Tasmania, particularly Nerida Cook and the late Bob White, who helped me formulate the research and carry out the first comparisons between Japan and Australia. I extend special thanks to Masahiro Hanada and Limi Hagiwara-Sabbatini for their help in planning and carrying out my research in Japan, and Yuko Katabami for assistance with translation. Next, I am grateful to the faculty of Bradley University who have commented on chapters, especially Brad Brown, Rustin Gates, Susan Smith, and Lizabeth Crawford, and the students who have assisted me with coding, Lynn Carew, Katie Lopuszynski, Jessica Nadler, and Jacob Rosser. I also thank Deborah Buffton, Simon Cordery, Martin Crotty, and Deepa Kumar who offered their carefully considered suggestions for the manuscript.

This kind of cross-national research is quite time and resource intensive. I could not have completed this project without the generous financial support of the following: the University of Tasmania Faculty of Arts, the Japan Foundation, the Sherry Endowment, and the Bradley University Research Excellence Committee. I am very grateful for their investment in this project.

Finally, I offer heartfelt gratitude to my friends, colleagues, and family, who have given me their unwavering moral support over the course of this long journey. And to my greatest supporters, Leo, Michael, and Zoe, thank you for tolerating my many lengthy research trips and for offering both clarity and welcome distractions when they were most needed.

1 Nations of Flesh and Blood
Gender and Race in the National Imaginary

Nations are more than geopolitical bodies, more than collections of people and institutions within defined sovereign territories. Nations are discursive constructs, created and sustained, in part, through "stories, images, land-scapes, scenarios, historical events, national symbols and rituals which . . . give meaning to the nation" (Hall 1992, 293). To borrow Anderson's (1983) aphorism, nations are "imagined communities," and in this communal imaginary the nation is almost inevitably gendered and racialized. That is, the icons, experiences, traits, and contexts central to notions of nation-ness come to be symbolically linked to individuals and groups with distinct gender and ethnoracial identities.[1] The imagined community is, in other words, a nation of flesh and blood. While such meanings are most clearly distilled in national archetypes such as Uncle Sam or Britannia, gender, race, and ethnicity often more subtly inflect narratives of national belonging by portraying certain characteristics, activities, and affiliations as natural, normal, and preferred.

Such gendered and racialized imaginings are of consequence because they both mirror and mold material relations. Groups which are politically and economically marginalized on the basis of such characteristics as race, eth-nicity, gender, class, or sexuality, tend also to be marginalized within the national imaginary. Their contributions, their histories, and sometimes their very existence are symbolically muted or disparaged. This discursive margin-alization in turn helps reproduce long-standing inequalities by reinforcing the Otherness of such groups, and thereby sustaining material and symbolic barriers to their full and equal participation in the life of the nation.

It is crucial, therefore, to place national imaginaries under the micro-scope to expose their ideological inner-workings. The ultimate goal of such an undertaking is to chip away at mechanisms of oppression which, for the most part, remain hidden in taken-for-granted understandings of and attachments to the nation. It would be virtually impossible for a single vol-ume to address all of the interconnections between symbolic renderings of the nation and the material inequalities they reflect and reinforce. The more modest aim of this work is to examine the complex ways nations are dis-cursively gendered and racialized, and the grounding of such discursive pro-cesses in material relations.

To this end, in this volume I examine the linkages between gender, race, ethnicity, and national identity in a range of texts drawn from four nations, Australia, Japan, the UK, and the US. The book has a broad empirical base, with data from sporting spectacles, television advertisements, letters to the editor, national broadsheet reporting, travel brochures, national museums, and living history sites. Each empirical study included here is cross-national in scope, comparing constructions of national identity in two or more of the nations under consideration. This comparative approach is intended not only to provide rich empirical detail on a variety of national settings, but to contribute to a fuller theorization of the dynamics of national identity in contemporary societies.

While the texts selected for analysis here are largely drawn from the realms of the mass media and popular culture, these are not the only realms implicated in the articulation of national identities. Indeed, until relatively recently, scholars of national identity have focused their analyses primarily on grand state spectacles and on the texts of high art and academia: monuments, rallies, coronations, paintings, operas, official histories, and so on. Although such texts have much to reveal, particularly about elite constructions of nation-ness, in reality most people have only limited contact with such official discourses of national identity—an occasional trip to a national monument, a coronation perhaps once in a lifetime. By contrast, we encounter more mundane expressions of national identity on a daily basis, as we affix a postage stamp to an envelope, glance at billboards on our morning commutes, or watch the sporting highlights on the evening news. Mundane texts such those analyzed in this volume provide a window on everyday experiences of national identity. It is such concrete and quotidian articulations of national identity that most powerfully connect individuals to their nations, giving them a sense of national belonging.

I wish to stress that the aim of this volume is not to identify "true," "authentic," or somehow fraudulent discourses of national identity. Rather, the volume provides insights into the dynamic construction of national identity at particular points in time, in particular sociohistorical contexts. The empirical data analyzed here were collected in all four nations over a ten year period, from 1996 to 2006. While all of these nations have experienced considerable social changes over this period, the earlier data are as relevant as the most recent data to an understanding of national identity, for discourses of national identity are inherently unstable; they are constantly in flux, being reshaped by changing social conditions. This being the case, any particular textual articulation of national identity is dated the moment it is generated. For even as it takes a concrete form (as a photograph, a newspaper article, a museum exhibit, and so on), it is incorporated into the larger, and ever-changing flow of discourses of national identity.

Furthermore, I acknowledge that all research accounts are inherently partial, in both senses of that word: both fragmentary and incomplete, and shaped by the values and experiences of the researcher. It would be presumptive to suggest that any single volume could provide a comprehensive account of discourses of national identity in the four nations examined here. Such is not my goal. Likewise, it would be disingenuous to claim that my own value commitments to social justice have played no part in this research. I have quite consciously focused on the ways dominant and subordinate social groups are portrayed in discourses of national identity. While I hoped to find less powerful groups being presented in sensitive and balanced ways, and did indeed find some examples of this, the case studies here suggest that in the four nations examined discourses of national identity are still largely gendered and racialized in ways that naturalize the continued subordination of women and ethnoracial minorities.

CONCEPTUALIZING NATIONAL IDENTITIES

Over the last two decades, in the context of accelerating globalization and rising ethnic nationalism, there has been increasing scholarly interest in the subject of national identity. As a broad index of this change, the catalog of the Library of Congress shows more than a tenfold increase in publications on national identity in the last twenty years.[2] Nonetheless, despite this increased scholarly attention, the field still lacks a rich and explicit definition of national identity.

Some authors seem to assume that national identity is a kind of national essence that exists in the very fabric of the nation's land, culture, and people. Others conceptualize national identity as an individual's affective ties to a (sometimes subnational) social collectivity based on attributes such as shared ethnicity, language, or territory. National identity is also frequently conflated with nationalism and nationality, concepts which are related to national identity, yet analytically distinct. While there are numerous and varied definitions of nationalism, the term is generally taken to mean a devotion to the nation, a belief in the primacy of nations, and the actions designed to protect and promote the interests of a nation. Nationality, on the other hand, is the legal status of citizenship which is granted to individuals by the state.[3]

I argue that national identities are most usefully conceptualized as widely circulating discourses of national belonging: representations of what a nation is and is not; of the nation's character, its accomplishments, its defining traits, and its historical trajectory. These discourses of national identity are neither top-down constructs imposed on the masses by controlling elites, nor spontaneous outpourings of popular sentiment. Rather, they are continually and collectively constructed in a complex process of discursive exchange. Discourses of national identity are not immutable, univocal, or unidirectional; rather, they are fluid and flexible, and always in the process of articulation. In fact, while I use the term "national identity" for the sake of brevity, it is less than ideal to speak in the singular, for multiple and competing discourses of national identity inevitably coexist.

This conceptualization of national identity is informed by a broad and diverse scholarly literature. Researchers from the social sciences, humanities, international relations, and fields such as postcolonial studies, gender studies, and cultural studies among others, have made valuable contributions to the study of national identities and nationalisms. While any overview of this vast literature can be only cursory, it can serve to attune the reader to ongoing debates about the nature of national identities.

National Identities as Social Constructs

For present purposes, I begin my review with three groundbreaking volumes: Benedict Anderson's (1983) *Imagined Communities*, Ernest Gellner's (1983) *Nations and Nationalism*, and Eric Hobsbawm and Terrance Ranger's (1983) *The Invention of Tradition*. Each volume introduced significant theoretical innovations which have shaped the way scholars understand national identities today.

Perhaps no single work has done more to reshape our understandings of national identity than Benedict Anderson's *Imagined Communities*. Anderson argues that nations are constituted, in part, through representational practices, principally through the written word. He notes that in Europe, for instance, improvements in print technology led to the standardization of national vernaculars, to the rise of such early mass commodities as newspapers and popular novels, and to increased literacy. These developments facilitated the formation of national-level identities by giving the disparate groups within the nation a common language and shared knowledge that allowed them to both participate more effectively in broader collective action and to imagine themselves as part of a national collectivity, an "imagined community."

I share Anderson's conviction that nations are discursively constructed. Although we will never meet all the members of our national community, we are in some sense bound together by our shared symbolic system. However, while Anderson focuses primarily on printed texts, I argue that discursive constructions of the imagined community can be found in a wide range of cultural productions, from advertisements and television dramas, to folk dances, football matches, parades, and public statuary, among others. Because not all people read newspapers and novels, it is crucial to consider the ways other cultural forms articulate national identity.[4]

Like Anderson, Gellner's *Nations and Nationalism* highlights the importance of common linguistic and cultural systems to the formation of national identities. Gellner argues that nationalism is essentially a modern phenomenon which arose in the context of industrialization. The industrial mode of production, he explains, requires a docile and dependable pool of workers with certain basic skills. Workers in an industrialized society, at a minimum, must be able to understand and convey information essential to their employment tasks, so they need a common language. They must follow basic workplace rules and procedures, so they need to respect authority and accept hierarchy. Depending on the particular workplace, they may also need at least basic literacy and numeracy skills. Gellner argues that modern states founded a number of institutions aimed at creating productive workers and responsive citizens to serve their industrializing nations. First and foremost, mass public education programs ensured that everyone spoke, more or less, the same language. Furthermore, elite state-supported institutions of higher learning and the arts gave official endorsements to particular forms of high culture and knowledge, setting standards to which all in the nation were meant to aspire.

In Gellner's view, then, the state (responding to the demands of industrialization) laid the foundations of nationalism by stamping the citizenry with a common vernacular, common values and aspirations, and common experiences. These commonalities forged a sense of national belonging, indeed forged the nation itself, which did not exist and effectively *could not* have existed previously. Gellner's work highlights the extent to which nationalism and narratives of nation are underpinned by material relations. Likewise, a key theme in this volume is that discourses of national identity matter because they reflect, contribute to, and sometimes even challenge material inequalities. Gellner's work can be criticized, however, for an overemphasis on top-down constructions of national culture and national identity. In his formulation, state elites have a virtual monopoly on discourses of national identity, and the masses uncritically accept such dictates. My work, by contrast, suggests that narratives of nation emerge out of more complex interactions between elite and non-elite actors.

Gellner's work also presents the student of national identity with an illustration of the ways scholarly treatises themselves both mirror and contribute to gendered and racialized discourses of national identity, as he consistently refers to the national citizenry in the masculine, the "man" or "men" of the nation. In an oft quoted passage he writes, "A man without a nation defies the recognized categories and provokes revulsion. . . . A man must have a nationality as he must have a nose and two ears" (1983, 6). One is left to wonder just where women fit into Gellner's conception of nations and nationalisms. This is not mere semantic hairsplitting, as some might argue. Rather, Gellner's work provides just one illustration of the ways nations are gendered— casually, implicitly, subtly, but in ways that make it clear that men are the natural proprietors of the nation; women are, at best, an afterthought.

Hobsbawm and Ranger's *The Invention of Tradition* has obvious overlaps with the work of both Gellner and Anderson. Through detailed historical case studies of so-called national "traditions" in Europe and its colonies, the authors in this volume demonstrate the degree to which national self-conceptions can be engineered to serve particular political and economic ends. Practices which today are accepted as ancient and organic are often relatively recent productions: folk costumes and dances, royal rituals, tribal customs, and national heroes, among others, have been selectively identified and refashioned to suit the tastes and needs of the day. Such invented traditions, the authors argue, are most often designed to promote social cohesiveness, legitimate social hierarchies, and promulgate particular values and norms.

Hobsbawm and Ranger offer invaluable insights into the processes by which narratives of nation are generated and the power relations that sustain them. However, while they acknowledge that invented traditions are seldom fabricated out of thin air, and that many officially elaborated traditions have a basis in long-standing popular custom, like Gellner they emphasize the top-down manipulation and imposition of national narratives. My own analysis suggests that discourses of national identity are more dynamic and collective constructions. Ordinary people are more astute than scholars of national identity sometimes assume. They are often keenly aware that so-called national traditions and national identity have been staged in particular ways to bolster national chauvinism, encourage compliance, and legitimate power hierarchies. When given the opportunity, these people will critique widely circulating narratives of nation and even articulate alternative discourses of national belonging.

Building on the work of Anderson, Gellner, and Hobsbawm and Ranger, scholars of national identity and nationalism have begun to explore the ways these phenomena play out not only in official texts and spectacles but in everyday texts and practices. Billig (1995) and Edensor (2002), for instance, examine the many mundane practices through which we construct our nations. When we use pronouns such as "us" and "them" in ways that mark the boundaries of the national community, when we send a picture postcard of a national landmark, or watch the national sport on television, for instance, we are participating in an ideological system based on the principle of national belonging.

As Billig points out, such "banal" constructions of the nation are not necessarily benign. On the contrary, they often sustain social inequalities and serve to justify the use of violence against those excluded from definitions of the national community. As the case studies in this volume will demonstrate, the discursive marginalization of women and ethnoracial Others in narratives of nation is undoubtedly implicated in the ongoing material disadvantages experienced by these groups.

GENDERED AND RACIALIZED DISCOURSES
OF NATIONAL IDENTITY

I am not the first to suggest that discourses of national identity are gendered and racialized in ways that reflect and reinforce hierarchies of power.[5] The bourgeoning scholarly literature on this topic suggests a growing commitment to exposing the many ways narratives of nation are implicated in ongoing social inequalities.

Gender and Nation

McClintock (1993) and others have suggested that in contemporary nation-states, men are typically constructed as the natural builders and rulers of the nation, while women represent in more abstract ways the flesh, the soil, the hearth, home, and traditions of the nation. In other words, men *create* the nation, while women simply *symbolize* the nation. At first glance, this argument seems intuitively correct. In the popular imagination, women are strongly linked to nature and to the home, two powerful symbols of nation. Moreover, because women bear the new members of the nation, women's bodies serve as markers of national boundaries (Yuval-Davis and Anthias 1989). This is seen perhaps most clearly in cases where the rape of a woman by a foreign male is perceived as an assault on the nation itself (Peterson 1996). Such attacks may be seen to shame not only the woman who was violated and the men who failed to prevent her violation but also the whole national community, which is both humiliated and polluted by the violence.

As compelling as such examples are it would be overly simplistic to suggest that nations are always discursively gendered in the feminine. It is not difficult, after all, to find both male and female national archetypes even within a single nation. Both Uncle Sam and Lady Liberty in the United States, for instance, or John Bull and Britannia in the United Kingdom undeniably embody what are perceived to be some of the most cherished characteristics of their respective nations. And, while Motherland imagery is widespread, so are references to the Fatherland. Rather than suggesting that women have come to symbolize the nation, it is more useful to examine the complex ways gendered imagery is employed in discourses of national identity.

It is clear, for instance, that in many contemporary nations, women are discursively constructed as the conservators of tradition, particularly in periods of rapid change. Sen (1993) for instance, has examined the ways women, in their roles as wives and mothers, were used as potent symbols of Bengali identity as India struggled for independence from Britain. Likewise, it is not unusual for women's equality, liberation, education, and political participation to feature prominently in national imagery where the intent is to stress the nation's modernity and its commitment to Western notions of justice and equality, as De Groot (1993) demonstrates in her analysis of pre-revolutionary Iran.

Even within a single nation, discourses of national identity may become masculinized or feminized in response to changing material conditions and political exigencies. Morris-Suzuki demonstrates, for instance, that national imagery in modern Japan has been alternately masculinized to emphasize the nation's industriousness, its dynamism, and its martial and economic power, and feminized to emphasize its gentility and benign intentions (Morris-Suzuki 1998, 110–139). Likewise, Jeffords (1989) has detailed the rise of masculine imagery in the US after the Vietnam War. While Jeffords avoids reductionist explanations, there is convincing evidence that the increased valorization of masculinity and the concomitant devaluation of the feminine in the post-Vietnam era have their origins in the emasculating military failures of the 1970s.

It is clear, then, that national imagery is seldom gendered in simple, consistent, or straightforward ways. Any analysis must therefore account for the subtleties and the oscillations of such gendered discourses. To date, much of the scholarly literature on gender and nation has focused on historical examples, particularly on articulations of national identity in the context of war, colonialism, or other social upheavals. Such studies offer invaluable insights into national identities in particular historical contexts. All too often, however, the reader is left with the impression that gendered national identities were created (or emerged organically) at some tumultuous point in the past, and exist relatively unchanged today. On the contrary, because discourses of national identity are inherently unstable and subject to revision, and because they are produced not only in dramatic historical circumstances but through mundane activities, it is essential to examine the ongoing construction of gendered national identities in contemporary everyday settings, such as those analyzed in this volume.

Race and Nation

For a full and nuanced understanding of the ways discourses of national identity are implicated in the politics of inclusion and exclusion, it is crucial to recognize that national imaginaries are not only gendered but also racialized. While many scholars of national identity acknowledge this fact, few analyze more than a single dimension of the national imaginary. Banet-Weiser's (1999) analysis of American beauty pageants is one of the few recent studies to examine in detail both the gender and ethnoracial dimensions of discourses of national identity.[6] The author traces the historical origins of beauty pageants in the US, and ably demonstrates the ways such competitions have reflected both changes in gender and race relations over time, and shifts in American discourses of national identity.

Such work builds on a rich and diverse scholarly literature on race and nation. In analyses of race and national identity, perhaps no single scholarly work has had a more profound intellectual impact than Edward Said's (1978) *Orientalism*. Said examines the ways Western nations have historically defined themselves against the essentialized Other of the East. The West has consistently characterized itself as civilized, rational, humane, free, and peaceful, while representing the East as the polar opposite—barbaric, fanatical, cruel, oppressive, and violent.

Certainly Said's analysis highlights the extent to which discourses of national identity are as much constructions of the Other as constructions of the national self. More importantly, however, Said argues persuasively that such symbolic constructions of self and Other have serious material effects. Specifically, the West has long used such stereotypes to justify everything from the imposition of unequal treaties, to military invasion and colonization of Oriental lands. According to the logic of Orientalism, the West has both the right and the responsibility to subdue and civilize "inferior" peoples. Clearly then, symbolic and material practices have worked in tandem to maintain the dominance of West over East.

Said's concept of Orientalism sheds light on any number of power hierarchies beyond the specific dynamics of the East–West relationship. Negative stereotyping of the essentialized, usually racialized, Other has long served to justify not only conquest and colonization, but even slavery and genocide, in a variety of settings. And powerful Western nations have not been the sole perpetrators of such symbolic and material violence against the Other. In the 1930s and 1940s the Japanese set out to rule all of Asia through violent invasion and occupation; in the 1990s Hutus turned against Tutsis in Rwanda, and Serbs attempted to "cleanse" Bosnia of its Muslim population. Racialized or ethnicized constructions of the national imagined community were implicated in these and other fatal moments, in ways consistent with the practices of Orientalism. That is, in each case, notions of essential differences and natural hierarchies were employed to justify bloody acts of domination.

The concept of Orientalism has also been applied to the construction of what I will call internal Others. These are marginalized groups within a nation who are represented as significantly different from, and often inferior to, the dominant group. In some contexts, these internal Others are constructed as quaint anachronisms and pleasurable spectacles for members of the majority. Other times, these groups are represented as threats to the national order. In some cases, internal Others are positioned both as a desirable novelty and a danger to society. In contemporary Australia, for instance, Aboriginal Australians are generally constructed as harmless and picturesque when they stage cultural performances for white tourists, but when they congregate in low-income urban neighborhoods they are represented as a source of crime and disease. Both types of representation help perpetuate prejudice and discrimination against these groups.[7]

Recent scholarship also reminds us that the marginalization of internal Others is not only accomplished through overtly racist discourses and practices, but also potentially through discourses of antiracism. In describing contemporary Australia, for instance, Hage (1998) argues that national calls for cultural and racial "tolerance" implicitly position whites as the dominant group, the natural rulers of the nation, those with the power to magnanimously tolerate interlopers.

It is crucial to recognize, however, that internal Others are not helpless dupes accepting and abetting their own marginalization. Because discourses of national identity are inherently labile, subordinated groups can potentially write themselves into the national imaginary by constructing "counter-narratives of nation" (Bhabha 1990), alternate visions of national belonging that may eventually shift widely circulating discourses of national identity.

GLOBALIZATION AND THE
CRISIS OF NATIONAL IDENTITY

No discussion of contemporary discourses of national identity would be complete without considering globalization.[8] Globalization is not new; however, while people, goods, and ideas have roamed across vast distances for millennia, true global integration has dramatically accelerated over the last three decades, primarily due to innovations in computing, communication, and transportation technologies. This intensifying globalization has prompted scholars and opinion leaders in a variety of nations to warn of an impending crisis of national identity.

Several predictions feature prominently in this crisis rhetoric. Some fear that exposure to other cultures and peoples will change national ways of life; that the influx of immigrants will undermine national solidarity; that the consumption of increasingly standardized products and experiences will eviscerate distinctive national cultures and lead to the development of a homogenized global monoculture; and that multinational corporations and transnational political bodies will render national boundaries, allegiances, and identities obsolete.

Certain globalizing transformations are readily observable. For instance, blue jeans, Big Macs, and Hollywood blockbusters have by now insinuated themselves into almost every corner of the world, and nation-states are increasingly ceding certain powers to supranational organizations such as the European Union and the United Nations. But such changes do not necessarily signal the waning significance of the nation or of national identities.

First, it must be remembered that even supranational organizations such as the EU or UN are in fact grounded in the nation-state system. The nation-state and its representatives are still the primary actors on the global stage—making decisions on behalf of national populations, working to protect national interests and ensure national security, and forging agreements *between* nations. Globalization and internationalism do not render the nation-state system obsolete; they sustain and are sustained by it. Second, it is essential to recognize that superficial material changes do not necessarily translate into deeper transformations of culture or identity. The fear that Big Macs or a European Parliament will undermine national identities is grounded in the notion that such identities are somehow both immutable and fragile—that they have existed more or less unchanged since time immemorial, and yet can be shattered beyond recognition or repair by alien influences. In reality, however, national identities are inherently changeable and almost infinitely adaptable.

A number of recent studies, including my own, suggest that the strength of national affiliations is not waning under the pressures of globalization.[9] In fact, globalizing social changes may even prompt a defensive strengthening of discourses of national belonging and national distinctiveness. Predictions of the crisis of national identity notwithstanding, empirical evidence of such a crisis is hard to find.

DISCOURSES OF POWER
AND THE POWER OF DISCOURSES

My analysis in this volume is premised on the notion that discourses of national identity are discourses of power, and as such, these discourses matter. In a more general sense, discourse matters because it shapes social worlds and social interactions. As Yeatman puts it, "Discourse is the power to create reality by naming it and giving it meaning" (1990, 155). Specifically, discourses of national identity do not merely reflect the national social order; they help create that order. When widely circulating narratives of nation discursively marginalize women or ethnoracial minorities, they both mirror and help sustain the inequalities faced by these groups. Likewise, when counternarratives of nation challenge the symbolic marginalization of women and ethnoracial minorities, they both reflect and contribute to the changing status of these groups.

I use a number of conceptual and methodological tools to reveal patterns of representation and meaning in the texts I analyze. While I do not adopt in a wholesale fashion the conventions of any single disciplinary perspective, my approach borrows generously from semiotics, Critical Discourse Analysis (CDA), Foucauldian theory, and traditional content analysis.[10] I propose that social reality is discursively constructed, that discourses reflect and sustain relations of power, and that power relations can and should be exposed through critical analysis of widely circulating discourses. To this end, I undertake detailed analyses of both the manifest and latent content of specific texts, scrutinizing them for gendered and racialized constructions of national identity.

Basic descriptive statistics are used as a way of identifying overarching representational conventions. The value of quantitative textual analysis is that it points us in the direction of the most significant patterns of meaning. However, numbers alone cannot capture crucial nuances in discourses of national identity. Therefore, I give more attention to subtle qualitative readings of the texts I analyze, and where possible introduce interview material to more accurately gauge popular conceptions of national identity.

Some readers will undoubtedly challenge the usefulness of any form of content analysis. Hermes (1995, 10), for instance, argues that "texts acquire meaning only in the interaction between readers and texts and . . . analysis of the text on its own is never enough to reconstruct these meanings." I readily acknowledge the limitations of content analysis, particularly where the researcher's reading of the text fails to account for the conditions of the text's production and consumption. However, if Hermes' argument is taken to its logical conclusion, all texts are rendered innocent and neutral; they become no more than Rorschach tests from which readers construct idio-syncratic meanings. This denies the social ramifications of demeaning and exploitative representations, and places responsibility for such representations on readers, who themselves may be the demeaned or exploited parties. I argue instead that the texts analyzed here carry dominant meanings, which audiences interpret in a variety of ways. The primary aim, then, is to lay bare these patterned meanings and the material relations that sustain, and are sustained by, them.

KEY PROPOSITIONS

Nine key propositions emerge out of the scholarly literatures and debates reviewed above. Because these propositions are central to the analysis throughout this volume, it is worthwhile reiterating them here.

1. Nations are more than collections of people and institutions within bounded territories; they are integrated symbolic systems.

2. As such, nations are constituted and sustained in part through stories and images that convey a sense of national belonging, of the nation's character, its accomplishments, its defining traits, and its historical trajectory. These stories and images are what I refer to as discourses of national identity.

3. Such discourses take myriad forms ranging from the verbal, to the visual, aural, and experiential. For the purposes of this analysis, specific articulations of national identity are treated as texts, even if they are ephemeral, improvisational, and fluid.

4. While states and other elite institutions are an important source of official discourses of national identity, individuals are perhaps most powerfully connected to their nations through mundane, everyday practices and texts. Not only do we encounter everyday texts more frequently than official ones, but we also might view them with less critical awareness because they appear to be politically innocent or neutral, beyond the reach of state manipulation and therefore more authentic. Mundane texts, such as those analyzed here, thus provide invaluable insights into taken-for-granted notions of national belonging.

5. Discourses of national identity are not immutable, univocal, or uni-directional. Rather, they are inherently fluid and unstable, constantly being reshaped by changing social conditions.

6. National identities are neither top-down constructs imposed on the masses by controlling elites, nor spontaneous outpourings of popular sentiments. Rather, they are continually and collectively constructed in a complex process of discursive negotiation.

7. Discourses of national identity are frequently gendered and racialized in both latent and often blatant ways. The imagined community is, in other words, a nation of flesh and blood, imagined through categories of race and gender.

8. Discursive practices and broader material practices are inextricably intertwined. Discourses of national identity reflect existing social hierarchies when dominant groups are featured more prominently and more favorably than subordinate groups. Moreover, the frequent repetition of such discourses further entrenches notions of who belongs to, and who rightfully controls, the nation. Nonetheless, because there are always multiple and competing discourses of national identity in circulation, counternarratives of nation have the potential to disrupt dominant discourses and reframe the national imaginary.

9. Because the analysis of discourses of national identity reveals power relations, such analysis plays a part in exposing and challenging social inequalities. It would be overly simplistic in the extreme to blame discourses of national identity for the long-standing disadvantage of women and ethnoracial minorities in the nations studied here. Nonetheless, only by dissecting narratives of nation can we reveal the politics of inclusion and exclusion that underpin them.

While these propositions hold true when applied to the nations studied here, and I surmise to national identities in all contemporary nation-states, it is crucial to examine the way national specificities inflect discourses of national identity in a variety of national settings. For a fuller understanding of the dynamics of national identity, it is crucial to avoid overgeneralizations and the creation of sterile typologies that fail to account for the diversity of national cultures, histories, and sociopolitical landscapes worldwide. To this end, Part I of this volume discusses the specific people, ideas, and experiences which have shaped discourses of national identity in the four nations under consideration. Part II consists of six cross-national case studies, each examining gendered and racialized discourses of national identity in a particular cultural form.

The four nations have been selected both for their similarities and their differences. All are well-established nation-states with stable forms of governance and advanced industrial (some would argue postindustrial) economies. We might therefore reasonably expect to see certain similarities in these nations' discourses of national identity. Specifically, under such conditions, we would expect extreme and more blatantly jingoistic articulations of national identity and "bloody nationalism" to fall out of favor, while forms of "banal nationalism" (Billig 1995) become the primary source of a sense of national belonging.

The four nations also offer useful points of contrast, however. The US, UK, and Australia are all Anglophone nations with ethnically and racially diverse populations. However, while the US is currently the world's sole superpower with unparalleled cultural, economic, and political influence, the UK is a former imperial power with more symbolic than material capital, and Australia, with its relatively small population and limited global economic and political influence, occupies a paradoxical position as a Western nation located in the Asia-Pacific region. Likewise, Japan presents a useful contrastive case. It is relatively racially and ethnically homogenous compared with the other three nations studied here, and it occupies a somewhat ambivalent position, being culturally and geographically part of Asia (and historically subject to the forces of Orientalism), yet with its advanced industrial economy, highly mobile population, and media-intensive society, some have argued that it is not only more Western than Eastern, but that it has become an exemplar of a kind of global postmodern culture.

I also chose these four nations for analysis because these are the nations I myself have called home. I was living in Sheffield, England, when the Hillsborough stadium disaster claimed ninety-six lives and the bombing of Pan Am Flight 103 over Lockerbie, Scotland, left 270 people dead. I was living in Japan during the *Aum Shinrikyō* sarin gas attacks on the Tokyo subways, and the devastating 1995 Great Hanshin earthquake that left more than six thousand dead. I became a naturalized citizen of Australia just as the nation was preparing to celebrate both the centenary of its Federation and the Sydney Olympic Games. And I had just returned to the US, the country of my birth, when the attacks of September 11, 2001, shook the nation and the world. Living through these monumental events, some tragic and some joyful, both intensified my own attachment to my native and adopted nations and prompted me to delve more deeply into the stories, images, and experiences that bind us together as members of national communities.

Comparative analysis of these nations within a single, consistent theoretical framework provides us with a unique opportunity to examine contemporary dynamics of national identity. Only through such efforts can we challenge the ideologies that underpin gendered and racialized notions of national belonging.

Part I

2 Discourses of National Identity in Australia

All too often discussions of national identity revolve around what are essentially national stereotypes: the easygoing Australian, the polite Japanese, the reserved Englishman, the brash American. Much intellectual energy has been expended in the attempt to define the national character and explain how it has developed over time. In this volume, on the other hand, I am not concerned with testing the veracity of such stereotypes or with charting their origins. For if there are always multiple and competing discourses of national identity, as I contend, and if these discourses are constantly in flux, any effort to describe and dissect the national character is both misguided and futile.

Nonetheless, because this is a cross-national study and because few readers will be equally familiar with all of the nations under consideration, it is worthwhile to review certain national archetypes and events that inform present-day articulations of national identity in Australia, Japan, Britain, and the US. The discussion here is by no means an exhaustive catalogue of the people, traits, images, and experiences that figure in current discourses of national identity; rather it is a selective and narrowly focused review of the themes and symbols that are inflected with gendered and racialized meanings in the discourses examined in this volume. While I chronologically organize the discussions below for the sake of convenience, I am not of the opinion that national identities develop in simple linear progressions; rather, discourses of national identity frequently both reach deep into the past and project forward to an imagined future. Neither does the chronological ordering here imply that the historical events and characters not mentioned had no effect on national identity. Rather, this overview presents select cases that exemplify themes in current discourses of national identity.

PRE-1788 AUSTRALIA

The most recent physical evidence suggests that indigenous peoples inhabited Australia for at least fifty thousand years before the first permanent settlers arrived from Europe in 1788 (Bowler et al. 2003). Although early European settlers rarely recognized the great cultural and linguistic diversity among indigenous groups, there were at least 250 distinct languages spoken across Australia, each representing a distinct cultural grouping (Schmidt 1990). While no population figures exist for the period before the arrival of Europeans, scholars estimate that the indigenous population exceeded three hundred thousand people, with perhaps as many as one million Aboriginal inhabitants of Australia (ABS 2002). Today, those who self-identify as Aboriginal or Torres Strait Islander people constitute approximately 2 percent of the population of Australia.

Symbols, experiences, and individuals from indigenous Australia rarely featured in early discourses of national identity, except perhaps when indigenous groups were portrayed as "primitive," "feeble," or "debased" people who were distinctly un-Australian. However, with a strengthening of the Australian indigenous rights movement since the 1970s, discourses of national identity now frequently include references to indigenous cultures. In one recent example, discussed here in Chapter 6, indigenous music, dance, and imagery featured prominently in the opening ceremony of the 2000 Sydney Olympic Games. This is not to suggest that native elements are always used in sensitive, culturally appropriate, or politically innocent ways. Indeed, indigenous (or faux-indigenous) motifs are frequently used to sell everything from t-shirts and tourism packages to state policies and programs, often with no discernible benefit to the indigenous peoples from whom such elements are appropriated.

THE ARRIVAL/INVASION OF EUROPEANS

Although Europeans first charted parts of "*Terra Australis Incognita*" (the unknown southern land) in the early 1600s, it would be almost two hundred years before the first permanent settlers arrived from Europe. The First Fleet from Britain arrived in Australia in mid-January of 1788, with eleven ships carrying more than 1,300 people. Some 750 of the new arrivals were convicts, three-quarters of them men, being transported abroad in part to ease the strain on England's overcrowded prisons.[1] The remainder of the settlers were officers and administrators and a small number of their family members. Free settlers began arriving in the 1790s, establishing farming and especially sheep-grazing enterprises. By the 1820s, pastoralism was such a crucial part of the colonial economy that it was said that Australia was rising to prosperity "on the sheep's back," an expression that still remains popular. From the beginning of European settlement the vast majority of both convicts and free settlers in Australia were men.[2] Not surprisingly, therefore, early discourses of national identity were dominated by masculine archetypes, many of which endure today. Furthermore, current discussions of the national character frequently evoke Australia's convict heritage when asserting that Australians today are antiauthoritarian, irreverent, and fiercely egalitarian.

It was 26 January 1788 when Captain (soon to be Governor) Arthur Phillip planted the British flag at Sydney Cove, establishing British sovereignty over much of the eastern Australian mainland. Today, 26 January is celebrated as Australia Day, a national holiday marking the birth of the nation. Among indigenous Australians, however, the day is known as Invasion Day or Survival Day, a day for mourning the lands, family members, and ways of life lost to European colonization, and a time to recognize the survival of native peoples in spite of the hardships they have faced since displacement by Europeans.

GOLD RUSH

In 1851 alluvial gold was discovered in rural Victoria, sparking a gold rush that would bring profound economic, political, and social changes to Australia and be remembered as a defining moment in the nation's history.[3] The fever for gold both prompted a massive internal migration toward the gold fields and attracted waves of enterprising migrants from abroad. In ten short years after the discovery of gold, Australia's population tripled (McCalman, Cook, and Reeves 2001, 1). In Melbourne alone, the population increased from 30,000 in 1851 to 125,000 ten years later (Davison 2001, 53). The social and environmental transformations set in motion by the gold rush were no less dramatic than the demographic transformations.[4] In addition to the quite devastating ecological effects of the gold rush (McGowan 2001), some of the most prominent and enduring social effects were seen in the areas of political rights and political consciousness, race and gender relations, and the emergence of themes and icons still prominent in discourses of national identity today.

The gold rush brought sweeping material changes to the colonies.[5] The sudden and dramatic generation of wealth increased demand for goods and services, leading to the rapid expansion of industry, and improvements to urban infrastructure and civic facilities. At the same time, the stampede to the goldfields led to labor shortages in Victoria and New South Wales, ultimately driving up wages for laborers, increasing the standard of living for the working class, and giving rise to the notion that Australia was a "working man's paradise."

Much has been said about the levelling and democratizing effects of the Australian gold rush, and no event better illustrates such tendencies than the uprising at the Eureka Stockade. On the Ballarat goldfields of 1854 there was growing discontent among gold prospectors, or "diggers," regarding oppressive licensing fees, government corruption, and voting restrictions.

After months of collective action by an estimated ten thousand miners, a group of some five hundred lightly armed diggers barricaded themselves on a section of the Eureka goldfield to make their stand. Government troops quickly overpowered the rebels. However, substantial reforms resulted from the investigation into the Eureka Stockade. The allegedly corrupt Gold Commission, the main body regulating the goldfields, was abolished; licenses were replaced by a more modest and equitable Miner's Right fee; and voting rights were expanded. While historians continue to debate the material effects of the Eureka uprising, it has entered the national mythology as a defining moment in the forging of the Australian character.

Although the gold rush was no doubt one among many factors that contributed to the development of a democratic political consciousness and an egalitarian ethic in Australia, the culture of the goldfields was also racist, misogynist, and xenophobic,[6] and the effects of the gold rush for indigenous Australians, women, and Asian immigrants were far from positive. Indigenous inhabitants were once again displaced as prospectors for gold moved further into the continent's interior, appropriating native lands and their precious natural resources.

Even as European domination of indigenous peoples was intensifying, the gold rush was strengthening an already firmly entrenched patriarchy among the colonizers. Digging was an almost exclusively male occupation, so few women made their way to the goldfields. Those few who came as wives and daughters of prospectors were frequently the victims of male violence; and those who came alone had little hope of supporting themselves independently, except as "sly-grog" (illicit alcohol) sellers, itinerant entertainers, or prostitutes, occupations which left them vulnerable both to the population they served and to law enforcement officials. And even while miners were advocating for manhood suffrage, there was little support for, and indeed fervent opposition to, women's suffrage.

At the same time, the gold rush reinvigorated anti-Asian sentiments. As large numbers of Chinese migrants arrived to mine for gold or fill the positions vacated by Australian laborers,[7] anti-Chinese rhetoric heated up, with prominent political leaders calling for the exclusion of the "abhorrent mass of foreign Paganism, festering with all incestuous and murderous crimes," the "yellow slaves from a land of lies, infanticide and heathenism" (quoted in Pickering 2001, 41). Such sentiments underpinned routine discrimination and violence against the Chinese in gold rush Australia.

The gold rush period has left a rich legacy of images and icons that feature prominently in contemporary discourses of national identity.[8] The Eureka rebel, the digger, and the "working man" more generally have come to exemplify hardiness, ingenuity, self-sufficiency, male camaraderie ("mateship"), and egalitarianism, all cherished traits in national self-conceptions. On the other hand, women, indigenous peoples, and nonwhite migrants remain on the margins of discourses of national identity, just as they were on the margins of society in gold rush Australia.

THE CREATION OF "AUSTRALIAN" CULTURE

The discovery of gold diversified the once limited Australian colonial economy, opening up the possibility of achieving independence from Britain. Not surprisingly then, the late nineteenth and early twentieth centuries witnessed the flowering of a distinctly and self-consciously Australian culture. Writers such as Henry Lawson and A.B. "Banjo" Paterson, and landscape painters from the so-called Heidelberg School[9] helped forge a national imaginary based on a romanticized notion of the Australian bush and the (white) bushmen who survived and tamed it.

In the lead-up to Australia's national federation, the shearers, stockmen, jackaroos, swagmen, and drovers immortalized in works such as Paterson's *Clancy of the Overflow*, Lawson's *The Drover's Wife*, and Roberts' *The Golden Fleece* rapidly became exemplars of Australianness. Even notorious bushrangers such as Ned Kelly became folk heroes embodying the national character. The national type, later described by Ward (1958) in *The Australian Legend*, was

> rough and ready in his manners ... a great improviser ... taciturn rather than talkative, one who endures stoically rather than one who acts busily ... sceptical about the value of religion and of intellectual and cultural pursuits generally ... a fiercely independent person who hates officiousness and authority ... very hospitable and, above all, will stick to his mates through thick and thin. (Ward 1958, 2)

At the same time, Australian sportsmen were enjoying great successes in international competitions, and Australian sporting prowess was being used by an increasingly Australian-born population to distinguish this young, robust, and manly culture from what was seen as an overly civilized, prudish, and effete Motherland (Crotty 2001). With the prominence of such rugged and spirited icons from the realms of sport and the bush, it is hardly surprising that discourses of national identity generated during this crucial period of national formation were unapologetically masculine and almost exclusively white Anglo-Celtic.[10]

Women seldom featured in discourses of national identity during this period, except, perhaps as characters who thwarted the Australian man's true nature. As Crotty (2001, 22) notes, "Women represented restrictive morality, law, Christianity and respectability, or could be the sexual possessions of men. But they were not active participants in the national legend. The 'real' Australian was male." Likewise, indigenous Australians and nonwhite migrants were all but invisible in nationalist discourses. Acknowledging the existence and rights of these Others would have challenged the white male proprietorship of the nation. The *Bulletin*, a leading newspaper of the day, made this explicit in its masthead, which carried the slogan "Australia for the White Man."

The marginalization of women and nonwhites from discourses of nationhood was, and arguably still is, obscured by pervasive and enduring notions of Australian egalitarianism, the principle of "a fair go" (equal opportunity for all). In the lead-up to Federation, as nationalists attempted to draw stark distinctions between Britain and Australia, the British were portrayed as slavish adherents to class boundaries while Australia was celebrated as a classless society in which, as the still-current aphorism reminds us, "Jack is as good as his master."

FEDERATION

1 January 1901 marked the Federation of the Commonwealth of Australia, when six separate states were united under a single constitution. The first substantial legislation passed by the new Commonwealth Parliament was the Immigration Restriction Act of 1901, designed to prevent nonwhite migrants from entering Australia. Parts of this so-called "White Australia Policy" would remain in place until the 1970s. An overriding fear among the white inhabitants of the young nation was invasion from Asia, whether by military force or by means of immigration. Such fears have proven so pervasive and enduring that recent commentators have identified Australia's "invasion complex" as a crucial factor in contemporary politics and national self-conceptions (Papastergiadis 2004; Elder 2007).

Hard on the heels of the Immigration Restriction Act came other discriminatory statutes such as whites-only labor laws, tariffs calculated according to the race of the producers, a statute preventing nonwhites from receiving old-age and invalid pensions, and a pronatalist policy that granted a maternity allowance only to white women (Commonwealth of Australia 2000, 8–10). At the same time, mass deportations of nonwhites began under statutes such as the Pacific Island Labourers Act of 1901, which resulted in the forcible repatriation of an estimated 7,500 Pacific Islanders who had been employed on the sugar plantations of Queensland.

Federation brought an expansion of women's rights to Australia. In 1902 white women won the right to vote in federal elections and sit in federal Parliament. However, Aboriginal Australians still lacked even the most basic civil rights. Section 127 of the new Constitution excluded indigenous Australians from the Census, an exclusion that would remain in place until 1967. Although Aboriginal voting rights varied from state to state, indigenous Australians only gained the Commonwealth vote in 1962, and it was not until 1965 that all states granted them the right to vote in state elections. In addition, at least through 1967, state-based Aboriginal "protection" agencies continued to closely regulate the lives of indigenous Australians, limiting their mobility and relations with non-indigenous people, and even forcibly removing so-called "half-caste" children to be raised by white Christian missionaries (Commonwealth of Australia 2000),[11] a practice resulting in what are known today as the Stolen Generations.

While state-sanctioned discrimination against indigenous Australians and nonwhite migrants was formally outlawed with the Racial Discrimination Act of 1975, the legacy of that discrimination has left a lasting imprint on Australian discourses of national identity. Periodic panics about the "Asianization" of Australia are inextricably bound up with national self-conceptions. It is geographically part of the Asia-Pacific region, but most closely culturally allied with Britain. Some of the most heated debates over national identity in the past two decades have centered on the question of whether Australia should be considered part of Asia. In addition, tensions between indigenous and non-indigenous Australians continue to inflect contemporary discourses of national identity. Aboriginal athlete Cathy Freeman provoked an uproar among many Australians when she chose to carry the Aboriginal flag on her victory lap after a win at the 1994 Commonwealth Games.[12] And yet, six years later Freeman was chosen to light the Olympic Cauldron at the Sydney Games.

WORLD WAR I

Roughly 417,000 of Australia's three million men enlisted to fight in World War I, with at least 330,000 embarking for duty abroad. Some sixty thousand died, and more than 150,000 were wounded or captured. Many contemporary discourses of national identity date the true birth of the nation to its participation in the conflict. Soldiers of the Australia and New Zealand Army Corps, or "Anzacs," became national icons embodying courage, self-sacrifice, ingenuity, and "mateship."[13] The soldiers came to be known as "diggers," a term deriving perhaps as much from the goldfields digger archetype as from the troops' trench-digging duties. The campaign in Gallipoli, in particular, features prominently in contemporary narratives of nation.

In early 1915, amid rising concerns for the security of the Suez Canal and British interests in the Middle East, Britain directed a large contingent of Anzac troops to invade Turkey at the Gallipoli Peninsula. After a protracted and devastating campaign, the Anzacs retreated in defeat with more than twenty-six thousand casualties including 8,700 Australian dead.[14] Although the Anzacs were defeated in the Gallipoli campaign, the Australian troops are said to have fought bravely, proving both their manhood and Australia's nationhood under enemy fire. Today 25 April, the day of the landing at Gallipoli, is celebrated in Australia as Anzac Day, a time of remembrance for not only the "diggers" of World War I, but for all of Australia's war veterans.

Australia's participation in war has long been central to national self-conceptions. Veterans of virtually every conflict in the nation's history have been celebrated as exemplars of Australianness.[15] Nonetheless, discourses of Australian national identity have been conspicuously silent on the only war to be fought wholly on Australian soil, a war spanning more than a century and claiming an estimated twenty-two thousand lives: the war between European colonists and Aboriginal Australians (Broome 1988; White 1988). While Australian soldiers are routinely lauded for their bravery in the face of overwhelming odds, Australia's own frontier wars do not readily allow for such heroic narratives. In incidents like those at Myall Creek (New South Wales), Warrigal Creek (Victoria), the Wonnerup House region (Western Australia), Battle Mountain (Queensland), Rufus River (South Australia), and throughout Tasmania, indigenous people were subjected to exile, abduction, rape, poisoning, and bloody massacre. These realities sit uneasily alongside twenty-first-century narratives of Australian egalitarianism, cultural pluralism, and military heroism, and so they are largely ignored.

WORLD WAR II

Nearly one million Australian men and women enlisted in the military during World War II, with some 575,000 deployed to the European, North African, and Pacific theatres, and thirty-four thousand killed (White 1988). While Australia had previously fought as an ally in Britain's wars in Western Europe, the Mediterranean, and Africa, World War II brought modern warfare to Australia's doorstep for the first time. In 1941–1942 as the Japanese Imperial Army invaded and occupied territory throughout the Asia-Pacific region, fears of a Japanese invasion of Australia grew. The stunning fall of Singapore in February of 1942, along with the capture of fifteen thousand Australians there, was followed quickly by aerial attacks on Darwin and later submarine attacks on Sydney Harbour. While Japan never attempted a large-scale land assault on Australia, the nation's long-standing distrust and dread of Asia seemed to be justified by the events of the Pacific war.

Anti-Asian sentiments were further fuelled by developments later in the war. In 1944 more than four hundred Japanese detainees escaped in an uprising at the Prisoner of War Compound near Cowra in New South Wales. While all of the escapees were eventually recaptured, the uprising resulted in the deaths of 231 Japanese and four Australians (National Archives of Australia 2006). At the same time, the nation was hearing reports of the high mortality rates for Australian POWs in Japanese custody in the Asian-Pacific theatre. 36 percent of Australians taken prisoner by Japanese forces died in custody, in what were reported to be cruel and inhumane conditions. By the close of the war, some eight thousand Australians had died in Japanese POW camps.

Even as World War II more firmly entrenched anti-Asian sentiments in Australia, it challenged long-standing gender ideologies. Women were called into military support duty with the newly created Women's Auxiliary Air

Force, Australian Women's Army Service, and Women's Royal Australian Naval Service, and when large-scale troop deployments led to a shortage of male labor on the home front, Australian women were actively encouraged to enter the paid workforce. Women entered male-dominated employment sectors, took up trade union membership in record numbers, and won wage concessions that lifted the female wage from the standard rate of 54 percent of the male wage before the war to 75 percent at war's end (see Beaton 1982; White 1988; Elder 2007). These gains were reversed somewhat in the immediate postwar period as women were urged to surrender their jobs to men and return to their "natural" roles as wives and mothers.[16] In the wake of the wartime threat of Japanese invasion, Australians readily adopted the notion that white Australia must "populate or perish." It was therefore seen as white women's patriotic duty to procreate, to safeguard the nation against Asian invasion.

World War II had not introduced any new national archetypes to rival the "digger" or Anzac icons. Instead, the conflict seemed to reinforce long-standing discourses of national identity. At the end of the war, dominant discourses of Australian identity were consistent with Prime Minister John Curtin's wartime characterization of the nation as a "British community in the South Seas."[17] In the national imaginary, then, Australia was a white, Christian, English-speaking community regulated according to naturalized gender and ethnoracial hierarchies.

POST-WORLD WAR II PROSPERITY AND CONSERVATISM

The radical social disruption of World War II was followed by a period of economic prosperity and social conservatism. Following the dictate to "populate or perish" the Australian government actively recruited migrants from war-ravaged Europe. In the years immediately following the war, only white migrants from Britain and northern Europe were recruited. However, when the flow of these migrants slowed to a trickle, migrants were recruited from southern Europe and eventually Turkey, Syria, and Lebanon (Lack and Templeton 1995, 74–75). Policy makers reassured the white English-speaking population that, under a policy of assimilation, these ethnically diverse migrants would blend seamlessly into white Australian society.

With plentiful migrant labor at its disposal, the government embarked on large public works and industrialization projects, the most famous of which was the Snowy Mountains Scheme, a water and power generation project built with the labor of more than one hundred thousand workers over a twenty-five-year period. The postwar decades brought increased affluence, a dramatic rise in home ownership, a demographic shift toward the suburbs, and the emergence of a new Australian ideal: the single-family home on a quarter-acre block. National pride was bolstered by the 1954 visit of Queen Elizabeth II, the first visit by a reigning British monarch, and by Australia's performance at the 1956 Melbourne Olympics, the first Olympic Games to be held in the Southern Hemisphere.

By the time it hosted the Melbourne Games, Australia had firmly established its international reputation as a "sporting nation." As early as 1877 Australia had proven its sporting prowess in rowing and test cricket among other sports, and in the 1930s, the Australian-trained racehorse Phar Lap dominated international racing and was widely embraced as a symbol of Australian "heart."[18] But one twentieth-century sporting figure, Donald Bradman, would rise above all others in the postwar years, being hailed as a national hero and an exemplar of Australianness. An extraordinarily talented batsman, Bradman's professional cricket career spanned more than twenty years and included the captaincy of the record-breaking 1948 Australian Test team known as "The Invincibles." Revered not only for his athleticism, but for his self-effacing humor and gentle manner, Bradman was knighted in 1949, and in 1997 he became the first living Australian to be featured on a postage stamp.[19] Today Bradman, "The Don," remains a common point of reference in discourses of national identity.

MULTICULTURALISM AND THE
RETREAT FROM TOLERANCE

By the late 1960s and early 1970s, there was a growing awareness in Australia that migrants were not assimilating as flawlessly as government rhetoric had promised. Social scientists highlighted the problems of migrant poverty and lack of access to social services, and urged a reconsideration of assimilationist policies.[20] At the same time, indigenous groups were staging increasingly visible protests, raising public awareness of the continuing marginalization of Aboriginal Australians. In the early 1970s, the government dropped the model of "assimilation" and adopted "multiculturalism," a term borrowed from Canada (Lack and Templeton 1995, 90). Successive governments focused multicultural discourses and policies on fostering cultural diversity in Australia, promoting social justice and political engagement for all Australians, and fully utilizing the skills of the diverse population to enrich the nation both culturally and economically.

Soon after its adoption, multicultural policy came under fire from a number of quarters. In response to increased Asian immigration stemming from the Indo-Chinese refugee crisis of the late 1970s, political conservatives decried the "Asianization" of Australia. Geoffrey Blainey, perhaps the most high-profile critic of Asian immigration, argued in his widely discussed *All for Australia* (1984), that Asian immigration was socially disruptive because of irreconcilable cultural differences between Asians and Australians (conceived as separate and monolithic groups), and because Asian migrants increased the competition for scarce jobs. As global economic restructuring led to widespread deindustrialization and rising unemployment in Australia in the late 1980s and 1990s, other conservative critics of multicultural policy echoed Blainey's arguments. Such rhetoric was rekindled in the 1990s in what some have called a "retreat from tolerance" in Australia (see Adams 1997).

In the lead-up to the national elections of 1996, there was a discernible backlash to the strong multicultural ethic of the previous two decades. A number of candidates from mainstream political parties campaigned on anti-immigration and anti-multiculturalism platforms (Kalantzis and Cope 1997, 69–70). National Party candidate Bob Burgess referred to citizenship ceremonies as "de-wogging" ceremonies ("wog" being a derogatory term for nonwhite migrants), while fellow National Party candidate Bob Katter derided "femo-Nazis" and "slanty-eyed ideologues." Graeme Campbell, running against the tide of his own ruling Labor Party, spoke out against multiculturalism. And Pauline Hanson, a Liberal candidate, spoke passionately about the unfair advantages enjoyed by migrants and Aboriginal Australians at the expense of "the whites." Although Hanson lost the endorsement of the Liberal Party, she went on to win her election as an independent and to found the One Nation Party, which continues to actively seek electoral support for its protectionist and xenophobic platform.

The backlash against multiculturalism has not been confined to a few marginal political figures, however. For instance, the Liberal Party under Prime Minister John Howard (1996–2007) demonstrated a distinct lack of sympathy for indigenous rights. In 1998, the administration's Native Title Act amendments reversed hard-won indigenous land rights. In 2000, it rejected the recommendations of the *Bringing Them Home* report (Human Rights and Equal Opportunity Commission 1997) and Howard himself refused to issue a formal apology for the long-lived policy of removing indigenous children from their families. In 2004, the administration oversaw the dismantling of the leading indigenous representative body, the Aboriginal and Torres Strait Islander Commission (ATSIC). And in 2007, in the wake of alleged child sexual abuse in Northern Territory indigenous communities, the administration passed the National Emergency Response Act, which allowed for the federal take-over of certain Aboriginal lands and institutions in the Northern Territory, the shutdown of government-supported employment programs, and the suspension of protections under the Racial Discrimination Act of 1975.

Just as the last decade has seen a retreat from multiculturalism, state policy during the period has been marked by growing conservatism in regards to gender and sexuality. Most notably, the Howard administration instituted the Family Tax Benefit Part B, widely understood as an attempt to encourage married women to become stay-at-home wives and mothers. Moreover, with echoes of the post–World War II "populate or perish" doctrine, Federal Treasurer Peter Costello exhorted all Australians who could have children to "have one for your husband, one for your wife and one for your country" (ABC 2005). And in 2004, an amendment to the Marriage Act effectively barred same-sex marriage in Australia. Such recent policies can be understood as a reassertion of heteronormativity and traditional gender roles.

MILLENNIAL DEBATES ON NATIONAL IDENTITY

Three major events taking place around the millennium sparked heated and widespread debate on Australian national identity: the 1999 Constitutional referendum; the 2000 Sydney Olympic Games; and the 2001 centenary of Federation. Each event demanded detailed consideration of the nation's history, its future, and its identity.

First, the Constitutional referendum. Two related questions appeared on the ballot in the 1999 referendum. The citizenry was first asked to vote on whether to retain Constitutional ties with the British monarchy or "to establish the Commonwealth of Australia as a republic with the Queen and Governor-General being replaced by a President appointed by a two-thirds majority of the members of the Commonwealth Parliament" (Australian Election Commission 1999). While there was some consideration of this issue even before Federation, it became a serious matter for public debate after stunning political developments in 1975. Then Prime Minister Gough Whitlam had come to power in 1972, leading the first Labor Party government in twenty-three years. In November of 1975, the Senate was in deadlock with opposition politicians blocking consideration of a crucial supply bill. In response, Governor-General Sir John Kerr, the Queen's representative in Australia, dismissed the government and installed Liberal-Country Opposition leader Malcolm Fraser as caretaker Prime Minister. The dismissal, perhaps the nation's most dramatic political event of the twentieth century, featured prominently in debates on the 1999 Constitutional referendum. A central issue was whether Australia should stand as a mature and fully independent nation, or whether it should remain subject to the will of the Crown and its representatives. However, no less salient was the issue of Australia's cultural heritage and national identity. Cutting ties with the monarchy was viewed by some to be abandoning the nation's Anglo-Celtic roots.

The second question in the referendum was whether to insert a preamble into the Australian Constitution. While the precise text of the Preamble was not included on the Ballot, drafts of the proposed text had been widely circulated by the government and the media in the months leading up to the referendum. Two elements of Prime Minister John Howard's draft Preamble generated intense public debate: references to the indigenous peoples of Australia and to "mateship."

While many Australian Aboriginal leaders strongly advocated Preamble acknowledgment of Aboriginal custodianship of the land, the initial draft Preamble noted simply that, "Since time immemorial our land has been inhabited by Aborigines and Torres Strait Islanders, who are honoured for their ancient and continuing cultures."[21] The use of pronouns was telling. In its reference to "*our* land" and "*their* cultures," the document constructed non-indigenous Australians as "us," the rightful owners and governors of the nation, and reduced indigenous Australians to "them," passive subjects in a system of naturalized white rule.

The draft Preamble further sparked debate with its assertion that Australians "value independence as dearly as mateship." At issue was the use of the term "mateship" which women's groups argued was "at the core of women's exclusion from business and public domains," and a "symbol of discrimination against women."[22] Linguists and historians were called on to clarify the origins and meaning of the term, but the country remained split on whether the term referred primarily to the bonds between white males, or to a more general sense of community and loyalty. Ultimately the term was dropped from a revised draft of the Preamble. While the change represented a victory for those Australians who objected to enshrining such masculinist imagery in the Constitution, indigenous leaders suggested that the document only further weakened the status of the indigenous peoples of Australia (ABC 1999c). This raises the question of whether the battle against the marginalization of women in the Preamble was won at the expense of the further marginalization of Australia's indigenous peoples. The electorate ultimately voted against both proposed Constitutional changes. However, the debates leading up to the referendum demonstrate that gendered and racialized discourses of nation are hotly contested in contemporary Australia.

The second millennial event sparking discussions of national identity in Australia was the 2000 Sydney Olympic Games. Because this event is covered in considerable detail in Chapter 6, only two general points about the Olympic opening ceremony will be raised here. First, in this telling of the story of the nation, every point in the narrative was framed by images of nature: the sea, the bush, the red earth of Australia, the "sunburnt county."[23] This is a reminder of the centrality of the natural landscape in discourses of national identity, not only in Australia but in the other nations considered here. Second, the opening ceremony featured many of the archetypes and characteristics already discussed here: the stockman, the bushranger, the working man, exemplifying ingenuity, self-sufficiency, mateship, and youthful exuberance. The overriding effect was a celebration of white male achievements and archetypes. Nonetheless, women, nonwhite migrants, and indigenous Australians appeared in large numbers in the ceremony, a reflection of changing power relations in the nation. In particular, the selection of Aboriginal runner Cathy Freeman to light the Olympic cauldron was seen by many as an important moment in the so-called "reconciliation" between indigenous and non-indigenous Australians.

"Reconciliation" is closely linked with the last of the major millennial events to prompt consideration of Australian national identity, the centenary of Federation in 2001. In 1991, the Commonwealth Parliament established the Council for Aboriginal Reconciliation with the goals of improving communication between indigenous and non-indigenous Australians, fostering understanding and mutual respect between the two groups, and improving on the material disadvantages still facing Aboriginal Australians, all by the centenary of Federation in 2001. While the efficacy of the program is a matter of considerable debate, particularly in the area of material improvements to the lives of indigenous Australians, and although the Council itself was dissolved in 2001, the Reconciliation movement unquestionably raised the profile of indigenous issues in Australia. So much so, in fact, that centenary events around the nation not only celebrated the accomplishments of Australia's settler population, but often reflected on the ways indigenous peoples have been quite intentionally and explicitly excluded from membership in the nation-state.

The centerpiece of the official state celebrations on 1 January 2001 was a parade in Sydney with some 6,500 parade participants and up to a half-million spectators. Many elements of the celebrations were consistent with state-sponsored grand spectacles across the globe. Royal Australian Air Force jets flew low over the parade route, a reminder of the nation's martial power. There were military marching bands and people in period costumes. Elaborate floats represented each region of the nation and each branch of the military. Fallen soldiers were celebrated for their sacrifice. And speeches by politicians, including Prime Minister Howard, stressed the national "spirit" and character, national accomplishments, and "faith under God" for a promising future (Howard 2001a). Parade organizers were also careful to include images of diversity and equality. Floats celebrated military nurses, Australia's indigenous peoples and diverse migrant groups, and even the pacifists and peacemakers of the nation, represented by a float in the shape of a naked infant.

It would be naïve to suggest that the centenary parade is a true reflection of a society characterized by gender and ethnoracial equality. Indeed, centenary events held throughout 2001 often highlighted ongoing inequalities grounded in gender, race, ethnicity, class, religion, sexuality, and disability.[24] So much so that many conservatives decried the "political correctness" or "black armband view of history" contaminating Australian narratives of nation. Such debates over critical interpretations of national history reached such a fevered pitch in the lead-up to centenary that they were dubbed "the history wars" (Macintyre 2003).

One prominent battlefront in the history wars was the new National Museum of Australia in Canberra, timed to open during the nation's centenary year. The Museum, discussed in greater detail in Chapter 11, opened in March 2001 to wildly mixed reviews. Where supporters saw a balanced and richly detailed story of the nation (NMA 2003), critics saw "a monument to horrendous political correctness" (Stead 2004, 390) demonstrating "sneering ridicule for white Australia" (Devine quoted in Macintyre 2003, 195). The Museum approached national history as a dynamic construction, constituted in and through a multitude of voices and experiences. It sought to both educate visitors and challenge them to reexamine their assumptions about the nation's past, present, and future. Ironically, although much has been made of the undue prominence afforded to women and ethnoracial minorities in the Museum, as Chapter 11 demonstrates, white males still overwhelmingly dominate its telling of the Australian story.

THE *TAMPA*, CHILDREN OVERBOARD, AND POST-9/11 FEARS

Just weeks before the 9/11 attacks on the United States, Australia was facing its own "invasion" crisis, a seemingly increasing number of illegal migrants, mainly refugees of Middle Eastern descent. In late August of 2001, an overloaded fishing vessel carrying 438 people began to sink in international waters between Indonesia and Australia. The passengers were mainly Afghan refugees. A Norwegian ship, the MV *Tampa*, rescued the passengers and crew of the vessel, and, in compliance with maritime law, proceeded to the nearest port for medical assistance. That port was on the Australian territory of Christmas Island. The Howard administration denied the *Tampa* permission to land and deployed Australian troops to intercept the ship in an apparent attempt to prevent the refugees from setting foot on Australian soil and claiming asylum. When the captain of the *Tampa* declared a state of emergency and entered the port without permission, most of the refugees were transferred to the HMAS *Manoora* and transported to detention camps on the island nation of Nauru, an action the Howard administration termed the "Pacific Solution."[25] Australia was reported to the UN Commissioner for Refugees and widely criticized for its failure to comply with its obligations under international human rights agreements. But the Howard government used the event to justify tightening border security against an anticipated wave of illegal migrants.

A little more than a month later, another vessel overloaded with asylum seekers was intercepted by the HMAS *Adelaide* in the waters off Christmas Island. In what came to be known as the "Children Overboard Affair," Immigration Minister Philip Ruddock and other officials in the Howard administration claimed that the refugees had thrown their children into the water in an attempt to force the Australians to rescue them and grant them asylum. The story understandably sparked outrage in Australia and arguably contributed to already rising anti-immigrant sentiments. In the election held soon after the incident, the Howard administration capitalized on such sentiments to win another term in office. Subsequent inquiries determined, however, that the "Children Overboard" story was false and that the government *knew* it was false even as they repeated it in the lead-up to the 2001 election (Parliament of Australia 2002).

Prime Minister Howard was in Washington, DC on September 11, 2001, when the World Trade Center and the Pentagon were attacked. In his first public address after the attacks, Howard characterized the events of 9/11 as an attack upon both the American and the Australian "way of life." He further promised that Australia would "cooperate within the limits of its capability concerning any response that the United States may regard as necessary" (Howard 2001b). That response included sending Australian troops to support the American-led invasions of Afghanistan and Iraq.

Despite massive anti-war demonstrations in Australia and around the world, the Howard administration seemed determined to prove its solidarity and parity with the US and the UK by joining them in the "global war on terror." Judging from media accounts, however, the effect in Australia seems to have been quite the opposite. Australian participation in the invasion of Iraq in particular sparked countless political cartoons portraying Prime Minister Howard as the lapdog, puppet, or menial servant of George Bush and Tony Blair. The term "cultural cringe," long understood as Australia's sense of inadequacy relative to Britain and America, has made a comeback.

It is crucial to note here that the September 11 attacks on the US occurred between the *Tampa* incident and the "Children Overboard" incident. The three events together undoubtedly contributed to a resurgence of fear and xenophobia in Australia, this time with an emphasis on the imagined Muslim Other. Such sentiments were only strengthened in October of 2002 when eighty-eight Australian tourists were killed by "Islamic terrorists" in a Bali nightclub bombing, an event sometimes referred to as "Australia's 9/11." In 2005 tensions between native-born Australians and more recent immigrants from the Middle East erupted into the racially charged Cronulla riots, discussed in more detail in Chapter 8. Such developments reveal lingering notions that Australia is, and should remain, a "white nation" (Hage 1998).

"ENDLESS AND AGONISED NAVEL-GAZING ABOUT WHO WE ARE"

Prime Minister John Howard, in his 1996 Sir Robert Menzies Lecture, castigated the left-wing intelligentsia for distorting Australian history by dwelling exclusively on "imperialism, exploitation, racism, sexism and other forms of discrimination" (Howard 1996). This "pre-ordained pessimism," he asserted, led only to "endless and agonised navel-gazing about who we are;" and for the good of the nation, such exercises in national self-flagellation must be abandoned. As Howard suggested in the lead-up to his 1996 election victory, Australians deserved to feel "relaxed and comfortable" about the nation's history, its achievements, and its place in world. In essence, then, one of the central promises of his government was to resuscitate traditional notions of national identity.

At the dawn of the new millennium, the Australia Day Council, seemingly working toward this same goal, commissioned historian John Hirst to "examine the nature and roots of our national character" (Pearson 2007, vii).[26] In the introduction of the resulting volume, Hirst asserts that there *is* an essential and enduring Australian character. And, perhaps not surprisingly, this state-endorsed vision of the national character centers on many of the same (largely white, masculine) archetypes and traits discussed here: bushmen, diggers, bushrangers, Anzacs, sportsmen, mateship, and, above all, egalitarianism or "a fair go."

While such discourses still dominate contemporary discussions of the Australian character, national identity remains a contested issue in Australia today, a contest that revolves around three issues in particular. The first is Australia's paradoxical position as a Western nation located in the Asia-Pacific. How should Australia "imagine" itself? What political and economic alliances should it cultivate? What is the ideal balance between British, American, and Asian influences in Australia? Certainly both the "Asianization" and "Americanization" of Australia are ongoing topics of public concern, while there is no equivalent discussion of "Anglicization."

The second issue is white Australia's relationship with its internal Others. Just after World War II, 90 percent of Australians were of Anglo-Celtic descent. Today, they constitute just 70 percent of the population, and demographers suggest that this will fall further to 62 percent of the population by 2025 (Price 1999). Additionally, today more than 40 percent of Australians were born overseas or have at least one parent born overseas. In this increasingly racially and ethnically diverse society, what attempts, if any, should be made to preserve or prioritize Anglo-Celtic traditions, particularly the English language and the tenets of Christianity?

The third issue is the status of indigenous Australians. What special claims, if any, do indigenous peoples have over the nation? Can any special claims be addressed symbolically (for instance, by featuring indigenous people more prominently in national iconography) or must they be addressed legislatively and economically? How should the nation address the issue of autonomy and self-determination for indigenous peoples? Is genuine reconciliation between indigenous and non-indigenous Australians possible when so many past wrongs go unaddressed, and so many drastic inequalities persist?

Notably absent from most current debates is the place women occupy in the national imaginary. In what ways do the near total absence of women as national icons and archetypes and the marginalization of women's contributions in stories of the nation reflect and contribute to ongoing gender inequality?

Treatises on the Australian character continue to find an eager market today. Australian national identity is still keenly debated. The question remains, however, what shape discourses of national identity will assume in the twenty-first century. Will traditional white, masculine pursuits and personae continue to dominate narratives of nation, or will countercurrents introduced by multiculturalism, feminism, the indigenous rights movement, and globalization among others substantially change national imaginings?

3 Discourses of National Identity in Japan

Evidence indicates that prior to contact with Europeans, few Japanese conceptualized Japan as a distinct and cohesive nation, and the notion of "the Japanese" as a national people had little meaning (Morris-Suzuki 1998, 13–14). However, the arrival of European traders and Christian missionaries in the sixteenth century sparked an intense national introspection in Japan that in some form or another has persisted ever since. In their exploration of national identity, Japanese intellectuals and, more recently, popular writers have both reached back to the dawn of time in search of essential and authentic national traits and looked abroad to determine which of these traits are unique to Japan and the Japanese.

In the modern era (circa 1868 forward), discourses of national identity based on notions of *kokutai* (literally the national body), *kokusui* (the national essence), *Nihon no kokoro* (the Japanese spirit), or simply "*ware ware Nihonjin*" ("We Japanese" as an organic category) have been used to explain and justify national actions.[1] This chapter offers a brief survey of historical developments in Japanese discourses of national identity; however it is not intended as a comprehensive catalogue of such discourses. While a vast scholarly literature exists on each of the developments noted, to remain within the scope of this book, I discuss only those points which bear most directly on contemporary gendered and racialized discourses of Japanese identity.

THE AGE OF THE GODS

The *Kojiki* (*Record of Ancient Matters*) and the *Nihon shoki* (*Chronicles of Japan*), both written in the Nara Era (710–784), are widely regarded as the earliest surviving texts concerned with the origins of Japan and the Japanese.[2] While the details of Japan's beginnings differ in the two texts, they largely agree on the matter of the imperial line. In the age of the gods, the Sun Goddess Amaterasu ruled the earth on her parents' authority. One of her direct descendents became *Jinmu Tennō*, the first human ruler of the earth and the founder of the Japanese imperial family. When the texts were first produced, their imperial genealogies served to legitimate the rule of the Yamato clan by linking them with the Sun Goddess and thus imbuing them with divine authority. Such authority was useful as they sought to standardize, centralize, and strengthen their rule (Kōnoshi 2000, 51–55).[3]

In later periods, however, the *Kojiki* and *Nihon shoki* would be used for other purposes. In the medieval period (circa 1150–1550), as power shifted away from a limited imperial system to the military rule of the Shogunate, interpretations of the two texts tended to de-emphasize the centrality of the divinely sanctioned imperial order. Later, as Japan's ruling elite sought to insulate the nation from foreign influences in the Edo Era (1600–1867), nativist scholars reassessed and even retranslated the two foundational texts in an attempt to remove alien (largely Chinese) influences and reveal an authentically Japanese essence (Kōnoshi 2000, 62–64).

Not surprisingly, in the Meiji Era (1868–1912), as Japan made the transition to a modern centralized nation-state unified under the authority of an emperor, the *Kojiki* and *Nihon shoki* were used once again to legitimate the imperial system by elevating the emperor to the status of *hitogami* (human-divine). At the height of twentieth-century Japanese militarism, the Ministry of Education made the lessons of the *Kojiki* part of the national curriculum. The 1935 *Kokutai no hongi* (*Fundamentals of the National Essence*) reminded students that, "The Great Japanese Empire is forever ruled by the emperor of a single and unchanging imperial line by virtue of the divine decree of the Imperial Ancestress. This is our eternal, unchanging national essence" (Kōnoshi 2000, 66).

After the emperor was compelled by the Allied Occupation authorities to publicly deny his divinity in 1946, the *Kojiki* and *Nihon shoki* came to be regarded more as national myths than literal histories. However, this did not diminish their contributions to contemporary discourses of national identity. In the postwar era, folklorists continue to probe the texts for what are considered to be the nation's most authentic traditions, values, and beliefs.

Today, these foundational texts provide Japan with a powerful symbol of nation, the Sun Goddess, and this symbol is clearly gendered. As the mother of the nation, she is a powerful creative force, but she also embodies certain stereotypically feminine traits: she is nurturing but temperamental, timid but vain. Likewise, stories of her divine forbearers convey powerful messages about the rightful gender order. According to origin myths, when the goddess Izanami first saw the god Izanagi, she proclaimed her delight only to be chastised by Izanagi. "I am a man and by right should have spoken first," he asserted, in a reminder of Japan's divinely sanctioned patriarchy.

Thus, the texts make it clear that men are the rightful rulers of the land. In fact, the emperor not only rules the nation but, through his descent from the Sun Goddess, he is both father and mother to the nation, both the masculine and the feminine (Morris-Suzuki 1998, 118–119). Just as the Emperor is symbolically both male and female, historically, discourses of Japanese national identity have been both masculinized and feminized, depending on the discursive context (Morris-Suzuki 1998, 110–139). Such discourses have been alternately masculinized to emphasize the nation's industriousness and its military and economic power, and feminized to emphasize its gentility.

In terms of racialized discourses of national identity, arguably at the time the *Kojiki* and *Nihon shoki* were written, there was no clear sense of the Japanese as a biologically distinct race. Rather, Morris-Suzuki (1998, 32) argues that notions of the "Japanese race" only developed in Japan out of encounters with Western theories of race in the Meiji Era (1868–1912). She suggests that prior to the Meiji Era, Japanese notions of identity centred primarily on ways of life, rather than on biological heredity. Nonetheless, in the modern era ethnic nationalists have drawn on the *Kojiki* and *Nihon shoki* to support their claims of Japanese uniqueness and innate superiority.

SHIFTING NATIONAL OTHERS

As noted earlier, the development of identities, both individual and collective, depends inherently upon notions of the Other. From the earliest stirrings of national consciousness, Japan has defined itself in relation to powerful national Others. The first of these was China, the "Middle Kingdom," recognized in ancient Japan as a superior civilization and the primary source of learning, high culture, and political legitimacy. While exchanges between the two lands likely extend well into prehistory (Denoon et al. 1996), between AD 600 and 839 those relations were formalized by regular Japanese tribute missions to China (Beasley 1999, 48). Japanese rulers, often declared "kings" by the Chinese emperors, sent delegations with gifts and pledges to China's imperial courts, and in return the delegations were allowed to study Chinese arts, religion, philosophy, and governance and bring valuable Chinese goods back to Japan.

While Chinese influence in Japan went through periods of ascendency and decline, at least through the eighteenth century Japanese elites subscribed to the *ka-i* (civilization-barbarianism) conceptual model in which China and Japan were at the core of civilization. The further away from the core, the more barbarous the culture. Even within what would become modern Japan, the indigenous *Ainu* of the north (present-day Hokkaido) and the *Ryūkyū* of the south (present-day Okinawa) were regarded as less civilized than the "mainland" Japanese, though not as barbarous as those in other parts of Asia or further afield (Morris-Suzuki 1996, 83–84).

The latter half of the Edo Era saw a waning of Chinese influence in Japan as scholars of the *kokugaku* (National Learning) school set out to cleanse Japanese language and learning of Chinese elements. Due to the close and extended links between the two cultures Japan inevitably retained deep Chinese influences, particularly in language, religion, arts, and governance. However, the notion of China as Japan's civilizational superior was losing its hold, a hold that was broken definitively with Japan's defeat of China in the Sino-Japanese War of 1894–1895.

Even before that conflict, however, Chinese influence in Japan was further weakened by the arrival of Westerners on Japan's shores.[4] Although a relatively small number of European traders and Christian missionaries arrived in Japan in the sixteenth century, Edo leaders grew sceptical of their political motivations and eventually either expelled them or strictly circumscribed their activities. However, when US Commodore Matthew Perry arrived with his gunships in 1853, the national Others against whom Japan defined itself radically shifted from China and Asia to the Western powers. Under the threat of superior martial force, Japan agreed to unequal treaties with a number of Western nations. Thus began the first great wave of Westernization in Japan. Arguably it was during this period that Japan first developed what is still commonly referred to as a *konpurekusu* (an inferiority complex) toward the West. While things Western fell from fashion and in some cases were formally banned during the years leading up to and including World War II, Western, especially American, culture was again enthusiastically embraced in the postwar period.

HEIAN COURTLINESS AND THE RISE OF THE SAMURAI

The Heian Era (794–1185) saw the development of two ways of life that would inflect discourses of national identity with gendered meanings even in contemporary Japan: a refined courtly culture and the rise of the samurai. In many ways, the two are in opposition. The Heian court tradition, as captured in the writings of Heian ladies of the court, is most often associated with femininity, gentility, elegance, and emotional sensitivity (Suzuki 2000). By contrast, in the modern national imagination at least, the samurai warriors of the period were characterized by physical strength, courage, austerity, fierce loyalty, and honor. Both of these strands of Heian experience have provided rich and enduring symbols of Japaneseness.

Today, Heian court culture as portrayed in the women's diary literature and novels of the period is often said to epitomize Japanese tastes, values, traditions, and the national character more generally. Works such as *The Pillow Book* (*Makura no sōshi*) and *The Tale of Genji* (*Genji monogatari*) de-emphasized the realm of masculine bravery and heroism, and instead celebrated passion, indulgence, a profound connection with nature, and the beauty of ephemeral experiences—a fleeting glance, a falling cherry blossom, a drop of dew on a kimono sleeve.

Significantly, these were among the first literary works to be written in Japanese script. Through the feudal period, Chinese script was used for scholarly and artistic discourse. However, because Chinese learning was largely considered inappropriate for women, elite women composed their literary works in Japanese phonetic script, then considered an inferior form of expression. However, in the early twentieth century, the Heian courtly literature was celebrated anew for its authentic Japaneseness (Suzuki 2000).[5] This was partly due to the devaluing of the male-dominated Chinese literary tradition after Japan defeated China in the Sino-Japanese War. But the popularity of the Heian women's writings was no doubt also a response to the rapid pace of social change and at least two cataclysmic events, the Great Kantō Earthquake of 1923 and the world economic crisis of 1929–1930.

The first two decades of the twentieth century had seen enormous technological and cultural changes in Japan as it embarked on a project of modernization. It also saw the emergence of the *moga* (modern girl), with her short-cropped hair, her Western-style dress, and her nontraditional attitudes and pursuits. To many social conservatives, the *moga* was both a symptom of Japan's cultural disintegration and a threat to the social order (Menzies 1998). Adding to fears of decline and disorder, the Great Kantō Earthquake claimed an estimated one hundred thousand lives and destroyed roughly 40 percent of the Tokyo metropolitan area. Many Japanese considered the earthquake to be "divine retribution" (*tenken*) for the decadent lifestyle of modern Japan (Weisenfeld 1998, 125). A mere six years after this disaster, the economic crisis of 1929–1930 placed added stress on a nation already burdened with earthquake recovery efforts. All of these developments contributed to a nostalgic turn in Japanese society, a longing for simpler and better days and for the elegant traditions of earlier eras. The Heian courtly literature not only provided an escape from the stresses of modern life, but was held up by some as a model for natural and correct social relations and gender roles (Suzuki 2000, 88).

Although the Heian literature was used to promote conservative notions of the social order early in the twentieth century, it was used in the postwar period as a model for women's liberation and social change more generally (Suzuki 2000, 91). That is, some postwar scholars saw the Heian women writers as paragons of resistance, as an oppressed group who made their voices heard. As dissident postwar intellectuals struggled to forge a more active and politically engaged civil society, the Heian writers served as admirable exemplars, perhaps especially because as elegant ladies of the court they were nonthreatening symbols of resistance and change.

Just as the ladies of the Heian court continue to serve as symbols of authentic Japaneseness, another figure of the period plays a central role in the contemporary national imaginary, the samurai. The samurai emerged as professional warriors during the Heian Era, became the ruling elite under the Tokugawa Shogunate of the Edo Era, and fell from power with the return of the Meiji emperor to the central position of authority. While the structural position of the samurai in Japan changed over time, both the samurai and the notion of *bushidō*, the samurai "warrior code," feature prominently in contemporary discourses of national identity.

Today, certain principles associated with *bushidō*, including courage, discipline, collectivism, loyalty, self-sacrifice, and honor, are commonly claimed as core components of the Japanese national character.[6] Not surprisingly, in the post-World War II era the martial aspects of *bushidō* are typically glossed over or used only metaphorically to describe the "fighting spirit" of the Japanese. Notwithstanding the centrality of notions of *bushidō* in the national imaginary, historical records indicate that this samurai "code" is in fact a more recent invention.

The historical record suggests that during the feudal era when the samurai ruled supreme, there was no unified samurai code of conduct (Hurst 1990; Friday 1994). Only after the samurai became more bureaucrats than warriors did the idea of a warrior's code emerge, and that code was based more on imagination and abstract ideals than on the actual practices of samurai warriors. As Friday (1994, 340) asserts, the retrospective invention of *bushidō* was indicative of "a search for the proper role of a warrior class in a world without war."

Today, the figure of the samurai is a staple of Japanese popular culture. Samurai appear in the staid and stylized productions of *kabuki* theatre and in period films, but also in television soap operas and historical dramas, cartoons and comics, and advertisements for everything from instant noodles to energy drinks and digital cameras. Whether they are presented as moral exemplars or as figures of fun, samurai in contemporary popular culture typically serve as symbolic bearers of national traits. This is easy to see in the samurai epics of contemporary film and television, which tend to have obvious *bushidō*-inspired themes: honor, bravery, selflessness. However, even in comic representations the samurai often embody supposedly national characteristics, including single-minded determination, the ability to endure and persevere, and adherence to strict behavioral codes.

EDO: THE "HIGH-WATER MARK OF JAPANESE CULTURAL TRADITION"

So many of the cultural forms now widely regarded as authentic and distinctive Japanese traditions were developed or elaborated during the Edo Era that historians often consider the period the "high-water mark of Japanese cultural tradition" (Beasley 1999, 171). Not surprisingly then, many aspects of Edo society feature in recent discussions of Japaneseness. While the arts, literature, and leisure pursuits of the period are certainly the hallmarks of the Edo Era, the political, intellectual, and demographic developments of the period have also left a deep mark on contemporary discourses of Japanese national identity.

The Edo Era experienced dramatic urbanization as the Tokugawa Shogunate set up court in Edo (Tokyo) and demanded that regional lords reside for extended periods of time in the new capital city.[7] This urbanization prompted a flowering of urban culture with its teahouses, theatres, and pleasure districts. The gaiety and decadence of this "floating world" (*ukiyo*) of ephemeral pleasures was immortalized in Edo Era woodblock prints (*ukiyo-e*), an enduring source of images of "traditional" Japan. The geisha with her ornate kimono and elaborate coiffure is a frequent subject in the prints, as is the *kabuki* actor striking his dramatic poses. However, while many *ukiyo-e* artists focused on urban life, others also turned to the natural world, perhaps most famously Hokusai Katsushika (1760–1849) in his now-iconic *Thirty-Six Views of Mount Fuji*. Likewise, it was during the Edo Era that Bashō Matsuo (1644–1694), often considered Japan's greatest poet, turned to the natural world for inspiration in his *haiku* poems.

Geisha, *kabuki, ukiyo-e, haiku*. These are but a few of the cultural forms associated with the Edo Era and with Japanese distinctiveness in the popular imagination today. However, the political and intellectual developments of the period also register in contemporary narratives of nation. Politically, the Edo Era saw the fullest development of Japan's feudal system. Although the Emperor maintained a court in Kyoto, real power was in the hands of the Shogun, his administration (*bakufu*), the regional feudal lords (*daimyo*) and their samurai retainers. Today, historians debate the lasting effects of Japanese feudalism. However one prominent view is that part of Japan's cultural uniqueness lies in its continued adherence to elements of feudalism, including rigid social hierarchies, a strong emphasis on shame and honor, and a complex system of duties and loyalties.[8] Whether or not this is actually the case, such arguments have made their way into contemporary discourses of national identity.

Likewise one of the Shogunate's most far-reaching policies, *sakoku*, the "closed country" policy (circa 1640–1854), has left its mark on contemporary national imaginings. Between 1574 and 1580, the *daimyo* Ōmura Sumitada put Nagasaki under the control of Jesuit missionaries and ordered his subjects to convert to Christianity. The Tokugawa Shogunate, sensing a new threat to its power, began expelling foreign priests, executing Christian proselytizers, and barring foreign traders from Japan's ports. By 1640, the *bakufu* had placed strict limits on contacts with the outside world. With a few exceptions, Japanese subjects were forbidden to travel or live abroad, in some cases under penalty of death; virtually all Westerners were expelled from Japan; and most trade with the West was prohibited (Beasley 1999, 136–151). As recent scholars have pointed out, even during this period of self-imposed national isolation, Japan maintained links with China, Korea, and the *Ryūkyū* Islands, so the nation was never truly secluded from outside contact. Nonetheless, contemporary discussions of Japaneseness often suggest that Japan developed a unique culture and a racially and linguistically homogenous population during this period of isolation. Some contemporary authors have even claimed that the Japanese retain a "*sakoku* mentality" which hampers their ability to interact with foreigners and prevents their full participation in globalization (Itoh 1998).

Recent discussions of Japanese distinctiveness often naturalize this isolationist mentality with the claim that because Japan is an "island nation" (*shima guni*) it has developed a particularly original, exclusive, and cohesive insular society. This now widespread and well-accepted proposition can be traced back at least to one of the Edo Era's leading intellectuals, Motoori Norinaga (1730–1801) who drew on the creation stories of the *Kojiki* to suggest that the Japanese had a special relationship with nature. As descendants of the creator deities, he suggested, the Japanese people were one with the land itself, and therefore had a deep, innate, and unique sensitivity to the natural world (Morris-Suzuki 1998, 47–49).[9]

Motoori's ideas are reflected in the writings of twentieth-century philosophers and folklorists who assert that Japan's unique social structure and national character have been profoundly shaped by its natural environment, and specifically by its reliance on rice paddy agriculture which demands synchronized communal activity.[10] While such assertions are not always framed in explicitly racial terms, in contemporary discussions of Japanese national identity there is often a fine line between a kind of environmental determinism and the biological determinism characteristic of ethnic nationalism.

The arts, literature, scholarship, and politics of the Edo Era have left a rich legacy for gendered and racialized discourses of Japanese national identity. Perhaps the two most abiding icons of the era are the geisha, symbolizing the "floating world" of Edo's vibrant urban culture, and the samurai, the key representative of militarized feudalism. Both national icons carry with them a clear and conservative gender ideology. At the same time, the Edo Era policy of national isolation (*sakoku*) is often understood today to have created a monoracial, monolinguistic, monocultural nation. While some Japanese scholars have seen this as a source of Japan's strength (even superiority) and others have seen it as an impediment to national progress in a globalizing world, most have considered this homogeneity itself to be a fact beyond dispute.

MODERNIZATION AND THE INVENTION OF TRADITION

Japan's national isolation came to an abrupt end in 1853–1854 when US Commodore Perry arrived to forcibly open Japanese ports and markets to the West. This dramatic development set in motion events that would lead to the creation of Japan as a modern nation-state and a national imagined community. The Tokugawa Shogunate collapsed under pressure from those who were angered by the Shogun's capitulation to foreign powers. With the demise of the feudal order and the ascendency of the Meiji emperor, the nation rallied around the slogan "Rich country, strong military" (*fukoku kyōhei*), hopeful that rapid modernization and social and political reform would allow Japan to stave off foreign encroachment and compete with the West as a nation among equals. The new Meiji state quickly recognized the need to forge national consensus and unity, and toward this end they set about revising, elaborating, and inventing a national symbology and mythology. Many of these symbols, myths, and invented traditions are evident in today's discourses of national identity.

Establishing the legitimacy of the emperor and the imperial system was seen by Meiji ruling elites to be crucial to the unification of the nation. Drawing on ancient texts such as the *Kojiki* and *Nihon shoki*, imperial scholars stressed the semi-divine status of the emperor, his descent from the Sun Goddess, and his role as the high priest of Shinto.[11] New rituals made him a key figure in seasonal Shinto rites to ensure the fertility and safety of the land and its people (Amino 1996; Ohnuki-Tierney 1993). The new concept of Japan as a "family state" (*kazoku kokka*) positioned the emperor as the father of the nation. Certainly in a culture which had historically embraced the Confucian value of filial piety, transforming the emperor into the national patriarch was a politically shrewd way to strengthen the allegiance and loyalty of the people. Moreover, the *kazoku-kokka* ideology, perhaps unintentionally, promoted the notion of the Japanese as a biologically distinct group, with all members of the national community linked through national kinship. Consequently, both the people and the nation itself were biologized and conceptualized as a "national body" (*kokutai*).

Increasing acceptance and reverence for the emperor system (*tennōsei*) was just one of the Meiji state projects designed to centralize authority and therefore strengthen the nation. Under the banner of "civilization and enlightenment" (*bunmei kaika*), ruling elites launched comprehensive reforms of criminal, commercial, and family law, of taxation, of the military, of the education, banking and class systems, and of industry, among others (Beasley 2000, 210–229). Japan rapidly modernized and became at least superficially Westernized. Western-style clothing, hairstyles, music, leisure activities, and food began to displace older Japanese forms. Arguably the enormity of such changes only further fuelled the simultaneous quest for "authentic" Japanese traditions, which the state readily supplied.

In one prominent example, the Meiji Crown Prince was married in 1900 in a Shinto ceremony, with ritual sake drinking, offerings to the Shinto deities, and elaborate Heian-style twelve-layered kimono (*jūnihitoe*). While the ceremony was promoted as an ancient tradition of the imperial family, most of its elements were recent innovations by Meiji elites who felt that the wholly secular weddings customary in Japan lacked the solemnity and grandeur of Western religious ceremonies.[12] Subsequent imperial weddings have incorporated these same elements, and as a result today they are widely viewed as ancient practices. After the 1993 wedding of the Crown Prince, for instance, newspapers in Japan and worldwide reported that the wedding followed a 1600-year-old tradition.

Just as the Shinto wedding is now widely believed to be an ancient tradition, Japan's *ie* family system is popularly regarded as an ancient institution. The *ie* family system is a hierarchically organized system of stem and branch families, each of which is ideally headed by a patriarch. Prior to the Meiji Era this family system was found only among the wealthy ruling elites to whom succession and inheritance were matters of utmost concern. However, the Meiji state made the *ie* family mandatory for all Japanese. This standardized system facilitated more accurate public record-keeping, which in turn increased the efficacy of taxation and conscription programs. It also placed all family members more firmly under the control of the male head of household, and put the househead more firmly under the control of the state.[13] While the *ie* system is no longer mandatory, it continues to be seen as an ancient and authentic Japanese tradition and an ideal to which to aspire.

The mandatory adoption of the *ie* family system in the Meiji Era had particularly significant effects on the status and roles of Japanese women. With the formalization of male authority in the household, women saw their rights and autonomy eroded in matters such as choosing a spouse, initiating divorce, and owning property, and female sexuality was closely monitored. At the same time, as part of the emphasis on hearth and home in the "family state," Meiji elites promoted a gender ideology that defined women as "good wives, wise mothers" (*ryōsai kenbo*) above all else. The public school curriculum, government pamphlets, and many newly emerging women's magazines reinforced the notion that women should place husband, children, and home above all else. Much of this ideology was adapted from the so-called "cult of domesticity" predominant in Victorian Britain and America.

The Meiji Era produced many of the symbols, icons, and ideologies that still feature in discourses of national identity today. While the emperor is no longer represented as a human-divine, the imperial family remains a powerful symbol of Japan's ancient cultural heritage. The depth of the nation's history features prominently in contemporary discourses of national identity. Japan, an old, venerable, and unchanging nation, is contrasted with the young, brash, energetic, and highly changeable nations of the West, exemplified by the US. Today, a foreigner's inquiry about Japanese national identity is likely to elicit an explanation beginning with the simple expression *mukashi kara*—"since ancient times" it has been so.

Meiji innovations likewise inflect current racialized and gendered imaginings of the nation. While few today would refer to Japan as a "national body" (*kokutai*) or suggest a close organic kinship among all Japanese, the notion of Japan as a monoracial nation is widespread (Hogan 2002).[14] In terms of gendered national imaginings, while the roles of women have changed dramatically in the postwar period, much of the gender ideology assiduously cultivated by Meiji elites is still in evidence today. In-depth interviews with Japanese respondents in the late 1990s revealed a strong association between "Japaneseness" and what is essentially the "good wife, wise mother" archetype—kimono-clad, gentle and elegant, a woman devoting her life to family and home (Hogan 2002). Likewise, although the *ie* family is no longer the dominant family form in Japan, it persists as an ideal in the popular imagination. The widespread belief that the *ie* family is an ancient and authentically Japanese tradition both reflects and naturalizes patriarchal social relations.

MILITARISM, EMPIRE BUILDING, AND ULTRANATIONALISM

As the nineteenth century drew to a close, Japan embarked on roughly fifty years of warfare, beginning with the Sino-Japanese war (1894–1895) and ending in 1945 with defeat in World War II. The period was characterized by militarism and nationalism made possible by reforms instituted by the Meiji state. Most obviously, the state reformed the military, incorporating Western technology and training, introducing conscription, and building a well-equipped modern navy. However, these changes also required a reformed taxation system to raise revenue, a reformed census to keep track of possible recruits, and improved coordination between industry and state. In addition, public support for the frequent wars was cultivated through a newly established public education system and an expanding mass media. Images and experiences from this tumultuous period in the history of modern Japan have had lasting effects on national self-conceptions.

The Sino-Japanese War (1894–1895) and the Russo-Japanese War (1904–1905) redefined Japan's relationship with its two most powerful Others, China and the West. With Japan's definitive victory in the Sino-Japanese War, China lost forever its once-dominant position in Japan's national imaginary, a position that had been gradually eroding since the Tokugawa period. In addition, Japan imposed an onerous settlement on the Chinese, reaping substantial territories and large compensation payments which the Meiji state used to further strengthen its military (Beasley 1999, 230–234). Similarly, victory over Russia in 1905 was both symbolically and materially significant. For the first time since being forced to sign unequal treaties with the Western powers in the mid-nineteenth century, Japan was in the position to dictate to a Western nation. The Meiji state's dream of competing with the West as an equal seemed to be coming true. In material terms, the Russo-Japanese War gave Japan control over southern Manchuria with its vast mineral reserves and its crucial position as a gateway to China. The acquisition provided much-needed raw materials for Japan's rapidly expanding industrial sector, enhanced its status as a regional power, and provided Japan's leadership with both the confidence and the means to embark on what would become a massive empire-building project.

In the Taishō Era (1912–1926), while Europe and the US were embroiled in the First World War, Japan devoted itself to industrialization and foreign trade, and was able to move effectively into markets temporarily abandoned by the West. By the close of the war, Japan's economy was robust and many Japanese, particularly in the younger generation, were enjoying fashions and fads imported from the West. But doubt and discontent grew with the global economic crisis of the late 1920s and early 1930s, providing an opening for nationalist and militarist factions to gain popularity with calls to reject decadent Western ways, take pride in Japan's ancient traditions, and assume leadership of the Asia-Pacific region.

As part of Japan's efforts to consolidate its influence in Asia, in 1940 the Shōwa state introduced the notion of the Greater East Asia Co-Prosperity Sphere (*Daitō-A Kyōeiken*). Even as Japan was invading and colonizing territories throughout Asia and the Pacific, it was legitimizing its expansionism with claims that it was actually liberating and protecting its Asian neighbors from the West. Successful attacks on Western powers in Pearl Harbor, Singapore, Hong Kong, Manilla, and Kuala Lumpur stoked Japanese national confidence and gave the Co-prosperity Sphere an air of inevitability.

Nationalist ideology and symbols were in crescendo: the emperor was a benevolent human-divine guiding Asia toward its destiny; military heroes were fighting for the just cause of resistance against the West; and the honest farmer and the "good wife, wise mother" toiled on the home front to support the war effort. Cherry blossoms (*sakura*), which had featured prominently in the national symbology at least as far back as the *Kojiki* and *Nihon shoki*, were increasingly employed to symbolize both the nation and its military defenders.[15] The fleeting beauty of the blossoms was a poignant metaphor for the young lives given in service of emperor and nation. At Yasukuni Shrine, erected during the Meiji Era to commemorate fallen soldiers, the weeping cherry trees were said to shelter and comfort the souls of the war dead. The cherry blossom was incorporated into Japanese military insignia and became closely associated with the euphemistically named Special Attack Forces (*tokkōtai*), the suicide attack squads commonly known as *kamikaze* in the West. The term *kamikaze* (or *shinpū*) is usually glossed in English as "divine wind," a concept dating back to the attempted Mongol invasion of Japan in 1281 when the enemy forces were decimated by a typhoon, seen by many in Japan as divine intervention. This use of images and icons sacralized the war effort: the soldiers, the emperor, and the nation were fulfilling a divine mission to unify and stabilize the region.[16]

The Western enemy, on the other hand, was demonized, sometimes quite literally, as in the case of propaganda cartoons that represented enemy troops as devils (Nornes, Komatsuzawa, and Yamane 1994a, 192). While Japanese representations of the Allies were not as explicitly racist as the American anti-Japanese propaganda of the time, the enemy was consistently portrayed as cruel, rapacious, and without honor (Nornes, Komatsuzawa, and Yamane 1994b, 240). Such representations were strategically used by the military to terrify civilians, making it unlikely that they would collude with the enemy, and increasing the likelihood that they would commit suicide rather than risk capture by foreign troops. This was most pronounced in Okinawa where 160,000 civilians lost their lives, many to so-called honorable mass suicide (*shudan jiketsu*).[17]

Honorable suicide, whether by civilians, *kamikaze* (*tokkōtai*) pilots, or ground troops, was in a sense legitimated by beliefs that in the *bushidō* tradition, the samurai were required to take their own lives rather than dishonor themselves, their families, or their lords. However in the postwar period, wartime suicides have often featured in constructions of Japan and the Japanese as victims of the war.[18] This national sense of victimization is most evident today in discussions of the atomic bombings of Nagasaki and Hiroshima in August 1945. Photos, film footage, artefacts, and eyewitness accounts are vivid reminders of the horrific deaths suffered by tens of thousands of Japanese civilians in the attacks.[19] Such images feature prominently in competing discourses of national identity today, both those generated by ultranationalist groups who deny that Japan was an aggressor in the war, and those by pacifist and antinuclear groups who focus on the unique capacity of Japan, as the only nation to have experienced an atomic attack, to serve as a world leader of peace and nuclear disarmament movements.

This extended period of warfare left its mark on gendered and racialized discourses of national identity. Both masculine and feminine national archetypes were strengthened during this period, most prominently the heroic soldier and the "good wife, wise mother." Such figures reinforced a conservative gender ideology in which men were public and active and women were domestic and passive. This was reflected to some extent in the labor trends of the period. Women textile workers had constituted more than 80 percent of Japan's early industrial workforce. However as Japan's militarist expansion increased, the textile factories were replaced by heavy industries, and female workers were replaced by male workers. By 1940, 60 percent of workers in the industrial workforce were men (Brinton 1993, 113–118). Women were encouraged to return to the home and contribute to the war effort by bearing sons, being thrifty homemakers, joining patriotic societies, and maintaining hearth, home, and tradition while their men served in the military. The image of the self-sacrificing, self-deprecating wife and mother still features prominently in discourses of Japaneseness.[20] The heroic soldier, on the other hand, has been transformed into the hardworking businessman (*sarariman*) of the postwar period. His military uniform and weapons have been replaced by a business suit and briefcase. But he still sacrifices his own health and welfare for the greater good, sometimes even suffering death by overwork (*karoshi*).

Japan's modern wars also reshaped the nation's conceptions of race in complex ways. On one hand the rhetoric of the Greater East Asia Co-Prosperity Sphere encouraged the Japanese to recognize an ethnic, and sometimes racial, affinity with the peoples of Asia. On the other hand, Japan's colonial policies and practices were often brutal, both reflecting and further fuelling a sense of natural superiority over the rest of Asia. At the same time, the Allied forces were a powerful Other, and were at times dehumanized or racialized in wartime propaganda. However, Japan simultaneously cultivated alliances with Germany and Italy. Such alliances no doubt complicated representations of the Western Other in wartime Japan, perhaps explaining why images of the enemy tended to be less racialized than American images of the Japanese.[21]

On the home front, representations of the *Ryūkyū* people were likewise complex. Long considered racially inferior outsiders by the Japanese, they were subjected to harsh treatment by the Japanese military. Nonetheless, stories of civilian deaths, especially honorable suicides, in Okinawa became metaphors for the nation's suffering and sacrifice. Meanwhile, with a growing need for troops, the Japanese state decided to conscript soldiers from two marginalized groups within Japanese society, the indigenous *Ainu* of the north and the *Burakumin*, or "untouchables," who had previously been barred from serving in the imperial forces. The change in policy somewhat reduced the Otherness of these two groups (Ohnuki-Tierney 2002, 81).

POSTWAR RECONSTRUCTIONS

Along with the reconstruction of Japan's physical infrastructure, economy, and political system in the postwar period, discourses of national identity underwent substantial renovations. Many of the icons, symbols, and ideologies dominant from the Meiji Era through the end of World War II were rendered meaningless or distasteful by the nation's defeat. This sparked far-ranging transformations of national self-conceptions in the postwar period.

From God to Man, From Heroes to Criminals

The Emperor, constructed since the Meiji Era as father of the nation, head of both state and Shinto, and direct descendent of the Sun Goddess, was forced by the Allied occupiers to publicly deny his divinity. State Shinto was dismantled and the Emperor was stripped of political authority. While he remained a symbol of the nation, both his mystique and his material power were greatly diminished.

At the same time, many of the nation's wartime leaders, who had served as national exemplars in the mould of the samurai and Shogun, were now disgraced. Their policies and pronouncements during the war were increasingly regarded as violations of the public trust and demonstrations of a callous disregard for the lives of both soldiers and civilians. Twenty-five leaders, mainly cabinet members and military commanders, were convicted as Class A war criminals by the International Military Tribunal for the Far East, and seven of them were executed. Wartime heroes and national icons such as General and Prime Minister Tōjō Hideki were transformed into symbols of shame.

From Militarism to Pacifism

Other key national symbols, such as the national flag (the *Hinomaru*) and the national anthem (*Kimigayo*) became subjects of contention due to their association with Japanese militarism. After fifty years of war, the Japanese people were embracing Article IX of the new Constitution, which renounced war and pledged not to maintain any armed forces for the purposes of waging war. In this context, national icons such as the cherry blossom were stripped of their martial associations to become the symbolic bearers of Japanese "tradition," reminders of a simpler time, of natural beauty, of purity and quietude, of an idealized ancient Japan.

From Repelling to "Domesticating" the West

At the height of Japan's ultranationalism, once popular Western imports were shunned or even banned. Western popular music and cinema all but disappeared and the Japanese language was, as much as possible, cleansed of Western loanwords. The "modern girl" (*moga*) and "modern boy" (*mobo*) with their Western fashions and fancies were objects of ridicule for their decidedly un-Japanese ways. The postwar period saw a dramatic reversal of this anti-Western orientation. While consumption of Western goods in the immediate postwar years was limited by financial constraints, once Japan's economy strengthened, Western and particularly American imports were enthusiastically embraced. From fashion to pop songs, from home furnishings to whiskey to automobiles, Western goods and practices were associated with modernity, affluence, and cosmopolitanism.

In the West, Japan gained a reputation as a great imitator, or in less flattering terms, a thief of other nations' intellectual and cultural property. However, as Tobin (1992) has pointed out, such borrowing was not so much wholesale adoption of Western ways as the adaptation of selected practices and products to the Japanese context, a process he calls "domestication." This very adaptability itself was soon identified by Japanese scholars as a national trait which helped explain the nation's extraordinary economic success in the postwar period (Dale 1986, 51).

From Imperialism to International Engagement

With the failure of Japan's plan to integrate and rule the Asia-Pacific region by force of arms, the postwar Japanese state adopted new strategies for rebuilding and strengthening the nation: democratization (*minshuka*) in the 1950s, modernization (*kindaika*) in the 1960s, and, finally, internationalization (*kokusaika*) from the 1970s onward.[22] In 1984, Prime Minister Nakasone Yasuhiro declared Japan an "international state" (*kokusai kokka*) (Itoh 1998); and, since that time, *kokusaika* has become a cherished slogan of state, business, and academic elites, as well as the popular media. The public has embraced Japan's new internationalist identity through practices such as foreign language learning, travelling and studying abroad, sampling foreign cuisine, and avidly consuming foreign films, music, and fashions (Hogan 2002, 2004).

From Demons to Guests,
From "Good Wives, Wise Mothers" to OLs

With intensifying internationalization, Japanese attitudes toward foreigners, ethnoracial minorities, and gender roles shifted dramatically. Westerners, once demonized in wartime propaganda, were now generally treated as guests, albeit often unruly and somewhat unwelcome guests. In areas with a high concentration of Westerners, such as in Okinawa with its massive American military presence, tensions between the two groups were palpable. However, throughout the nation, Westerners, particularly white Westerners, became increasingly accepted and even sought after. Advertisers, in particular, employed foreign models to lend Japanese products an air of Western glamor. Nonwhite and non-Western foreigners, however, were still largely regarded with suspicion, and associated in the popular imagination with crime, violence, and disorder (Hogan 2002).

Postwar internationalization also heightened awareness in Japan of issues related to racial and ethnic discrimination. Japan's main minority groups, the *Ainu*, *Burakumin*, and resident Koreans and Chinese, experienced some legal gains starting in the 1960s with the strengthening of indigenous rights and civil rights movements worldwide, but still faced substantial barriers to full equality.[23] In recent decades, the *Ryūkyū*, long considered "backward, lazy, inefficient, prone to insanity, irrational and unhygienic" by mainland Japanese, have promoted themselves as exemplars of internationalization, a people with a rich tradition of "bridging cultures" (Barclay 2006, 120, 126). In this way, the *kokusaika* project has somewhat reduced the marginality of the *Ryūkyū* in Japan. They still nonetheless remain on the geographic, economic, and cultural periphery of the nation.

Gender roles and gender ideology changed so dramatically in the postwar period that any discussion here can be only cursory.[24] In terms of shifting female archetypes, however, it is clear that in the postwar period women became less biologized. In feudal Japan elite women were known as "borrowed wombs" (*hara wakarimono*); that is, public discourse defined them almost exclusively in terms of their reproductive capacity. In the Meiji Era through the end of World War II, "good" women were "good wives, wise mothers" (*ryōsai kenbo*), combining their biological role with social roles including the nurturing and education of children, the organization and maintenance of the household, and participation in patriotic and civic activities.[25] In the postwar period, while the "good wife, wise mother" is still a powerful image in the popular imagination and in popular culture, it exists alongside images of working women, most prominently the *OL* (office lady) and the *paato* (part-time employee).

The *OL* is usually represented as young and single, carefree and consumerist, spending her salary on fashion and travel. While there is clearly a continuity between the *OL* and the earlier "modern girl," the *OL* is not considered radical, rebellious, or dangerous to the social order. Rather, *OL* is a temporary status, a stage in a woman's transition from parental control to the assumption of her role as wife and mother. The *paato*, on the other hand, is generally represented as a married woman with older children, working part-time both for personal satisfaction and to meet the children's extra educational and leisure expenses. So, while she is engaged in paid labor, she assumes this public role as part of her domestic responsibilities. The *OL* and *paato* do not, therefore, challenge the "good wife, wise mother" ideology; rather, the three archetypes work together to reinforce the primacy of women's domestic responsibilities.

From Ultranationalism to Cultural Nationalism

The vast cultural, political, and economic changes of the postwar period sparked a national quest for Japanese identity, partly out of fears that Japan was losing its cultural traditions, and partly out of a need to explain the nation's dramatic transformation from fallen empire to economic superpower. By the 1980s, with Japan at the apex of its economic miracle, the nation was in the midst of what Ivy (1995) has called a "nostalgia boom." Department stores stocked Japanese handicrafts and offered Japanese cultural enrichment classes; travel agencies offered silk-weaving holidays and tours of "exotic Japan"; and municipalities inaugurated festivals to celebrate rediscovered (or newly invented) local "traditions" (*dentō*).[26]

This growing nostalgia and search for cultural authenticity was at the same time reflected in the rise of theories of Japaneseness. The vast body of writing known as the *Nihonjinron* (discourses of Japanese uniqueness) encompasses the work of academics and popular writers alike. While some of the work is empirically based and some is merely speculative or moralistic, the writings all share a concern for the supposedly unique characteristics of Japanese culture and the Japanese people. Some of the treatises focus on biological traits: a uniquely Japanese nose that is more sensitive than that of other races; a uniquely Japanese digestive tract that has difficulty breaking down foreign beef; a uniquely Japanese brain that processes language differently than non-Japanese brains.[27] Others focus on the effects of climate, geography, and subsistence activities on social organization and social psychology: for instance, the notion that wet rice cultivation necessitated close cooperation and communal living to such a degree that Japanese people now intuitively understand each other, even without resorting to spoken language.[28]

Nihonjinron writings have been used both to explain Japan's postwar success and to justify certain national policies and practices such as restricting immigration to maintain racial and cultural homogeneity and limiting agricultural imports in consideration of the unique Japanese physiology. They have also served to combat the Orientalist stereotypes to which Japan has been subjected since it opened its doors to the West in the Meiji Era. The *Nihonjinron* are therefore usefully characterized as reverse Orientalist discourses. That is, they exoticize Japan and the Japanese through the typical Orientalist tropes identified by Said (1978), while inverting the effects of these tropes by making the "exotic" and "unique" a source of nationalist pride.

While some *Nihonjinron* authors focus on innate biological characteristics, Yoshino (1992) has argued that the *Nihonjinron* are, above all, implicated in rising cultural nationalism in postwar Japan. Cultural nationalism, he writes, "aims to regenerate the national community by creating, preserving or strengthening a people's cultural identity when it is felt to be lacking, inadequate or threatened" (1992, 1). Japan's cultural identity has been "threatened" in the postwar period by rapid modernization, Westernization, and internationalization. Assertions of Japanese uniqueness are a defensive response to these perceived threats, and the success of the *Nihonjinron* "industry" suggests a postwar shift from militarist ultranationalism to commercialized cultural nationalism.

NATIONAL AMBIVALENCE

Japan experienced an economic downturn in the 1990s, the effects of which has extended well into the first decade of the new millennium. The bursting of the "bubble" economy presented further challenges to national self-conceptions. The exceptionalism of the *Nihonjinron* was firmly predicated on Japan's extraordinary postwar successes. If Japan was no longer "Number One," as Ezra Vogel (1979) famously asserted, then claims of national uniqueness and even superiority rang hollow. It was in this context that national ambivalence over Japan's place in the world, and its very identity as a nation, came into sharper focus.

Perhaps the clearest instance of this ambivalence in contemporary Japan is the ongoing tug-of-war between particularism and universalism, and, more generally, between tradition and change. Postwar social changes have been so rapid and so dramatic that the older generation sometimes refers to younger Japanese as *shinjinrui* (a "new human species"). Discomfiture over these changes, as noted earlier, has led to a longing for "tradition," for simplicity and stability, for an idealized past. The *Nihonjinron*, with their emphasis on autochthonous Japanese traits help satisfy this nostalgic longing. While the particularist claims of the *Nihonjinron* appear to run counter to the universalist claims of the internationalization (*kokusaika*) project, the two are closely interconnected. That is, the process of internationalization has challenged long-standing notions of Japanese national identity and prompted a more earnest search for unique national traits. As Befu (1983,

241) has observed, ironically "the very processes of internationalization which are supposedly making Japanese more cosmopolitan have the unexpected effect of making Japanese more nationalistic. . . . Internationalization promotes 'anti-internationalization.' "

Ambivalence over Japanese national identity is also clearly evident in vigorous debates over the interpretation of Japan's role in World War II. The key question is whether Japan should remember the war as an act of aggression and expansionism, or as a failed but well-intentioned attempt to protect the Asia-Pacific region from predation by the Western powers. Domestic and international disputes focus most prominently on five issues: the continued use of the flag (the *Hinomaru*) and anthem (*Kimigayo*) that represented imperial Japan; the official visits of Japanese prime ministers to Yasukuni Shrine, dedicated to Japan's fallen soldiers and enshrining fourteen Class-A war criminals; the government censorship of school textbooks in ways that gloss over Japan's acts of aggression and wartime atrocities; the lack of official apologies to Japan's victims in the war, including prisoners of war and the so-called "Comfort Women" forced into prostitution by the Japanese military; and the perceived violation of Japan's Constitutionally mandated pacifism with the nation's recent military missions abroad, particularly the Self Defence Force (SDF) deployment to Iraq in 2004.

At the heart of these issues are questions of national self-image. Was Japan the prime offender or just another victim of the war?[29] How can it come to terms with its wartime actions without dishonoring its war dead? Should Japan still embrace the pacifism essentially imposed on the nation by the Allied powers, or should it now reassess Article IX in light of its new position in the world? Has Japan truly become a global actor, or does it remain an island nation with a "*sakoku* mentality"? And should it identify more closely with the West or with Asia? Specifically, should it ally itself with the US even though such an alliance provokes the fear and suspicion of its Asian neighbors?

National ambivalence is likewise apparent in discussions of the presumed homogeneity and collectivism of Japan and the Japanese.[30] Although the notion of Japan as a cohesive, organically connected unit is still widespread (Lie 2001; Weiner 1997a), recent developments have challenged this assumption. First, labor shortages in the 1980s led to an unprecedented wave of migration, mainly from elsewhere in Asia. Although the number of foreigners was small, reaching around 1 percent of the population in the early 1990s, and although migrants typically filled low-wage and undesirable jobs, immigration captured the popular imagination as one of the nation's most serious social problems (Lie 2001, 6–26). Foreigners, especially non-white foreigners, were believed to bring crime, drugs, disease, and disorder to Japan, and many Japanese began to fear an imminent "race problem" (*jinshu mondai*) as the result of miscegenation (Hogan 2002). The Japanese would eventually lose their distinctive traits, and social harmony would be undermined by increasing numbers of mixed-race children, who could not be regarded as truly Japanese. While such fears were unfounded, their widespread articulation reveals the power of the "illusion of homogeneity" in Japan (Weiner 1997).

Even more dramatically and traumatically, the 1995 nerve gas attacks on the Tokyo subway system by the *Aum Shinrikyō* doomsday cult exposed deep fissures in what many assumed was a unified society. The attacks which injured more than five thousand people and killed twelve, were carried out by a well-educated, well-funded, and tightly knit group of Japanese who shared the belief in an imminent global war that would destroy all but a chosen few. In the saturation media coverage that followed the attacks extensive attention was given to members' motivations for joining the cult. One of the most popular explanations was that in an age of weakening values, beliefs, and collective social life, *Aum* provided its members with meaning, structure, and a sense of community (Iida 2002, 237–244). The *Aum* attacks simultaneously provoked anxieties about postwar social changes, raised the spectre of "enemies within," and undermined the comforting image of Japan as a uniform and unified organic whole.

"ON SHAKY GROUND:" THE UNCERTAIN STATE OF JAPANESE NATIONAL IDENTITY

As the twentieth century drew to a close, Japanese people in a variety of social locations were expressing concerns about their nation's rapid cultural and demographic changes, changes perceived by some to threaten Japan's distinctive national identity. As Ms. Honda, a teacher, put it:

> A long time ago, in my grandmother's generation, there was a Japanese identity . . . But I think the kind of Japanese ethnic consciousness people used to have in common is now fading . . . I think the national identity of the Japanese is on shaky ground.[31]

The perilous state of Japan's national identity was most often associated with the growing numbers of foreigners in the nation. Certainly postwar constructions of the *Nihonjinron*, Japanese homogeneity, and the "foreign worker problem" reveal a strong ethnoracial component to national self-conceptions. Such racialized discourses of national identity obscure or problematize the presence of ethnoracial Others in Japan, and thus contribute to the continued marginalization of these groups. In addition, racialized discourses of Japanese identity ultimately serve the interests of the Japanese state, by making it possible to ignore the real material disadvantages facing these marginalized groups. If they are not acknowledged as part of the national community it is not necessary to address their needs (see Mouer and Sugimoto 1983, 1986).

While matters of race and ethnicity have featured prominently in recent discussion of national identity in Japan, there has been little explicit discussion of the contemporary gendering of Japanese identity in the scholarly or popular press.[32] Nonetheless, my own research in rural Japan found a strong association between perceived Japaneseness and "traditional" femininity (Hogan 2002). However, nontraditional women—for instance, those who choose not to marry or have children, or high-achieving career women— rarely feature in contemporary discourses of national identity, except perhaps as examples of particularly un-Japanese behavior, the kind of behavior commonly associated with the "shaky" state of Japanese national identity today.

4 Discourses of National Identity in Britain

Any discussion of British national identity is complicated by the frequent conflation of Britishness and Englishness. Certainly in the modern era with the political and economic ascendency of England over Scotland, Wales, and Northern Ireland, there has been a tendency outside the "Celtic fringe" to equate British national identity with English identity. Most recently, however, with political devolution, reassertions of Welsh and Scottish identities, ongoing disputes over the control of Northern Ireland, and a growing recognition of the multicultural and multiracial nature of British society, English dominance of the national imagery has been increasingly challenged. The discussion here focuses on discourses of British identity, the symbols and icons, epochs and experiences that have inflected discourses of belonging throughout the nation. Nonetheless it is crucial to acknowledge that multiple and competing discourses of nation are constructed in different regions of the country, and to some Britons regional symbols and stories may be more powerful markers of nation than those shared by the national community as a whole.

Of course the United Kingdom of Great Britain, as a national designation, dates back only to 1707.[1] But national imagery seldom confines itself to the actual period of nationhood. Rather, discourses of national identity routinely reach back into the primordial past seeking out the earliest imaginable traces of nation and national character. The deeper the roots, the stronger the tree.

Some of the earliest national archetypes, from Britannia to King Arthur and Robin Hood, have proven enduring and flexible signifiers of nation. Such icons still carry salient meanings about the land and its people, even as new symbols and discourses have become fixtures in the national imaginary. Again, what follows is not intended as an exhaustive survey of British national identity. Such an undertaking would be not only monumental but futile due to the inherent changeability of narratives of nation. Rather, this overview focuses on the gendered and racialized images reflected in current discourses of British national identity.

BRITANNIA AND JOHN BULL

As one of the oldest of British national icons, Britannia warrants consideration here. Britannia is best known today as the personification of Britain, typically portrayed as a woman dressed in flowing robes and carrying a shield and a trident. However, Britannia was originally simply the Latin name given to the British territories by Roman occupiers in the first century BC.[2] It was not until the rule of Hadrian (AD 117–138) that Britannia was represented in human form, usually as a goddess in Roman dress and a Centurion's helmet, and often in a submissive posture. Britannia regularly appeared on coins during the Roman period, but then virtually disappeared for almost a thousand years before enjoying a comeback in the eighteenth century.

It was common in eighteenth- and nineteenth-century Europe to personify nations in female form: "Marianne" of France, "Aura" of Finland, "Germania" of Germany. With the unification of England, Scotland, and Wales, Britannia became a symbol of the newly established national union. Later, as Britain expanded its empire to control roughly a quarter of the world's population, Britannia also became a symbol of the empire—an imperial mother, holding her colonial children in her embrace.

Britannia has long embodied national ideals. In her usual modern incarnations, she is a paragon of British femininity, beautiful, nurturing, and fair, while also exhibiting masculine agency, with her Centurion's helmet, her shield and trident symbolizing Britain's martial power. As Hunt's (2003) study of British caricature art and satire demonstrates, however, representations of Britannia have changed along with changing social norms. Hunt identifies the 1780s as a watershed moment for depictions of Britannia (2003, 140). In the lead-up to the 1784 Westminster election, Hunt explains, society women were playing an unusually active role in political campaigning, a role many considered unseemly for the "fairer sex." In the midst of concerns over women's expanding political influence, Hunt asserts, Britannia's more masculine, more agentic traits were deemphasized, and her feminine passivity and vulnerability came to the fore.

By the 1790s, Britannia "usually appeared as a helpless female needing masculine assistance" (Hunt 2003, 139), a beautiful damsel in distress, vulnerable to attack both by corrupt and incompetent politicians at home and by foreign invaders. In some cases, her rescuer came in the form of another national icon, John Bull. Satirist John Arbuthnot had first created the character of John Bull in 1712. While John Bull has assumed many forms over the years—a soldier, a sailor, a country rustic, a squire, and a member of the urban middle class, among others—he has consistently embodied what are presumed to be central traits of the English, or even the British, national character: loyalty, courage, common sense, and patriotism. At the turn of the nineteenth century, amidst rising concerns over women's engagement in the public sphere, John Bull could exemplify an active, assertive nation in ways that Britannia could not. Political cartoons of the period feature John Bull leaping boldly to the defense of gentle Britannia, representations which both reflected and endorsed conventional gender roles.[3]

KING ARTHUR AND ROBIN HOOD

As national heroes and national icons of Britain, perhaps none have been so enduring and so highly elaborated as King Arthur and Robin Hood. Arthurian tales date back at least to the ninth century, and the first written references to Robin Hood appear in the fourteenth century.[4] Sometimes tragic and sometimes comedic, the heroes have been staples in literature, pantomime, drama, songs, and most recently films. However the historicity of both figures is a matter of perennial debate. Although the British landscape is strewn with historical markers claimed as birthplaces, graves, and other places of note in the tales of these two men, scholars and devotees have not reached a consensus on when, where, or indeed whether the "real" Arthur and Robin Hood existed. Nonetheless, despite these historical uncertainties, Arthur and Robin Hood have proven impressively flexible archetypes of national identity, changing in response to alterations in national circumstances.

Early references to Arthur constructed him as a kind of Welsh warlord, a Celt battling against barbaric Saxon invaders.[5] Not surprisingly then, Arthur has served as a rallying point for Welsh nationalism through the ages. However, beginning with the Norman Conquest of 1066, the Welsh began to lose their exclusive claims on the legend. As the Normans displaced and dominated both Saxon and Celt, Arthur was transformed from a Welshman to a pan-national figure, and from a mere warlord to a king. After 1066, references to Arthur frequently evoked a prophecy that he would rise again when the nation was most in need. In the context of colonization by a foreign power, Arthur became the "once and future king," amalgam of Celt and Saxon, promising to defeat the colonizer.

Over time, however, Arthur began to shed his Celtic and revolutionary traits to become a symbol of ruling class beneficence and moral superiority.[6] The Arthurian romances of the twelfth through the fifteenth centuries, drawing on French literary conventions, portrayed Arthur as a chivalrous and selfless leader laboring for the good of his people and the glory of God. The romances also reflected the concerns of the day. Sir Thomas Malory wrote his celebrated *Le Morte d'Arthur* (circa 1470) in the midst of the War of the Roses. The chaos, violence, intimate betrayals, and social disintegration of the period are reflected in his Arthurian epic.

Subsequent elaborations of the Arthur legend likewise reflected the preoccupations and political needs of the day. When a protracted civil war for the crown culminated in the accession of Henry VII to the throne, he sought to strengthen his position by claiming descent from King Arthur. When James I of Scotland took the English throne, he claimed to have fulfilled the prophecy that England and Scotland would again be united, as they were under Arthur. As Britain expanded its empire, Arthur was deployed in defense of imperialism. Not only was he an exemplar of the civilized and godly society the British hoped to spread around the globe, but as a uniter of disparate peoples he offered a glorious precedent for benevolent British imperial rule.[7] In the modern era, the image of Arthur has been evoked by monarchists and populists, conservatives and radicals alike.

Although the Arthur legend has been coopted for quite varied purposes, we can observe a general tendency toward the use of Arthur to defend the establishment: the monarchy, the ruling class, the Empire. This stands in stark contrast to another enduring national hero, Robin Hood. Robin Hood, one of history's great bandit-heroes, has been portrayed through the centuries as a man who fights against tyranny and defends the weak. Although his most frequent targets include corrupt nobles, law enforcers, and clergy, he is not antiauthoritarian or anticlerical in a general sense. Rather, he is often shown to be pious, deeply spiritual, and devoted to his true and just king, Richard I.

Like King Arthur, Robin Hood has been evoked by different groups for different purposes. Radical reformers have seen him as a rebel, resisting authority and inverting repressive hierarchies. Moderate reformers have seen in him a rational actor who challenged corrupt power, but also gave his loyalty and support to moral and just rulers. Conservatives, while often critical of his flouting of the law, have also recognized him as a defender of traditional English liberties and institutions. Perhaps most strikingly, Robin Hood was evoked by both critics and defenders of the Empire.

Critics easily made the case that Robin Hood was forced into banditry and civil disobedience by the negligence of King Richard who had abandoned his kingdom to join the Crusades. For anti-imperialists the message was clear: a monarch who neglects domestic affairs to pursue an agenda abroad risks leading the nation to chaos, corruption, and decay. However, defenders of imperialism were quick to point out that Robin Hood supported King Richard in his efforts to civilize and save the "heathen," and in one Victorian tale he even joined Richard in the Crusades. Furthermore, even conservatives often offered Robin Hood as a British exemplar: hale and hearty, courageous and independent, just and generous. In short, Robin Hood embodied many traits imperialists hoped to cultivate in colonial subjects.[8]

In addition to bearing meanings about the British character and the British political and social order, the legends of King Arthur and Robin Hood convey powerful messages about gender and, to some extent, race. In both legends, the two heroes and their male companions, the Knights of the Round Table and the Merry Men, exemplify the best and most admirable traits of the British character. In a sense, these men come to stand for the nation itself. However, the women in the tales are often defined more by their Otherness than by their essential Britishness.

This is clearest in the Arthurian tales which, until recent feminist reinterpretations, have tended to portray the main female characters of Guinevere and Morgan Le Fay in overwhelmingly negative terms.[9] Guinevere, the selfish adulteress, betrays her husband and her nation, leading to the downfall of both, while Morgan Le Fay, a cruel and seductive witch, plots to destroy her half-brother Arthur and place the villainous Mordred on the throne. The tales thus reinforce a patriarchal social order in which women's sexuality, autonomy, and power must be strictly limited, and the violation of gender norms leads to both personal and national ruin. At the same time, not only do the Arthurian women fail to live up to the national standards established by the male heroes of the legend, but they prevent men from serving the nation. Women are constructed as deviant Others who threaten the well-being of the national community.

The female characters of the Robin Hood tales convey more complex messages about gender (Barczewski 2000, 162–200). Women most often appear as frail innocents in need of protection or rescue. However, one prominent female character, Maid Marian, defies such expectations. Active, independent, and outspoken, Marian takes up arms and fights in hand-to-hand combat beside Robin and his Merry Men. Periodically dressing as a man and even rescuing Robin and his men, Maid Marian blatantly violates gender norms. Yet she is represented quite positively in most of the tales. Barczewski (2000, 197) suggests that Marian is, in a sense, consistent with a British gender system that has generally demanded that most women confine themselves to the domestic realm and submit themselves to male authority, while a few women are celebrated as leaders, even warriors: Boadicea, Elizabeth I, and more recently the "Iron Lady" Margaret Thatcher.[10] Thus, the figure of Marian does not substantially challenge patriarchal hierarchies or the masculine nature of discourses of British identity found in the Robin Hood tales. However, expanding and changing representations of Marian through the ages serve as an index of women's changing roles in British society.

Just as national imagery is gendered in the Arthur and Robin Hood tales, it is racialized to some degree. Although the Arthur of early tales is a Celt, he becomes progressively more Anglo-Saxon in appearance and nature (Barczewski 2000, 124–161). Likewise, Robin Hood's pure Saxon blood gradually assumes more importance as his foes are increasingly identified as Normans.[11] At the height of nineteenth-century scientific racism, the legends of Arthur and Robin Hood reflected the racial stereotypes and racial hierarchies commonly accepted in England, if not in the Celtic territories. Anglo-Saxons were tall and fair, moral, rational, and godly. Celts were dark and craven, treacherous, violent, and generally heathen. Jews and "Orientals," although they seldom appeared in the tales, were portrayed as swarthy, venal, and villainous. Britain, as embodied by King Arthur and Robin Hood, was ultimately defined as white, Christian, and Anglo-Saxon.

THE FRENCH WARS

Antipathies between the English (later the British) and the French date back at least as far as the epoch-shattering Norman Conquest. However, the period between 1707 and 1837 was marked by frequent and intense martial conflict between the newly formed Great Britain and its Continental nemesis.[12] Colley (1992) has argued that this period was crucial to the formation of a British sense of national identity. It must be remembered that the Act of Union joining England, Scotland, and Wales was accomplished in 1707 with great ambivalence about older national identities and loyalties giving way to a new sense of belonging, a sense of Britishness. Ongoing conflicts with France helped smooth over perceived differences within Britain and forge a new communal identity in three important ways.

First, as Hobsbawm (1990, 91) has observed, "There is no more effective way of bonding together the disparate sections of restless peoples than to unite them against outsiders." Mutual suspicion and resentment, especially between the English and the Scots, were long-standing and often bitter. While many English considered Scots, particularly Highlanders, their racial and civilizational inferiors, many Scots well remembered their centuries of oppression at the hands of the English.[13] However, well-founded fears of French invasion and sustained military engagement with France in Europe and at sea, joined the disparate people in a common purpose and eventually a shared sense of national belonging.

Second, both in the French wars and in the American War of Independence, the Scots, with their strong martial tradition, quickly proved themselves able warriors for Britain (Colley 1992). The success of the Highland Regiments chipped away at English racist stereotypes of the Scots. Furthermore, both the Welsh and the Scots voiced strong support for Britain's actions in the American War of Independence, and both groups joined state-supported militias in higher proportions than the English (Colley 1992, 139–141, 293). So the wars of the period provided the people of Wales and Scotland with an opportunity to express patriotism and prove their loyalty to the new state of Great Britain.

Finally, as Said (1978) and others have noted, imagining a national "us" necessarily involves imagining a national "them." During these 130 years of warfare, Britain increasingly defined itself in opposition to France. And national differences were often imagined in gendered terms. The British considered their own culture to be "masculine," physically robust, logical and honorable, with simple tastes and habits. The French, by contrast, were considered "effeminate," overly cultured, vain, intellectually and physically indulgent, and preoccupied with the superficialities of food, fashion, and sexual gratification.[14] It can be argued, then, that discourses of British national identity which emerged at this time were strongly masculine, often centering on wartime heroes.

Just as Britishness was imagined in gendered terms, it was imagined in religious terms. While different forms of Protestantism were practiced in different regions of Britain, and some Catholic enclaves remained, England, Scotland, and Wales shared a strong commitment to Protestantism and a fear, even loathing, of Catholicism. The wars with Catholic France, therefore, were not simply seen as secular battles, but rather as battles for the one true faith; and military outcomes were interpreted in theological terms. Defeats suggested a nation that had offended the Lord, victories were proof of divine sanction. Britain's final victory over Napoleon at Waterloo was not only a triumph for the nation but for Protestantism. The French wars helped forge a solidly Protestant British identity, and fueled the notion that Britain's divine destiny was to spread Protestant civilization across the globe, a notion that would later serve Britain well in its pursuit of Empire.

"WORKSHOP OF THE WORLD"

Even as Britain was embroiled in a protracted war with its continental nemesis France, developments on the home front were transforming British society. New technologies, chief among them the steam engine, revolutionized manufacturing and transportation, and led to the massive demographic, economic, political, and other social changes now collectively known as the Industrial Revolution. By the mid-nineteenth century, Britain had become the world's leading producer of cloth, iron, and coal, and had come to see itself as the "workshop of the world."

Despite the fact that women participated in large numbers in the workforce of industrializing Britain, in the national imaginary, paid labor was increasingly defined as a male activity. Some scholars have suggested that the late Victorian "revival of patriarchy" resulted, in part, from the changing gender dynamics under industrial production (Rutherford 1997, 19–20). That is, as Britain industrialized, men became the main wage earners and the masters of public affairs, while women were relegated to the increasingly devalued domestic realm.[15] National showcases such as the Great Exhibition of 1851 celebrated the ingenuity and determination of Britain's men of science and industry and its working men, with the blackened faces of the colliery or the callused hands of the foundry. However, even in areas such as the West Midlands where by 1860 women made up roughly half of all ironworkers, women industrial workers were called "a gross outrage on civilization" and a "disgrace to the nation" (Morgan 2001, 99–111). While the nation prided itself on being "the workshop of the world" in the national imaginary, the workshop was staffed exclusively by men.

Also obscured behind the doors of the world's workshop was a history of racial exploitation. Specifically, Britain's industrialization was made speedier and more profitable by participation in the slave trade. Before Britain outlawed the slave trade in 1807, British merchant ships delivered millions of African slaves to the New World, and returned to Britain with commodities such as sugar and cotton. Thus, although British factories did not rely directly on slave labor, industrial enterprises nonetheless profited from the slave trade in that the traffic in human beings kept commodity prices low and colonial demand for manufactured goods high.[16] In today's multiethnic Britain, the nation's Abolitionist movement is frequently celebrated in public exhibitions, political speeches, and educational programming.[17] The story of the Abolitionist movement resonates well with contemporary representations of "New Britain" with its emphasis on ethnoracial diversity and equal opportunity for all. Less common, however, is the discussion of the ways the slave trade contributed to Britain's rise to global prominence. Such silences are a reminder that the construction of national identities is as much about forgetting inconvenient and inglorious facts as it is about remembering our proudest moments.

EMPIRE

British industrialization was inextricably bound up with British imperialism. Industrial expansion was facilitated by the flow of cheap raw materials from the colonies and by the increasing demand for British consumer goods among colonial populations. Moreover, the wealth generated by industrial enterprises buttressed the nation's political and military dominance worldwide.

In 1899, with the British Empire at its zenith, Rudyard Kipling opened *The White Man's Burden* with the following lines:

> Take up the White man's burden—
> Send forth the best ye breed—
> Go bind your sons to exile
> To serve your captives' need;
> To wait in heavy harness
> On fluttered folk and wild—
> Your new-caught, sullen peoples,
> Half devil and half child.[18]

One of the most fertile periods for the generation of gendered and racialized discourses of British identity was the heyday of the British Empire. The imperial project itself both reflected and reinforced hierarchies of gender and race. Kipling's words suggest how important representations of essentialized national Others are to the construction of national identities. Yes, discourses of national identity are stories of who we are, but they are also stories of who we are *not*.

While Kipling is perhaps the most prominent literary apologist for Empire, his work by no means stood alone in its racialized constructions of national Others. In the comic operas of W.S. Gilbert and Arthur Sullivan, the Sherlock Holmes mysteries of Arthur Conan Doyle, the fiction of Joseph Conrad, the boys' adventure magazines and school textbooks of the period, travel accounts and press coverage of colonial affairs, among others, representations of dark, childlike, and irrational (or bloodthirsty and treacherous) colonials were commonplace.[19] Although such representations were sometimes tempered with a heavy dose of anti-imperialist critique, the repetition of these national types both mirrored and sustained the image of Britain as a white Christian nation.[20]

The opening stanza of *The White Man's Burden* offers not only a racialized construction of national identity, but a gendered construction as well, for Kipling calls specifically on the white *man* to mobilize his *sons* to the service of nation and empire. Imperialism was a profoundly patriarchal project. Sons left the comforts of the motherland to prove their mettle on the frontiers of the Empire, and return physically invigorated and masculinized. Thus imperialism was a test of individual manhood, just as it was a test of national masculine agency—a way to prove the nation's muscularity, discipline, and dominance (Wilson 2003, 18–20). It was during this period that boys' public schools gained popularity and became "nurseries of empire," inculcating boys with respect for authority, hierarchy, and mastery over self and others, within environments that were at once homosocial, homophobic, and misogynistic (Rutherford 1997, 15–20). In the late Victorian period, in particular, masculinity and femininity became polarized. By virtue of their perceived strength and skill, men were defined as the natural leaders of nation and empire, while women's key contributions were in bearing sons and safeguarding British gentility, refinement, and morality (Wilson 2003; Rutherford 1997).

By the end of the Victorian era, Britain had so extended its global reach that it was said that "the sun never set on the British Empire." Britain's position as an unrivalled superpower fostered, at least among the privileged, an unmitigated confidence in the superiority of the British way of life. This confidence encompassed not only British political, administrative, and economic systems, but naturalized racial and gender hierarchies as well.

WORLD WAR I: NATIONAL TRAUMA, NATIONAL NOSTALGIA

The psychological and material effects of the First World War on Britain and its national identity can hardly be overstated. In the course of the war (1914–1918), six million British men were recruited into military service, and another three million men and women served in "reserved occupations" such as munitions manufacture. 750,000 British soldiers were killed in the conflict, 9 percent of British men under the age of forty-five. At least twice as many were wounded, many suffering permanent and debilitating injuries (Harrison 1984, 349). The war disrupted certain powerful notions about British national identity. The presumption of the innate superiority of white Britons over irrational Orientals was challenged by devastating losses against the Turks. The presumed necessity and propriety of rigid class hierarchies was challenged when the decisions of ruling class officers led to the battlefield slaughter of lower-status enlistees and conscripts, giving rise to the enduring image of "lions led by donkeys."[21] And the Victorian image of stoic British manhood was challenged by the reality of disabled, shell-shocked, and fragile men returning from the battlefront.[22]

At the same time, women entered the workforce in unprecedented numbers and in previously male-dominated sectors: industrial manufacturing, transport, commerce, and even the police. Eighty thousand women served in uniform as members of noncombatant military support units. In the face of such achievements, the anti-suffragist movement lost momentum and women over thirty won the vote in 1918. Although many women saw their jobs evaporate after the war as a traumatized nation reverted to comforting "traditions," women continued to make political gains during the interwar years, and women's and men's franchise was equalized in 1928 (Light 1991, 8).

Out of the trauma of war emerged a national nostalgia for simpler, happier times, for the unsullied countryside, for an authentically British way of life.[23] In H.V. Morton's best-selling (1928) travel diary, *In Search of England*, the reader senses both a pining for yesteryear and an active, at times even desperate, attempt to rediscover or redefine national identity. While Morton confined himself to exploring England, many of the sights and sounds, the tastes and textures and character-types he lovingly described have found their way into the British national symbology: thatched cottages and cobbled lanes, hearty country folk and stately manor houses, hedgerows and cream teas. And Morton's imagery is highly gendered and at least implicitly racialized.

While Morton never consciously reflects on the racial homogeneity of the nation, the people he describes are almost without exception white Anglo-Saxon in appearance. Where ethnoracial Others do appear they are described in disparaging terms, as is a "little Jew" who cunningly preys on guileless English girls (1928, 202). In Morton's nostalgic portrait of the nation, the true national character is deep and unchanging and carried in the blood and bones of an Anglo-Saxon people.

The nation itself is also clearly gendered in Morton's mind. He refers to England in the feminine and speaks, in rather sensuous terms, of his longing for her. Her cities are likewise gendered. Bath is "the dear old lady of Somerset," Clovelly is the "old-established beauty queen of England," Devonport is "mother to the Fleet," and York "is the lovely queen—as London is the powerful king—of English cities."[24] He happens upon a "feminine" street lined with tea shops where a lovely waitress distracts him from his "pilgrimage" and lures him into an "orgy" of tea and pastries (70–72). In the countryside, girls with flirtatious eyes become part of the pleasing bucolic scenery. In one encounter with a young woman whose car has run out of gasoline, Morton indulges in an extended fantasy in which he plays the chivalrous knight rescuing a "delicious" damsel (43–46). In other moments of fantasy, he sees manly ghosts in the mists and shadows—warriors, kings, knights, Crusaders—and he follows them through the landscape and the timescape of the nation.

What is the contemporary reader to make of Morton's gendered imaginings? It would be tempting, although ultimately limiting, to read his descriptions of doe-eyed maidens and their virile rescuers as the product of the repressive sexual norms of Morton's childhood years. Rather, after the bloodbath of the Somme and the humiliation of Gallipoli, Morton constructed a comforting vision of England with landscapes and social relations—including gender, class, and race relations—seemingly unchanged since time immemorial. Such nostalgic constructions of national identity offered the semblance of stability in the aftermath of the Great War and amidst the modernizing changes of the early twentieth century.[25]

WORLD WAR II: THE "ISLAND RACE" UNDER SIEGE

Because of their unambiguous geographical boundaries and their distance from other nations, island nations such as the UK, Australia, and Japan often imagine themselves to be utterly separate and utterly different from even their nearest neighbors. World War II, more than any other conflict, shattered Britain's comforting self-image as a "snug little island."[26] The scale of national mobilization in the war effort was staggering: 5.2 million men and women in the military, 7.8 million in civilian support positions, the conversion of industrial infrastructure to armament manufacture, and the implementation of massive rationing and national surveillance programs. Although the nation lost fewer soldiers than in World War I, the trauma of World War II was heightened by German aerial bombing campaigns which transformed Britain's home front into its battlefront (Harrison 1984, 360–367).

The nation suffered forty-three thousand civilian deaths and another fifty thousand serious injuries in the Blitz, and millions of people fled the cities, or evacuated their children to the countryside (Colls 2002, 125; Harrison 1984, 360–367).[27] In London, the main target of the attacks, residents spent their nights huddled in Underground stations, cellars, cinemas, and neighborhood shelters, and spent a portion of each day queuing for rations and serving in voluntary associations for national defense and readiness. Characteristics that in the Victorian era were identified strongly with British manliness—courage, stoicism, orderliness, rationality—were now applied to men and women alike by leaders such as Winston Churchill who aimed to inspire and fortify the people (Colls 2002, 124–130).

When St. Paul's Cathedral survived the bombs, leaders and ordinary Britons took it as a sign that God was on their side in the war (Colley 1992, 29). Such sentiments were consistent with long-standing discourses of the nation's divine mission to spread Protestant godliness and civilization throughout the world.[28] Even as the nation's Christian identity was being reconfirmed, however, the nation's racial and gender ideologies were being challenged.

Nineteenth-century racial hierarchies linked white Anglo-Saxon Britain most closely with the Teutonic and Aryan peoples, while Celts and darker-skinned colonial subjects were considered distinct and inferior "races." However, the war saw once-kindred Aryans transformed into the enemy Other, while Britons suppressed internal differences, such as those between Saxons and Celts, to unite against a common external enemy.[29] At the same time, Britain's armed forces were bolstered by colonial troops, especially Afro-Caribbean volunteers (Phillips and Phillips 1998). Amidst such changes, older racialist assumptions were more difficult to sustain.

Nonetheless long-standing racial and ethnic hierarchies persisted throughout the war. Overt anti-Semitism was a feature of the British wartime experience, particularly during the Blitz. The popular press accused Jews of selfishly monopolizing the safest bomb shelters, shirking wartime service, and profiting from black-market trade (Rose 2003, 92–104). While Britain faced pressure from the international community to accept Jewish refugees fleeing Nazi persecution, persistent anti-Semitism undoubtedly contributed to the state's decision not to substantially expand its refugee intake.

Discourses of national identity are often most vivid during times of war, when the nation defines itself not only against the enemy, but against internal Others perceived to be hampering the war effort or otherwise endangering the national community. Certainly, Jews in wartime Britain were constructed as internal Others, as were conscientious objectors and women who failed to conform to gender norms (Rose 2003). Of particular concern to wartime moralists were so-called "good-time girls" who pursued pleasure in the company of soldiers. The indiscretions of these "good-timers" were discussed in lurid detail in the media, serving as examples of selfish, unpatriotic and un-British behavior. Their actions were said to degrade the character, morale, and health of the nation, particularly when white British women chose to associate with "black" soldiers.

Even women who fulfilled their wartime duties and conformed to the rules of social propriety were sometimes constructed as unpatriotic "anticitizens" (Rose 2003, 79). Women were expected to work in essential wartime industries and serve in civil defense and readiness posts. To do so was to be a good citizen. However, women who sought equal pay for equal work, women whose work put them in the company of large numbers of men, and women whose duties kept them out at night or forced them to leave their children in the care of others, were open to charges of selfish, unseemly, and un-British behavior. Nonetheless, the shortage of male labor did lead women to enter the workforce in unprecedented numbers. And while the postwar period saw a nostalgic return to traditional gender roles, arguably wartime changes in gender roles eventually led to greater independence and autonomy for women.[30]

World War II reconfirmed certain long-standing national self-conceptions: Britain saw itself as a white Protestant nation, dedicated to justice and honor and characterized by the "stiff upper lip," courage, self-sacrifice and common sense celebrated in Victorian constructions of British masculinity. The conflict also reinforced a deep-seated mistrust of Europe. However, the conflict also challenged commonly accepted racial hierarchies and forced a tacit acknowledgement of the public contributions of women.

POSTWAR RACIAL TENSIONS

In June of 1948 the *Empire Windrush* arrived in Essex carrying some five hundred West Indian passengers, the first sizeable group of "black" colonials to arrive in postwar Britain.[31] Their arrival sparked public uproar and panicked rhetoric about an impending invasion of dark-skinned aliens stealing British jobs, increasing crime and violence, and overburdening the social welfare system. That no such outcry was sparked by the issuing of work permits to some three hundred thousand postwar migrants from Germany, Austria, Italy, and Belgium (Rutherford 1997), suggests that the clamor over *Windrush* had less to do with economic concerns and more to do with racialized notions of British national identity.

Over the next two decades a series of dramatic public events would keep the issue of black immigration in the limelight, and contribute to the construction of nonwhite Britons as a social "problem" (Gilroy 1987). First, in 1950, long-standing British assumptions about the innate superiority of white Britons over dark-skinned colonials were undermined when the West Indians beat the English at cricket, their own national sport, on English soil.[32] Amid mounting paranoia over perceived threats to white Britain, the 1950s also saw the rise of the Keep Britain White movement, the White Defence League, the violent antiblack gangs known as the Teddy Boys, and the first in a number of so-called "race riots," the most prominent in Nottingham and North Kensington in 1958. In 1962–1963, new public outrage was sparked by the Profumo Affair, in which Secretary of State for War John Profumo was found to have had an affair with Christine Keeler, a young woman who was also having affairs with Soviet Naval attaché Yevgeny Ivanov and two West Indian men, Johnny Edgecombe and Lucky Gordon. Profumo resigned amidst stories of sex, drugs, espionage, prostitution, and interracial sexual liaisons. When Edgecombe and Gordon later brawled over Keeler, the salacious media coverage reinforced widely held stereotypes about the hypersexuality and violence of Afro-Caribbean men.

It was in this context that Conservative politician Enoch Powell rose to prominence as an opponent of black immigration.[33] In 1968 he famously suggested that if immigration from Britain's former colonies continued unchecked, blood would soon run in the streets. Although he was dismissed from his Shadow Cabinet position after the so-called "Rivers of Blood" speech, both Powell and his ideas continued to enjoy broad public support.

The 1970s saw a strengthening of cultural pride and activism among Britain's Afro-Caribbean community. A Caribbean-style carnival, first organized by immigrants living in the downtrodden area of Notting Hill in the mid-1960s gained popularity, and today the Notting Hill Carnival is one of Britain's largest cultural festivals, attracting in excess of a half-million visitors each year and serving as a visible reminder of Britain's increasingly multiethnic population. This growing acceptance of racial and ethnic diversity did not go unchallenged, however. At the extreme end of reactions against ethnoracial diversity, organizations such as the National Front and the British National Party rose to prominence in the 1970s and 1980s, with goals ranging from reducing nonwhite immigration to expelling nonwhite migrants from the nation. In the realm of mainstream politics, the Thatcher/Major years were marked by a nostalgic (white) nationalism in many ways consistent with Powell's vision.

THE THATCHER/MAJOR YEARS: NOSTALGIC WHITE NATIONALISM

Margaret Thatcher assumed the leadership of the Conservative Party in 1975 and the Prime Ministership in 1979 determined, as she expressed it, to put the "great" back in Great Britain.[34] When she appealed to Britons to reclaim their pride in Empire and to support the Falklands War in defense of their far-flung "kith and kin," she was by implication addressing white Britons and excluding nonwhites from her conception of the nation. Conservative commentator Peregrine Worsthorne captured the racial tensions of the time when he wrote of the Falklands conflict,

> If the Falkland Islanders were British citizens with black or brown skins, spoke with strange accents or worshiped different Gods it is doubtful whether the Royal Navy and Marines would be today fighting for their liberation . . . Most Britons today identify more easily with those of the same stock 8000 miles away . . . than they do with West Indian or Asian immigrants living next door.[35]

Implicit in Worsthorne's statements, as in Thatcher's rhetoric, is the notion that real Britons are white. Those of West Indian and Asian descent might reside in Britain, but they are not truly British.

Likewise, John Major upheld his predecessor's white Anglocentric and nostalgic vision of the nation. Addressing those concerned that Britain's increasing engagement with Europe threatened British culture and identity, he famously asserted that

> Fifty years from now, Britain will still be the country of long shadows on county grounds, warm beer, invincible green suburbs, dog lovers, pools fillers, and—as George Orwell said—old maids bicycling to Holy Communion through the morning mist. (Lawson 1993: 20)

Major's vision of Britain, then, was overwhelmingly white, middle-class, and Christian, and the speech promised a continuation of these racial, class, and religious hierarchies. Often overlooked in the speech, however, is an implicit promise of conservative gender relations, with the figure of a quietly pious "old maid" played against the traditionally masculine realms of cricket, sports wagers, and the pub.

The Thatcher/Major years also witnessed the dramatic growth of the so-called "heritage industry," the commercial development and promotion of British historical sites as tourist attractions. Critics have complained that heritage tourism leads to historical revisionism, for instance by obscuring unpleasant realities to create a more pleasurable experience for tourists. Some have also suggested that the heritage industry creates an excessive focus on the past and is transforming the nation into a giant theme park of quaint thatched cottages and well-preserved manor houses, or as West (1988, 38) put it, Britain as "Ye Olde Leisure Park."[36]

In terms of national identity, heritage tourism has tended to focus on the experiences of wealthy and influential Britons, the royals, the gentry, the literary and artistic elites.[37] Even industrial heritage sites that focus more explicitly on the lives of working men and women routinely gloss over issues of class, gender, and racial inequality, while perpetuating such inequalities in the division of labor at the sites (West 1988; Bennett 1988). Consequently, the heritage industry as a whole has arguably contributed to nostalgic discourses of national identity, featuring a beneficent ruling class, a happy, industrious working class, ethnoracial homogeneity and naturalized patriarchy.

A central contention of this book is that discourses of national identity are inextricably bound up with material relations. During the Thatcher/Major years, as discourses of national identity were becoming increasingly nostalgic, white Anglocentric, and patriarchal state policies reflected and reinforced this growing conservatism. Although Thatcher made history when she became the first woman to serve as British Prime Minister, she was dismissive of the feminist movement and generally unsympathetic in regard to "women's issues" such as pay equity. Both in rhetoric and policy Thatcher's government promoted the traditional nuclear family as the primary social unit of British society. Acolytes of the Iron Lady argued that divorce, out-of-wedlock births, and even the entry of women into paid work threatened the family and the well-being of the nation.[38]

At the same time, Thatcher began dismantling or weakening organizations such as the Greater London Council and the Inner London Education Authority that had been active advocates of gender and racial equality and multiculturalism. She expressed sympathy with those (white) Britons who feared that the nation "might be rather swamped by people with a different culture," and she supported increasingly repressive policing practices that disproportionately targeted minorities (Alibhai-Brown 2000, 78, 81–85). Under her leadership, the national history curriculum was revised in ways critics claimed glorified the British Empire and stifled meaningful discussion of the racist underpinnings of imperialism (Grosvenor 1997, 191). And, in keeping with her anti-immigration stance, she oversaw the passage of the British Nationality Act of 1981, which created different categories of British citizenship and effectively limited the number of colonial subjects entitled to reside permanently in the UK.[39] In the throes of nostalgic white nationalism, state policies seemed designed to preserve Britain as a "snug little island" of white Anglo-Saxon Christians.

"COOL BRITANNIA" AND "CHILLY BRITANNIA"

The 1997 general elections seemed to signal a sea change for constructions of British national identity. Tony Blair's New Labour campaigned in part on its vision of "Cool Britannia," Britain as a progressive, exciting, and fashionable society on the cutting edge of creative pursuits, business practices, and social policies. Cool Britannia embraced multiculturalism and gender equity and rejected the patriarchal, white-Anglo nationalism of the Thatcher/Major years. The electorate agreed with this "re-branding" of the nation, giving Labour a landslide victory.[40] During the Blair years, the nation faced considerable challenges to national self-conceptions, chief among them increasing engagement with Europe, the devolution of power to Scotland and Wales, and participation in the global "war on terror." At the dawn of the new millennium, commentators began to speak of a "crisis" of British identity.

Certainly one of the fears of Britain's so-called Eurosceptics is that strengthening alliances with Europe—by joining the European Union (EU), adopting a single currency, and adhering to laws and policies framed in Brussels rather than in Whitehall—will fundamentally alter the British way of life, dilute British culture, and undermine British national identity. Although Europe's unification began some fifty years ago with the creation of the European Economic Community (EEC) in 1957, there is slim evidence that national identities have eroded under the strains of transnationalism (Deflem and Pampel 1996). Rather, the EEC and now the EU are still fundamentally bodies *of* and *for* nations, and citizens belong to their respective nations first and foremost. Likewise, there is little evidence that Britain's entry into the EEC in 1973 and the EU in 1993 precipitated a waning of a sense of British national belonging. On the contrary, vehement public debate over Britain's relationship to Europe has, if anything, prompted greater national introspection and attempts to describe, measure, and preserve a distinctively British identity.

A second perceived challenge to British national identity was political devolution. Referenda on devolution were passed in Scotland and Wales in 1997, with the first elections for the new parliaments being held in 1999. In the lead-up to devolution, critics of the change predicted that it would undermine British national identity and fragment and weaken the Union, perhaps marking the beginning of the end of Britain (Curtice 2006, 96). However, a recent analysis of broad-based surveys in England, Scotland, and Wales before and after devolution found only modest changes in respondents' national identifications (Curtice 2006). As Table 4.1 shows, among Scots, when respondents were forced to choose whether they identified as Scottish or British, there were no discernable changes after devolution. In Wales, contrary to critics' predictions, there was actually a slight decrease in claims of exclusive Welsh identity and a slight concomitant increase in British identity. Only in England did the regional (English) identity increase slightly while a sense of British national identity decreased.

However, clearly the majority of Britons do not conceptualize national identity in such exclusive terms. When allowed to identify as only British, as only English, Scottish, or Welsh, *or* as some combination of British and regional identity, the majority of respondents in all areas reported that they were both British and English, Scottish, or Welsh (Table 4.2). This was true both before and after devolution. With this more nuanced measure of national identification, we see slightly larger increases in exclusive English, Scottish, and Welsh identities after devolution. However, as Curtice (2006, 100–101) observes, these increases occurred directly after devolution and

Table 4.1 Forced-Choice National Identity

Region	Reported National Identity	1997	2003
England	English	34	38
	British	59	48
Scotland	Scottish	72	72
	British	20	20
Wales	Welsh	63	60
	British	26	27

Source: Adapted from Curtice 2006. Original data from quantitative studies with representative samples in England, Scotland, and Wales.

Table 4.2 Non-Exclusive National Identity

Region	National Identity	1997	2003
England	Only English	7	17
	Both English and British	76	63
	Only British	9	10
Scotland	Only Scottish	23	31
	Both Scottish and British	69	60
	Only British	4	4
Wales	Only Welsh	17	21
	Both Welsh and British	70	64
	Only British	12	9

Source: Adapted from Curtice 2006. Original data from quantitative studies with representative samples in England, Scotland, and Wales.

have held steady (or even weakened) in subsequent years, leaving no reason to predict that British identity will continue to decline.

A third challenge to the "re-branding" of British identity was the nation's entry into the so-called "global war on terror." After the September 11, 2001, attacks on the United States, Tony Blair not only offered commiseration on behalf of his nation, but declared the attacks an assault on the whole of "the free and democratic world," and pledged to "stand shoulder to shoulder" with America to "[drive] this evil . . . from our world" (cited in Coates and Krieger 2004, 44). Just days after making this pledge, Blair travelled to the US to consult with George Bush and attend the President's address to a joint session of Congress, an address in which Bush declared that "America has no truer friend than Great Britain."[41] Indeed Blair proved to be an indispensable ally in US-led attacks against Afghanistan and Iraq, vigorously lobbying world leaders and courting the world press on behalf of the US plan.

Although Blair faced some opposition to his decision to participate in attacks in Afghanistan, his support for an invasion of Iraq sparked massive public protests and Cabinet-level resignations.[42] By early 2003, he was defending himself against charges of turning Britain into America's lackey. He implied that rather than Britain serving a foreign master, it was quietly exerting its influence as an equal member in the "Coalition of the Willing."[43] On the eve of the Iraq invasion, Blair's address to the nation evoked images of earlier wartime or imperial sacrifices, when he observed, "As so often before, on the courage and determination of British men and women, serving our country, the fate of many nations rests" (quoted in Coates and

Krieger 2004, 62). Britain was once again positioned as a protector of the "civilized world."[44]

While Blair was always cautious not to conflate terrorism with Islam, the heated rhetoric of civilization versus fanaticism, good against evil, us and them, inevitably led to such conflation in the popular imagination. Islamophobia appeared to be on the rise, as non-Muslim Britons voiced concerns about the nation's Muslim population. Fears of the enemy within were only intensified by the 7 July 2005 London Underground bombings which killed fifty-six people, including four suspected suicide bombers. The men identified as the attackers were all Muslims, one an Afro-Caribbean convert to Islam. Following the attacks, multiculturalism and immigration policies came in for harsh criticism in the press, and the government instituted sweeping security reforms which critics claimed disproportionately affected Britain's Muslim and Asian populations (Sivanandan 2006).

Scholars have argued that the Blair years marked the transition from ethnic nationalism to civic nationalism in Britain (Billig et al. 2006a). That is, in most public rhetoric at least, white-Anglocentric notions of Britishness have given way to the idea that Britishness is defined not by skin color or even religion, but by shared civic values and ways of life. Racialist conceptions of Britishness are increasingly associated with fringe and extremist groups. However, in the midst of the global "war on terror," immigration, multiculturalism, and the treachery of enemies within, continue to be issues of heated debate and media scaremongering.[45] As Britain turns back toward the notion that a more racially or culturally homogeneous nation is a safer nation, "Cool Britannia" is seemingly becoming "Chilly Britannia," at least for the nation's ethnoracial minorities (Billig et al. 2006b).

"THE END OF BRITAIN?"

In a commentary entitled "The End of Britain?" the editors of *The Political Quarterly* observed, "The British have long been distinguished for having no clear idea about who they are, where they are or what they are" (Wright and Gamble 2000). While I would argue that British national identity is no more indistinct, muddled, or changeable than it is in most nationstates, the editors' observation certainly captures the sense of uncertainty about the nature of national identity at the turn of the new millennium. The last decade of the twentieth century saw increased examination of British national identity and its anticipated demise. As Britons continue to define and chart changes to national identity in the twenty-first century, several key questions emerge. One set of questions centers on the changing racial and ethnic composition of Britain's population. What is the place of the nation's white-Anglo-Saxon-Christian heritage in today's increasingly multiethnic society? If Britons can no longer consider themselves a homogeneous "island race," how should they conceive of their constituent populations?

How do ethnoracial minority communities think of themselves in relation to the nation? How are these communities constructed in relation to widely circulating discourses of national identity? Are they constructed as Britons or as internal Others?

A second set of questions concerns Britain's place in the world, its responses to globalization, and its status as a former imperial power. Should it accept an equal but non-privileged position as part of the European Union, or aspire to a separate and more dominant status? How closely can it ally itself with the US without being perceived as America's "fifty-first state"? And how should it regard its imperial past? With pride or shame? What residual rights and duties does Britain have to its former colonies? And how can Britain reconcile the reality of its current political and economic status with its former role as an unrivalled imperial power?

A third issue is the balance between regional and national identity. Does British identity supersede categories such as English, Scottish, and Welsh, or is it undermined by such identities? Is a truly national British identity even possible in light of Scottish and Welsh devolution and continuing instability in Northern Ireland?

Finally, despite the recent drive to define British national identity, little attention has been given to the place of women in the national imaginary. To be sure, British feminists continue to speak out about the ongoing material disadvantages facing women today, although, as Alibhai-Brown (2000, 187–221) points out, it is mainly white, middle-class feminists whose voices are heard. However, few scholars and even fewer popular commentators have examined the ways and the degree to which discourses of British national identity are gendered. Such silences are remarkable given the clear masculine bias in contemporary discourses of national identity, discussed in subsequent chapters here.

5 Discourses of National Identity in the United States

In 2004, Samuel Huntington described what he perceived as the mounting crisis of American national identity. He argued that America's "core" culture, Anglo-Protestant culture, has been dangerously eroded by decades of globalization, immigration, multiculturalism, identity politics, and programs such as affirmative action and bilingual education.[1] He warned of the dire consequences of this weakened national identity: collapse and breakup of the nation; a divide between English-speaking Protestants and Spanish-speaking Others; or descent into a kind of white supremacist nationalism leading to mass expulsions and isolationism. But Huntington, urging against despair, then offered a clear solution: Americans must recognize Anglo-Protestant culture as the true and natural culture of the land and insist that all ethnoracial Others assimilate to the Anglo-Protestant model.

Huntington's vision of the national community is clearly ethnicized and implicitly racialized. If only those who speak the English language and share a commitment to Protestant values are true Americans, then Muslims, Hispanic Catholics, and groups from other linguistic and religious backgrounds are rendered outsiders. Huntington's construction of American national identity is less explicitly gendered. He touches on gender only briefly when suggesting that feminism is among the forces that have destabilized American identity and challenged the rightful dominance of Anglo-Protestant culture. Of course, if the traditional cultural order has been undermined by feminism, we can only conclude that it is a patriarchal national culture to which Huntington aspires.

Huntington's impassioned call for a preservation of America's national culture highlights the extent to which American national identity has been and continues to be constructed as largely white, Christian, and masculine. While the discussion here is necessarily selective and therefore should not be taken as a comprehensive survey of American self-conceptions, it sheds light on certain themes and archetypes that have featured prominently in American discourses of national identity.

A FRONTIER SOCIETY

Looming large in discourses of American national identity even before the achievement of formal nationhood was the image of the frontier.[2] Not just the literal spaces of uncharted, unsettled lands, but the myths, mysteries, and emotions associated with the frontier. Frontier icons have been, and continue to be, deployed liberally in everything from political rhetoric to popular culture and scholarly treatises. The sturdy pioneer, the laconic cowboy, the enterprising prospector, the outlaw, the sheriff. These archetypes are among those commonly held to exemplify the national character. These figures are hearty and brave, independent and self-reliant, moral and progressive, not bound by convention, and not afraid to use violence in the service of a just cause. They are the founders of a new land, they are the fathers of a new people, and they are, almost without exception, white Anglo-Protestant males.

Certain frontier heroes have entered the national iconography: Daniel Boone, Davy Crockett, General George Armstrong Custer, Jesse James, "Buffalo Bill" Cody, and John Wayne, among others.[3] Each has served as a national exemplar, and each has been so mythologized that the line between fact and fancy is often indiscernible. John Wayne, the quintessential twentieth-century cowboy memorialized as such on a US postage stamp and a Congressional gold medal, never worked as a cowboy. And although he symbolized American military heroism, he never served in the armed forces. Likewise, these other frontier heroes have been transformed and rendered larger-than-life in paperback adventures, television, film, and live performances.[4] While the biographies of these men differ, history has condensed their lives and legends into paeans to American courage, ingenuity, loyalty and, perhaps above all, masculinity.

Women and ethnoracial minorities serve as foils to white male frontier heroes, though in different ways. Theodore Roosevelt, a fervent promoter of America's frontier identity, neatly summed up frontier gender roles when he described an ideal society of "fighters and breeders," men to build and defend the nation and women to bear its sons.[5] According to this ideal, women were not only there to breed, however. They were also there to exert a civilizing influence on men. While men were charged with taming the wilderness, only women, principally in their roles as wives and schoolteachers, were capable of domesticating it by bringing some degree of order, refinement, and godliness to a naturally unruly male domain. Of course, only the Good White Woman could exert such influence. Because frontier prostitutes and nonwhite women were not desirable as "breeders," there was little symbolic space for them in the national imaginary, except perhaps as examples of the forces that hindered national progress.

Good White Women also provided frontier men with opportunities for heroism; for a woman on the frontier was a woman in peril, vulnerable to accident, illness, and privation certainly, but above all else vulnerable to rape, captivity, and murder. From the earliest years of nationhood, the defense of women, especially against attack by "Red Indians," was closely linked to the defense of "race" and nation.[6] For Europeans struggling to gain a foothold on a new and vast continent, the viability of the colonies, and later the nation, depended absolutely on the ability to safeguard the reproductive capacity of white women.[7] When women and girls were killed or racially "contaminated" through rape, this threatened the nation in two ways. It directly compromised the ability of the white race to proliferate and therefore compete with its racial Others. But it also threatened to emasculate white men, who would become painfully aware of their inability to protect "their" women. Such anxieties no doubt account for the popularity of captivity and rescue narratives throughout the nation's history, from Mrs. Mary Rowlandson's best-selling captivity memoir of 1682 to the sensational US Army Special Forces rescue of Pfc. Jessica Lynch in 2003 (see Colley 2002 and Faludi 2007a, 2007b).

From early colonial captivity narratives and nineteenth-century dime-novel adventures through more recent Hollywood "Westerns," one racialized Other features most prominently in the American frontier myth, the Native American.[8] While Mexican renegades, Asian "coolies," Irish outlaws, and African-American cowboys appear periodically in frontier tales, Native Americans, represented as either "bloodthirsty savages" or "noble savages," are a constant feature of the mythic frontier landscape.

In representations of the "bloodthirsty savage," Native Americans are constructed as the antithesis of the white frontier hero and of civilization more generally. Crazed and cruel, godless and merciless, without shame or a sense of basic human decency, the "bloodthirsty savage" haunts frontier tales as a constant reminder that horror and death lurk near. The figure of the "noble savage," alluded to by Jean-Jacques Rousseau in the eighteenth century, popularized by authors such as James Fenimore Cooper in the nineteenth century, and romanticized in Hollywood films in the latter half of the twentieth century once the perceived threat posed by Native Americans had been thoroughly neutralized, also stands in contradistinction to white civilization. Instinctual, spiritual, honorable, untainted by greed and corruption, the "noble savage" often serves as a reminder of the failings of urban, industrial society and the folly of war, imperialism, and environmental destruction. Even in such sympathetic representations, however, Native Americans are still clearly racialized Others, at one with the land and yet on the symbolic margins of the nation.

GOOD WARS

A key feature of the frontier experience, and of frontier imagery, is the encounter with the Other: other peoples, other landscapes, other ways of life, even the Other within—one's darker, more elemental self, stripped of the trappings of civilization. Such encounters were fraught with violence, but violence held both peril and promise. While death and destruction might result, those who survived such violence would emerge stronger and revitalized. Frontier mythology promised that both individuals and the nation as a whole could experience "regeneration through violence" (Slotkin 1973, 1992).[9]

Judicious violence has been a strong theme in American discourses of national identity. Much national pride and countless national resources have been invested in fighting "good" wars, wars framed as morally justified, altruistic, and often divinely sanctioned. From the Revolutionary War through the Indian Wars, the Civil War, the World Wars, the Cold War, and wars declared on such social ills as poverty, drugs, and terrorism, the nation has constructed itself as a defender of freedom, justice, equality, morality, and democracy. America's military successes have fostered a national expectation that "War brings unity, efficiency, prosperity, security and victory" (Robertson 1980, 325) as well as glory and divine blessings to both the individual and the nation. Add to such positive associations the enormous economic impact of the US armaments industry and it is not surprising that American wars and warriors are celebrated throughout the nation in forms as diverse as public statuary, parades, textbooks, movies, and bumper stickers.

Not surprisingly, discourses of national identity are often intensified during times of war, as the national self is defined in stark contrast to enemy Others. One of the most recognizable icons of the United States, Uncle Sam, rose to national prominence through a World War I recruiting poster proclaiming "I WANT YOU" for the US Army. The poster featured an imposing Anglo man with white hair, a stern countenance, a red white and blue suit of clothes, and a star-spangled top hat. Four million copies of the poster circulated between 1917 and 1918. The image proved so popular that it was reprised for military recruiting in World War II, and continues to be used in everything from political cartoons to product advertisements with messages such as "I WANT YOU to buy a new mattress."[10] While the image has been variously used to promote national solidarity, to critique government policies, and to hawk any number of consumer goods, Uncle Sam's position in the national imaginary is clear: this unambiguously white male icon remains a definitive personification of the nation, both in times of peace and war.

Warfare is, of course, "one of the most rigidly gendered activities known to humankind" (Ehrenreich 1997, 125). While women have always participated in wars in a variety of ways, warfare has been defined almost exclusively as a masculine domain. With few exceptions, the military heroes celebrated in discourses of American national identity are men: the Minutemen, the Seventh Cavalry, the Roughriders, and a host of generals, from Washington to Grant, Lee, MacArthur and, more recently, Schwarzkopf and Powell. The real and the fictional, decorated officers and rank-and-file troops, are lauded as rugged, noble, courageous, and self-sacrificing. Never thirsting for blood, but never too timid to shed it in the name of the nation.

Few female soldiers have made their way into discourses of national identity. One exception is US Army Private First Class Jessica Lynch, discussed in detail in Chapter 9. In 2003, Lynch became a national hero when she was captured in Iraq and later rescued by US Special Forces in a dramatic midnight raid on a Nasiriyah hospital. Photos of a frail-looking Lynch wrapped in the US flag made newspaper front pages across the nation. In media constructions of her heroism it appeared that she was celebrated not so much for her own deeds on the field of battle as for her status as an attractive, petite, young blond who had been saved by elite male warriors. Ultimately the Lynch story both reflected and reaffirmed a vision of the national community in which women are the passive and grateful recipients of male authority.

Just as warfare often exposes assumptions about the national gender order, it brings widespread notions about race and ethnicity into clearer focus. From early European settlement, colonists and later the nation invested heavily in fighting "savage wars" (Slotkin 1992), wars against racialized, inferiorized Others. Native Americans were the earliest and arguably most enduring "savage" enemy, but in time other groups were constructed in similar ways: "Oriental" migrants to the American West, Filipino guerrillas in the Philippine War, the Japanese and Japanese-Americans during World War II, the Vietcong, Colombian "drug lords," Iraqi "insurgents," and "Arab terrorists," to name but a few. Although there are countless differences between these groups, in national discourses all were (and some still are) demonized as cruel, bloodthirsty, and lacking even basic human decency. Racial epithets for each of these groups have emphasized that differences between the national "us" and the enemy "them" are essential, biological, natural. Such representations reaffirm the white Anglo-Protestant character of discourses of American national identity.

The American Civil War deserves special consideration in any discussion of "good wars" and "savage" enemies, because opinion about the nature of the conflict and the enemy was, and to some extent still is, starkly divided. The Civil War epitomizes an enduring symbolic divide in the nation, the divide between North and South. This conflict in which three million soldiers fought, and some six hundred thousand died, continues to be a popular focus of fiction and nonfiction literature, film, historical reenactments, and historical tourism. While some Southern treatments of the conflict characterize it as a war for independence or a "War Against Northern Aggression," at the national level it is remembered as a war to end slavery, and thus a war of liberation, a "good war."

One legacy of the Civil War is that throughout the twentieth century the South itself has been represented as an internal Other of sorts. In Jansson's (2004, 2005) analyses of *National Geographic Magazine* and Hollywood film, he identifies a tendency to represent the South as antiquated, hierarchical, bigoted, oppressive, exploitative, and poor while the North is portrayed as modern, democratic, tolerant, free, equal, and prosperous. In what Jansson describes as "internal Orientalism," the values and qualities of the North are constructed as genuinely American, in opposition to those of an aberrant South. Because the South is constructed as the repository of outmoded racism, poverty, and oppression, the rest of the nation is, in a sense, absolved of such sins.

Constructions of the American Civil War are also significant in terms of racialized discourses of national identity. Although some 185,000 black soldiers fought in the conflict, they are seldom the focus of popular treatments of the event. Rather, where blacks appear in contemporary Civil War discourses, they are most often slaves, mere observers of a fight between white men. At best, such discourses marginalize African Americans in narratives of nation, rendering them passive objects in the white man's struggle for national determination. Far more damaging, such discourses construct African Americans as both the cause of the conflict and a reminder of the traumatic loss of Southern pride and autonomy. Lingering white bitterness over wartime defeat turned lethal in the postwar era when freed blacks were routinely subjected to white harassment, discrimination, and violence. Best-selling novels such as Thomas Dixon's *The Clansman* (1905) and films including D.W. Griffith's *The Birth of a Nation* (1915), an adaptation of Dixon's book, celebrated white Southern heroism and portrayed African Americans as intellectually and morally inferior brutes, as "savage" Others. Such views were both reflected and reinforced by Jim Crow laws, the rise of white supremacist groups such as the Ku Klux Klan, and the widespread use of lynching, cross-burning, and other forms of institutionalized terror against African Americans.

As much as war can intensify racial and gender inequalities, it also has the potential to challenge national gender and racial hierarchies. We have only to look to World War II for examples. With the unprecedented scale of the Second World War, demands for soldiers and civilian workers increased, creating new opportunities for women and ethnoracial minorities. More than six million women joined the civilian workforce during the war, and 350,000 women enlisted in the Women's Army Corps, seventy thousand as nurses and more than one thousand as Women's Air Force Service Pilots. At the same time, ethnoracial minorities were enlisting in the armed forces in record numbers. While some served in integrated units, segregated units were established for Native Americans, African Americans, and Asian Americans. One of these, the 442nd Regimental Combat Team, consisting mainly of Japanese-American soldiers, became the most decorated unit in US military history.

The war brought both opportunity and pressure for marginalized groups to prove their patriotism and their worth to the national community. In most cases their efforts and sacrifices did not result in immediate gains in status or power. At the end of the war, women workers were routinely fired or pressured to surrender their positions to returning soldiers, and female and nonwhite veterans were not extended equal benefits under the Servicemen's

Readjustment Act (the GI Bill) which gave financial assistance to veterans pursuing higher education, starting a business, or purchasing a home. Nonetheless, the noteworthy contributions of women and ethnoracial minorities during the Second World War undoubtedly contributed to the gains of the postwar civil rights and women's rights movements by challenging long-standing notions about the natural deficiencies of women and ethnoracial minorities.

THE "AMERICAN DREAM"

The end of World War II brought unparalleled economic growth and affluence to the nation. Consumer goods ranging from televisions and automatic washing machines to automobiles became increasingly accessible to a growing middle class. This, paired with rising levels of home ownership, seemed to millions of Americans to be a realization of the "American dream" of affluence and upward mobility. But this dream was not new to the postwar era. Rather themes of abundance and mobility have been prominent in the national mythology since the colonial period.

Although the earliest European settlers experienced extreme hardship, the "New World" was most often represented as a land of plenty.[11] Ample timber, water, game, mineral resources, and above all vast expanses of fertile land drew increasing numbers of colonists ever westward with a promise of independence and prosperity. The perceived natural bounty of the land continues to be celebrated today in cultural forms as diverse as Thanksgiving Day pageants and parades, landscape paintings, and songs such as "America the Beautiful" with its vision of "amber waves of grain" and the "fruited plain."[12]

Over time, the preferred path to the American dream has changed: homesteading, mineral prospecting, small business ownership, salaried employment, entrepreneurship. But in every period from earliest settlement onward, the American (or "Protestant") work ethic has been held up as the key to prosperity and advancement.[13] Horatio Alger brought the rags-to-riches theme to full fruition in his best-selling boys' books of the late nineteenth century. The "Alger hero" was the very embodiment of the American dream, a boy of humble birth whose industriousness, perseverance, and virtue were rewarded with wealth and status. The books are not only celebrations of upward mobility, but celebrations of white, American masculinity. Alger's female characters seem to exist primarily for his male heroes to rescue and thus to demonstrate their nobility of character, their competence, their manliness. Women and girls here do not participate in the American dream themselves, but rather are the passive recipients of its rewards. Even in contemporary politics, there is a tendency for candidates to stress their humble origins and downplay any inherited privileges they may have enjoyed.[14]

Alger's themes have a prominent place in American discourses of national identity today, and Algeresque narratives of nation have material consequences for women, ethnoracial minorities, the poor, and the marginalized. Given the historical period during which the books were written, it is not surprising that women and ethnoracial minorities were virtually absent from Alger's American success story. His American exemplars were almost without exception white males. More significantly, however, Alger's enduring message that anyone can achieve greatness through hard work and virtue implies that the failure to achieve greatness is largely due to one's own deficits. Widely circulating notions of a readily achievable American dream obscure the realities of institutionalized discrimination and a legacy of oppression which still disadvantage certain segments of the population.[15]

In American narratives of nation, social mobility has been strongly associated with physical or geographical mobility. Among the nation's most enduring foundational stories are those of pilgrims leaving the corruption and persecution of the "Old World" behind to build better lives for themselves in a new land. The national mythology is replete with images of mobility: pioneer families journeying West in covered wagons; the Alger boys moving from the mean streets or the impoverished countryside to boardrooms and townhouses; and later, the protagonists of prime-time dramas such as *Dallas* and *Dynasty* expanding their empires from the seats of their private jets.

There is perhaps no more potent symbol of American mobility than the automobile. Since the early twentieth century it has featured prominently in American advertising, popular music, literature, and film among other cultural forms.[16] The car has served as a vehicle, quite literally, for messages about American values, the American character, and American ways of life. In works such as F. Scott Fitzgerald's *The Great Gatsby* (1925), The Beach Boys' "Fun, Fun, Fun" (1964), and George Lucas' *American Graffiti* (1973), the car is associated with American affluence, liberation, and pleasure. In works such as John Steinbeck's *The Grapes of Wrath* (1939) and Ridley Scott's *Thelma and Louise* (1991) cars facilitate escape from oppressive circumstances, while in a host of "road trip" movies the characters' physical journeys mirror their journeys toward self-discovery, independence, reconciliation, and redemption.

While the automobile has symbolized bounty, independence, and mobility, key features in discourses of national identity, it has also symbolized social, moral, and environmental decay. The road trip in Vladimir Nabokov's *Lolita* (1955) is a journey into perversion and debasement. In Arthur Miller's (1949) *Death of a Salesman*, the mobility of the travelling salesman does not lead upward but to failure and despair. And in Michael Moore's documentary *Roger & Me* (1989) the filmmaker juxtaposes images of affluence and poverty in a General Motors factory town to critique the exploitative practices of big business and the disenfranchisement of the working class. This dark side of the American pursuit of mobility and affluence serves as a reminder of a crucial tension in national imaginings. A tension between a celebration of wealth, status, and pleasure on the one hand and a reverence for humility, hard work, and Puritanical restraint on the other.

Furthermore, the automobile as a symbol of American national identity has carried meanings not only about affluence and mobility, but about gender and to some extent race and ethnicity. Car advertisements have long featured eroticized women, appealing to the fantasies of heterosexual male consumers. As women's earning power has increased in recent decades, car marketing has begun to target women as well, but this has done little to challenge the widespread assumption that men have a natural mastery of automotive technology. At the same time, as car models have proliferated, certain models have become associated with specific racial and ethnic groups—the innocuous white middle-class minivan, the intimidating Latino "lowrider," and the ostentatious "pimped out" custom car popularized by African-American rapper Xzibit in the television series *Pimp My Ride*. So the automobile, as a symbol of American national identity, conveys a host of messages about not only class mobility, freedom, individualism, and pleasure, but about gender, racial, and ethnic hierarchies.

"ONE NATION UNDER GOD"

Huntington's recent plea for a resuscitation of America's "Anglo-Protestant culture" is an indication of the powerful and enduring presence of religion and the divine in American discourses of national identity. From the Puritans' dreams of founding a Zion in the New World, to the Declaration of Independence with its references to "Nature's God," the "Creator," and the "Supreme Judge of the world," many of the earliest national narratives constructed America as a land blessed, protected, and guided by God.

While the framers of the Constitution took care to build a "wall of separation between church and state," official and unofficial national imagery is replete with references to the sacred.[17] National crises have frequently prompted a strengthening of religious imagery in narratives of nation. In the midst of the Civil War, the phrase "In God We Trust" first appeared on American (Union) coins. The phrase was later adopted as the official national motto by the Eisenhower administration. In the throes of the Cold War, the Eisenhower administration also revised the Pledge of Allegiance in 1954 to include the words "one nation under God," in glaring contrast with the image of Soviet atheism. And in the months following the attacks of September 11, 2001, there was a dramatic increase in the popularity of the unofficial national anthem, "God Bless America," penned by Irving Berlin in an earlier period of crisis, the buildup to World War II.

It is not surprising that war, hardship, and uncertainty inspire individuals to turn to faith in a higher power for solace. But sacred imagery arguably serves another purpose in discourses of national identity. Not only does it legitimate the existence and actions of the nation with a claim of divine sanction, but in certain instances, it helps define the national community against real or imagined nonbelieving Others. Whether "heathen savages," "papists," atheistic Communists, or "Islamic terrorists," the figure of the dangerous nonbeliever has long reinforced the notion of America as a community of Protestants.

Although anti-Catholicism eased considerably in the twentieth century, dominant discourses of national identity still construct the nation as a Christian (or Judeo-Christian) community. The implications for non-coreligionists are clear: they are always outsiders to some degree. Even coreligionists may be constructed as apostate if they challenge traditional social hierarchies too significantly. In recent decades, American socialists, feminists, gay rights activists, environmentalists, "liberals," and intellectuals, among others, have been portrayed by conservative social forces as godless, un-American Others. The power of such imagery was evident in 2006 when Evangelist Jerry Falwell claimed that faithful Christians would react more strongly against Hillary Clinton running for President than against Lucifer himself seeking the office (Wallsten 2006). Although Clinton has publicly professed her deep Christian faith (Clinton 2003), to Falwell and his followers, Clinton's political and social commitments, her feminism and her liberalism, are incompatible with true Christian, and true American, values.

FROM "MELTING POT" TO MULTICULTURALISM

Even while American discourses of national identity have focused most prominently on the white, Anglo-Christian community, another vision of the national community gained popularity in the twentieth century: America as the "melting pot." Between 1890 and 1920 some eighteen million immigrants, mainly from Europe, arrived in America (Booth 1998). In 1908, one of these immigrants, Israel Zangwill, staged his play *The Melting Pot* in Washington, DC. One character declared that America was ". . . the great Melting Pot where all the races of Europe are melting and re-forming." He continued, "A fig for your feuds and vendettas! Germans and Frenchmen, Irishmen and Englishmen, Jews and Russians . . . ! God is making the American." (Zangwill 1909)[18]

This new American was expected to leave the ways of the Old World behind and adopt the language, values, and customs of his new homeland.[19] Not to do so, not to assimilate fully into white Anglo-Protestant culture, was to risk evoking resentment and suspicion. Amidst the Red Scare of 1919–1920 and the McCarthyism of the 1940s and 1950s, thousands of Americans, mainly immigrants, trade unionists, social activists, and suspected communists, were questioned and detained in an effort to stamp out radicalism and "un-American" activities. Such campaigns both reflected and fuelled fears about growing numbers of migrants from Southern and Eastern Europe, many of whom were Jewish or Catholic and darker-skinned than earlier migrants from Northern Europe. Enforced conformity to main-stream political views and Anglo-Protestant culture, it seems, offered an antidote for those fears.

Later in the twentieth century, as immigration patterns shifted and increasing numbers of migrants came from non-European nations, such assimilationist expectations gave way to the goals of pluralism. In the late twentieth century, the "melting pot" model fell out of favor somewhat, replaced by new metaphors, such as the "salad bowl" or "mosaic" society. "Diversity" and "multiculturalism" were the new national buzzwords growing out of the social changes of the 1960s and 1970s: the civil rights movement, the women's rights movement, the gay rights movement, the Watergate scandal, the Vietnam War, antiwar protests, and increasing immigration from non-European nations. While each of these developments had its own dynamics, each in its own way challenged the taken-for-granted authority and naturalized dominance of white, heterosexual males. Such shifting power relations ultimately reshaped American discourses of national identity.

Not surprisingly, the rising prominence and demonstrated equal competence of women and people of color led, over the last decades of the twentieth century, to the inclusion of at least some nonwhite and non-male imagery in discourses of American national identity.[20] In 1983, Dr. Martin Luther King Jr. became the only African American to be honored with a national holiday. And between 1976 and 1990 the federal government officially designated an annual Black History Month, Women's History Month, Hispanic Heritage Month, Asian American and Pacific Islander Heritage Month, and American Indian Heritage Month. While schools, libraries, civic organizations, and state bodies commonly sponsor displays or events to acknowledge the contributions of women and people of color during these designated months, such observances are typically quite modest and often pass without significant public comment. These dedicated months represent official attempts to shape more inclusive narratives of nation; however, they also reflect the widespread perception that "black history," "women's history," and the histories of the nation's other marginalized groups are somehow separate from "American history" as a whole.

While the sweeping social changes of the 1960s and 1970s ultimately created at least limited space in the national imaginary for the achievements of women and people of color, Jeffords (1989) has argued that the net effect of such changes was a "remasculinization" of American society. Specifically, she suggests that military defeat in Vietnam and the simultaneous rise of the US feminist movement presented a perceived double threat to American masculinity. As a nation that had long prided itself on its military manliness and heroism, the loss in Vietnam and a growing tendency to characterize the conflict as an unjust or shameful one were blows to masculine national self-conceptions. At the same time, the incursion of women into previously all-male domains seemed to be chipping away at male privilege. Jeffords suggests that a patriarchal backlash against this perceived national emasculation led to the "large-scale renegotiation and regeneration of the interests, values, and projects of patriarchy" (1989, xi).[21] While popular culture in the 1980s and 1990s celebrated such hypermasculine icons as Rambo and the Terminator, the state pushed the nuclear arms race with the Soviet Union to new extremes and attacked what were characterized as feminizing or "nanny state" programs including social welfare, and health and environmental protection programs.[22] Ronald Reagan, the "cowboy President," took a leading role in restoring the masculine agency of the nation.

HEROES AND SUPERHEROES

The "cowboy President" was, of course, more thespian than ranch hand. But over his long political career, he settled comfortably into a role seemingly tailor-made for him, that of the stalwart, plainspoken American hero. Some of the most enduring images of Reagan show him suntanned and physically vigorous, dressed in denim and a cowboy hat, and flashing an easy smile. Although not a young man himself, he exemplified the youthful vitality of the nation, and his relaxed cowboy persona was a visible reminder of American egalitarianism, self-sufficiency, and rugged (masculine) individualism. Such heroes have a long pedigree in the national imaginary, stretching from the larger-than-life frontiersmen discussed earlier through twentieth-century superheroes and beyond. Each in his or her (usually his) own way, distils what are widely considered to be quintessentially American traits.

Scholars of national identity and nationalism have largely ignored comic books, a cultural form characterized as lowbrow, juvenile, and disposable. But, as Dittmer (2005) argues, the messages conveyed in comic books may be all the more powerful because the medium is considered "innocent." The very ordinariness of the form makes its messages appear natural and normal. American comic book superheros exemplify national ideals and, in the case of a character like Captain America, literally "embody" the nation (Dittmer 2005, 627).

The Captain America character, initially created to appeal to rising nationalism in the lead-up to US entry into World War II, continues to attract a readership in the twenty-first century (Dittmer 2005). He is a blond-haired, blue-eyed, muscle-bound Anglo-American dressed in a red, white, and blue suit that clearly evokes the national flag. Readers are told that he used to be physically frail until he received a "super-soldier serum" developed by military scientists. Although the serum increased his size and strength, he can only maintain his powerful physique through rigorous training. Throughout the story lines, it is clear that while Captain America was created by the state he is not simply a servant of the state. Rather, he is guided by a natural sense of morality and justice. Likewise, although he is certainly capable of using force, he uses it reluctantly and only in defense of the nation. The Captain America comics celebrate hard work, moral action, the judicious use of violence, and patriotism. Moreover, they clearly celebrate Anglo-American masculinity.

Also making his debut in the lead-up to the Second World War, Superman has proven an enduring national icon. Unlike Captain America who was said to be an average American man before his transformation, Superman was said to have travelled to Earth from a distant planet. In a sense, Superman is the "ultimate American immigrant" (Dittmer 2005, 631). Coming from an alien land, he assimilated fully, passing as a "mild-mannered" citizen in his everyday life as Clark Kent, while becoming the greatest defender of the American status quo, constructed as "truth, justice, and the American way."

The forceful individualism of these iconic male superheroes is usefully contrasted with superheroines of the comic book genre. Characters such as Batgirl and Supergirl served in tagalong supporting roles to the real (male) heroes of their series, and were clearly subordinate and juvenile members of their respective teams, as indicated by their designation as "girls." Wonder Woman, on the other hand, was characterized by maturity, evidenced in both her well-developed physical and mental powers and in her curvaceous physique.

Like Superman, she was a recent arrival to the human world who assimilated fully to American life. Like Captain America, she literally wrapped herself in the colors of the nation, in her cleavage-baring star-spangled leotard. However, while Wonder Woman also debuted in the buildup to World War II, the powers she brought to the battle against the Nazi menace were stereotypically feminine. She could draw the truth out of even the most sinister villain with her Lasso of Truth, she could communicate with animals, she had healing powers, and she sought always to rehabilitate her enemies rather than to simply defeat them. Men were her weakness, however. If a man managed to link her golden bracelets together she was left powerless, and her love for a human man, Major Steve Trevor, led her to surrender her powers to become his helpmate and eventually his wife. So while superheroes such as Captain America and Superman have embodied cherished American traits, such as individualism, a strong work ethic, and the judicious use of violence, superheroines have embodied traits generally devalued in the culture, whether the immaturity of characters such as Batgirl and Supergirl or the vulnerability and emotionality of Wonder Woman.

Superhero imagery has by no means been confined to the pages of comic books. These national icons feature prominently throughout popular culture and even make their way into political discourse. In the wake of the attacks of September 11, 2001, for instance, President George W. Bush took a bellicose stand against those he labelled "evildoers." Assisted by Vice President Dick Cheney, Attorney General John Ashcroft, and Secretary of Homeland Security Tom Ridge, Bush pursued military and security policies that critics claimed violated both the US Constitution and international law. Supporters, however, praised these men-of-action as national saviors, and gave them monikers to match. *Vanity Fair* dubbed Cheney "The Rock," Ashcroft "The Heat," and Ridge "The Protector." And one syndicated columnist declared that she was expecting the President to "tear open his shirt and reveal the big 'S' on his chest."[23]

In times of uncertainty and perceived threat, American heroes and super-heroes have reflected the hopes of the nation. Whether real or fictional, these characters have embodied cherished national traits: assertiveness, strength, integrity, and individualism, among others. And, almost without exception, they have been white men.

"9/11 CHANGED EVERYTHING"

The facts of September11, 2001, have by now been widely reported. Four American airliners were hijacked and crashed into the World Trade Center, the Pentagon, and a field in Pennsylvania, taking nearly three thousand lives. While the human and financial toll of the attacks has been a regular topic of discussion, relatively little has been said of the ways 9/11 challenged Ameri-can discourses of national identity.

In the first days and weeks after the attacks, national grief, fear, and anger were mixed with variations of a single question: "Why do they hate us?" For Americans who had long subscribed to the notion that theirs was the most admired and beloved nation in the world, this was a confounding question. President George W. Bush provided an answer in his first Congres-sional address after the attacks. "They," the attackers and their supporters, hated American democracy, American "progress and pluralism, tolerance and freedom," and the American "way of life" (Bush 2001). "They" had declared war on America, on Christians and Jews, and on "civilization" itself (Bush 2001). Bush declared a "war on terror" that night, with rhetoric reminiscent of the nation's "savage wars" and "good wars" of the past. He characterized the enemy as brutal, cruel, fanatical, evil, a "dark threat" plot-ting to kill women and children. America, by contrast, was peaceful, just, loving, respectful of others, creative, hardworking, courageous, and godly. In this way, clear-cut dichotomies of us/them, good/evil, cruelty/justice were employed in the face of events that threatened to dramatically undermine America's long-held sense of exceptionalism.

In the immediate aftermath of 9/11 the US was the recipient of sympathy and support from around the world, reassuring many Americans of their nation's place in the hearts of the international community. However, when the Bush administration undertook military invasions of Afghanistan and Iraq, those same Americans were shocked and appalled at the refusal of most nations to support them. Arguably the most intense public outrage was directed at European allies who were characterized as turning their backs on the very nation that had rescued them in the Second World War. The French, in particular, were derided to such an extent that politicians in Washington,

DC, changed the menus in their Capitol Hill cafeteria to obliterate references to French culinary influences.[24] Censure was also extended to Americans who opposed military action or suggested that the nation examine the ways its own policies inspire resentment and violence around the world. Conservative commentators branded antiwar activists "un-American"; popular performers faced boycotts for their criticisms of American military actions; and dissenting scholars were publicly denounced as traitors.[25]

At the same time, American Muslims, those of Arab descent, and even individuals considered "Middle Eastern–looking" faced increasing hostility and discrimination. Under the hastily passed USA PATRIOT Act, the use of racial profiling was sanctioned in the interest of national security. In the months immediately following the 9/11 attacks, the administration detained 1,200 people and announced that they were pursuing another eight thousand individuals (mainly men of Middle Eastern descent) for questioning and possible detention in what the ACLU called "the first large-scale detention of a group of people based on country of origin or ancestry since the internment of Japanese-Americans during World War II" (ACLU 2004, 4–5). Not surprisingly, with the state at least tacitly suggesting a connection between ethnoracial background and terrorism, in the year following the 9/11 attacks, the FBI reported a seventeenfold increase nationwide in hate crimes against Muslims, people of Middle Eastern descent, and those mistaken for Muslims or Middle Easterners (Human Rights Watch 2002). As a further measure of increased national Islamophobia, the earnings of Muslim men in the US dropped 10 percent in the post-9/11 period (Kaushal et al. 2007).

Post-9/11 national security concerns and a general economic downturn have, at the same time, contributed to rising anti-immigrant rhetoric. In 2005, the US House passed the anti-immigrant Sensenbrenner-King Bill (HR 4437) which made rendering assistance to illegal immigrants a felony. Teachers, doctors, and clergy working in immigrant communities were among those likely to face felony prosecution under the legislation. While public protests led to the introduction of the slightly less punitive Hagel-Martinez Bill (S 2611), in the lead-up to the 2006 elections, the Congressional leadership staged a number of "Immigration Hearings," which seemed designed to showcase anti-immigration sentiment. It was in this context that President Bush signed into law the Secure Fence Act, approving the construction of a seven hundred-mile long barrier along America's southern border to contain the "menace" and "simmering powder keg" that fence supporters claimed lurk across the border.[26]

The proposed fence is just one recent manifestation of the nation's periodic isolationism. In times of economic or military crisis, American elites have often sought to minimize international political linkages and responsibilities while still pursuing economic opportunities abroad. Such tendencies have revealed tensions and contradictions in American discourses of national identity: the US welcomes the "tired ... poor ... huddled masses yearning to breathe free," but must be prepared to shut its doors for self-preservation.[27] The US is the "promised land," a land of opportunity for all, but it is also the land where self-interest will and should trump collectivism, to the extent that socialism, communalism, and above all communism are treated as social evils. The US is a land of immigrants, yet also a nation that prefers to cut itself off from the rest of the world and pursue unilateral policies. American isolationism and unilateralism are, in a sense, a natural extension of discourses of national identity which celebrate independence, self-reliance and individualism.

Since the September 2001 attacks, it has become commonplace to observe that "9/11 changed everything," usually with reference to matters such as security reforms, the curtailment of civil liberties, and escalating militarism. In regards to American discourses of national identity, however, another truism is more accurate: the more things change, the more they stay the same. The post-9/11 period has witnessed a marked reversion to older, less inclusive narratives of nation. The consciously pluralist and less patriarchal constructions of national identity which emerged in the last decades of the twentieth century appear to be fading amidst rhetoric of the "war on terror" (Faludi 2007a). Instead, images of "military manliness" (Funck 2002), of female vulnerability, of Anglo-Christian culture, and of the "dark threat" of nonwhite Others are in ascendancy: another cowboy president, another generation of soldiers, another "savage enemy" to fight against with the blessings of one true God.

"WHO ARE WE?"

At the turn of the new millennium and in the wake of 9/11, Huntington asked "Who are we?" As a nation, as a civilization, what distinguishes us from others, and how do we manage difference within our own society? As noted earlier, Huntington concluded that cultural diversity in the United States must be carefully circumscribed to ensure the rightful dominance of Anglo-Protestant culture and the peace, prosperity, and justice it engenders. Allowing too great a voice for religious minorities, non-English-speaking populations, and feminists, among other groups, will lead to the degradation and eventual collapse of the nation.

Huntington is certainly not the only one exploring these questions of national identity, however. Dramatic events in the global "war on terror" have many Americans today asking "Who are we?" or perhaps "Are we who we *thought* we were?" Several cherished assumptions about the nature of the nation's people and institutions have been challenged by recent developments.

"America is a land of plenty." Yet the gap between rich and poor is growing, the number of those living at or below the poverty level is growing, the number of those without even basic health care is growing, the number of home foreclosures is growing, and the demands on charity organizations are growing. So is this a land of plenty?

"America is free and just." Yet under the USA PATRIOT Act, the Protect America Act, the Military Commissions Act, and related legislative and policy reforms, the state can now intercept private communications without a warrant, arbitrarily designate detainees as "unlawful enemy combatants," and indefinitely detain prisoners without charge or due legal process. So is this a free and just nation?

"America is humane." Yet the state has redefined "torture" so as to allow extreme forms of physical coercion previously considered impermissible under the Geneva Conventions. In 2004, shocking photographs of detainee abuse at the US-run Abu Ghraib prison in Iraq sparked a public outcry in both the US and abroad, and yet reports of systematic prisoner abuse at Guantánamo Bay continue. At the same time, the "extraordinary rendition" program allows the transfer of detainees to foreign prisons that employ torture, and evidence obtained through torture is admissible in any legal proceedings against the prisoner. So is this a humane nation?

"America is a bastion of democracy." Yet irregularities in recent elections have undermined American confidence in the electoral process. At the same time, frequent invocation of executive privilege and state secrets provisions suggest a lack of transparency and accountability more commonly associated with dictatorships than democracies. Is this a democratic nation?

"America is tolerant and open." Yet since 9/11 hate crimes against Muslims and people of Middle Eastern descent have increased dramatically, the state has endorsed the use of racial profiling for the purposes of protecting national security, and lawmakers have voted to build a massive fence along the nation's southern border. Is this a tolerant and open nation?

"America fights good wars." Yet America's invasion and occupation of Iraq, almost universally derided outside the US, has steadily lost support at home. First, claims that Iraq possessed weapons of mass destruction proved false, then human rights violations by US soldiers began to emerge: the prisoner abuse at Abu Ghraib, the kidnapping and summary execution of a civilian in Hamdania, the mass killing of civilians in Haditha, the rape and murder of a teenaged girl in Mahmoudiya and the murder of her family. At the same time, thousands of US soldiers and tens of thousands of Iraqis have been killed in the conflict. It becomes increasingly difficult for Americans to see the war in Iraq as a "good" war.

With such challenges to long-standing national self-conceptions, it remains to be seen how Americans will answer the question, "Who are we?" Will narratives of nation be increasingly dominated by the images and agendas of the patriarchal, white Anglo-Protestant culture that Huntington defends? Will the pendulum swing back toward the ideals of multiculturalism and social equity? Or will an alternate vision emerge out of the complex negotiations that generate discourses of national identity?

Part II

6 Staging the Nation
Gender, Race, and Nation in Olympic Opening Ceremonies

International sport can usefully be conceptualized as symbolic warfare, a way for nations to sublimate their martial aggression, assert their will and power over others, and satisfy their most chauvinistic impulses.[1] At international sporting spectacles such as the Olympics, explicit articulations of national pride, loyalty, and attachment are *de rigueur*. And through the rituals of competition, ceremony, and spectatorship the national self and national Others are starkly delineated. Thus, the Olympic Games, the largest of international sporting events, are a rich source of discourses of national identity.

This chapter examines constructions of Japaneseness, Australianness, and Americanness in the opening ceremonies of the Nagano 1998, Sydney 2000, and Salt Lake City 2002 Olympic Games. Specifically, it considers how narratives of nation are gendered and racialized in ways that mirror, sustain, or challenge the subordination of women and ethnoracial minorities within these three nations.

The analysis here builds on the scholarship on sport and inequality.[2] Sport is often constructed as the great equalizer. That is, in the sporting arena each competitor is said to be judged on performance alone, rather than on traits such as gender, race, or class. However, critics have suggested that rather than breaking down social inequalities, sport in general and the Olympics more particularly serve to reinforce inequalities based on race, gender, and class. Many such critiques are class based, focusing on three principle ways sport serves the interests of capital and the state: by creating a self-disciplined, obedient, and physically robust workforce, thereby increasing worker productivity; by promoting the consumption of sport products and services, thereby maintaining exploitative economic relationships; and by pacifying the workforce with the pleasures of spectator sport and sheer physical exhaustion, thereby stifling dissent and distracting the masses from their own oppression.

In addition to reinforcing these class-based inequalities, however, contemporary sporting practice, including Olympic sport, is arguably implicated in continuing inequalities based on race and gender. Throughout the history of the modern Olympic Movement, Olympic teams have indexed the status of women and ethnoracial minorities in their respective nations. The exclusion of Jews from competition in Nazi Germany, the exclusion of people of color from South African and Rhodesian teams under those nations' racial segregation laws, and the exclusion of women, initially from all Olympic competition and today from participation on some national teams, have both reflected and reinforced the marginalization of women and ethnoracial minorities in these national contexts. However, recent racial integration of formerly segregated Olympic teams and increasing numbers of female Olympic competitors also reveal the gains made by subordinated social groups on both the national and international stage.

OLYMPIC OPENING CEREMONIES AS COMMERCIALIZED DISCOURSES OF NATIONAL IDENTITY

Olympic opening ceremonies in their current form are elaborately staged and commercialized narratives of nation. The ceremonies consist of a number of compulsory elements enumerated in the Olympic Charter, together with interpretive cultural performances by the host nation. Although the ceremony ostensibly celebrates all member nations, in practice both compulsory and interpretive elements mirror the values and experiences of the host nation. This narrative serves not only as an affirmation of national identity, but as an extended advertisement for the host nation, an opportunity to promote tourism, international corporate investment, trade, and political ideologies. Such commercialized national narratives serve as a reminder that discourses of national identity are not free-floating collections of signs, but are firmly grounded in material relations.

The commercial reality underpinning Olympic narratives of nation is that hosting the Games is an enormously expensive venture, not undertaken simply for the sake of global altruism or even patriotism, but with the expectation that the Games will result in a net economic gain for the host nation. From the very beginning of the modern Olympic Movement, the Games have been closely bound up with commercial interests. After a shaky start in 1896 when the inaugural Athens Games were nearly canceled for lack of financing, subsequent organizers took steps to ensure the economic viability of Olympic events. The next three Olympic Games were held in conjunction with international trade and cultural exhibitions, with sporting events at times staged amidst manufacturers' displays (Gruneau 1984). Commercial links have increased exponentially in the intervening years.

Today the economic impact of revenue-generating activities directly or indirectly associated with the Olympic Games is almost incalculably massive. Marketing has become the single largest revenue-generating activity associated with the Olympic Games. In the lead-up to the Sydney Games corporate "Olympic Partners" paid an estimated $579 million in exchange for permission to use the closely guarded Olympic logo during the Olympiad.[3]

Additionally, in the US alone, advertisers paid up to $600,000 per thirty seconds of airtime during Sydney Games telecasts, translating into an estimated $900 million in advertising revenue for NBC, the exclusive holder of Olympic broadcast rights in the United States (Fendrich 2000). The sale of Olympics broadcast rights is now the leading source of income for the International Olympic Committee (IOC) and national organizing committees. Between 1980 and 2000, the sale of Games broadcasting rights grew from $101 million to $1.3 billion worldwide, the revenue shared between the IOC and host Olympic committees.[4] These marketing and broadcasting agreements go some way toward offsetting the substantial costs of hosting the Games.

The 1984 Los Angeles Games marked a watershed in the commercialization of the modern Olympics. After the 1976 Montreal Games, when taxpayers had to meet a $1.2 billion dollar budget shortfall, public funding of the Games decreased substantially and subsequent Games organizers faced pressure to finance the event through private sector agreements (Preuss 1998, 201). Los Angeles Games organizers therefore established lucrative sponsorship and broadcasting arrangements that would ultimately change the look and feel of the Olympic Games. While Olympic pageantry had been intensifying since the 1970s, the Los Angeles Games took the mass-mediated spectacle to new heights, with all the costumes, choreography, and special effects of a Hollywood blockbuster film. A combination of unprecedented spectacle and political controversy (the boycott of the Games by the Soviet Union and its Eastern bloc allies) saw television audiences soar to an estimated 2.5 billion viewers in 156 nations (Toohey and Veal 2000, 131).

Following the striking commercial success of the Los Angeles Games, which generated a budget surplus of $225 million and an estimated $2.5 billion boost to the California economy, subsequent Games organizers have incorporated Hollywood-style opening and closing ceremonies into their Olympics programs and adjusted the timing and structure of events to maximize global viewership (Toohey and Veal 2000, 133, 217). In this way, the economics of a globalized mass media continue to shape Olympic stagings of the nation.

At the same time, as noted in Chapter 1, the cultural and political dynamics of globalization have created perceived threats to national self-determination, which in turn have sparked vigorous assertions of national identity around the globe. The modern Olympic Games, as both a product and promoter of economic, cultural, and political globalization, exemplify tensions between globalism and localism and provide fertile ground for articulations of national identity. As Tomlinson (1996, 601) has noted, "The study of Olympic spectacle offers a revealing basis for the comprehension of the complexities characteristic of the cultural expression of the persisting crises of modernity and globalization," perhaps chief among them, the so-called "crisis" of national identity.

IDEOLOGICAL TENSIONS OF THE OLYMPIC
MOVEMENT AND OLYMPIC OPENING CEREMONIES

The Olympic opening ceremonies analyzed here reveal the ideological tensions inherent in the modern Olympic Movement. The most prominent of these, and therefore the key focus of this analysis, are the tensions between universalism and nationalism, and the tensions between tradition and change.

The eighth Fundamental Principle of Olympism, as stated in the Olympic Charter, reads: "The practice of sport is a human right. Every individual must have the possibility of practicing sport in accordance with his or her needs" (IOC 2001, 9).[5] In adopting the language of human rights, the IOC constructs sport as a universal human desire and experience, a means through which one demonstrates one's humanity. The Olympic opening ceremonies examined here celebrate universalism both through compulsory rituals and through interpretive segments centering on themes such as the relationship between humanity and nature and the triumph of the human spirit.

At the same time, Olympic competition is competition between nations, and has the capacity to heighten national rivalries and alliances. Likewise, national-level specificities inflect virtually every aspect of the Olympic opening ceremonies described here. The consciously universalist rituals of the ceremonies are in a sense domesticated by the host nations and imbued with national meanings. The interpretive cultural performances dramatize national myths, experiences, and values, focusing on such themes as the antiquity of the nation and the struggles, triumphs, and character of its people.

A second ideological tension, that between tradition and change, is particularly evidenced in the interpretive performances of the opening ceremonies examined here. From the beginning of the modern Olympic Movement, Olympic rhetoric has been Janus-faced, gazing both back in time to ancient Greece, long constructed as an exemplar of Western culture, learning, and the arts, and forward in time to a world of change and progress. Opening ceremony interpretive segments exemplify this tension between tradition and change. As already noted, nations constantly invent and reinvent their "traditions" by drawing selectively on historical resources. The Olympic opening ceremonies examined here simplify, amplify, and depoliticize national (invented) traditions, and extend the narrative of nation back in time, to an age well before the official founding of the nation. However, the narrative of nation is simultaneously extended forward in time in a staging of national economic, political, and social progress.

The opening ceremonies of the Nagano 1998, Sydney 2000, and Salt Lake City 2002 Olympic Games consisted of both the mandatory Olympic rituals and interpretive cultural segments designed by the host organizers and approved by the IOC (Table 6.1). What follows is a critical reading of the content of each opening ceremony in order to identify underlying

Table 6.1 Sequence of Events at the Nagano, Sydney, and Salt Lake City Olympic Opening Ceremonies

Order in Program	Nagano 1998	Sydney 2000	Salt Lake City 2002
1	Coming Together	*Man from Snowy River**	Parade of Flags from Past Games
2	Raising of the Pillars	Entrance of Officials	Entrance of Officials
3	Entrance of Sumo Wrestlers, Emperor, and Empress	Host Nation's Anthem and Flag	Host Nation's Anthem and Flag
4	Dance of the Guardian Spirits	*Deep Sea Dreaming*	*The Fire Within* Part I
5	*Parade of Nations*	*Awakening*	*Parade of Nations*
6	Speeches by Officials and Opening Declaration	*Tin Symphony*	Native American Performance
7	Olympic Hymn/Flag, Host Nation's Anthem	*Arrivals*	Journey of the Pioneers
8	Olympic Torch/ Cauldron	*Eternity*	Salt Lake Olympic Anthem
9	Oaths and Dove Release	Marching Band	Speeches by Officials and Opening Declaration
10	*Ode to Joy* Finale	*Parade of Nations*	Olympic Flag and Hymn
11	—	*Dare To Dream*	*Fragile* and Dove Release
12	—	Speeches by Officials and Opening Declaration	Development of a Champion
13	—	*Heroes Live Forever*	Olympic Torch/ Cauldron
14	—	Olympic Hymn/Flag and Oaths	*The Fire Within* Part II
15	—	Olympic Torch/ Cauldron	*The Fire Within* Part III

* Segment titles in italics are the official segment titles or titles of artistic works.

patterns of meaning. As with any exercise in content analysis, this is not the only possible reading of these complex cultural texts. However, it is a reading that is grounded in the specific material and ideological contexts of the three host nations.

Domesticating Universalist Rituals

By IOC decree, all Olympic opening ceremonies currently must include the following elements: a parade of Games participants; speeches and declarations by local and international Olympic officials and the head of state of the host nation; the raising of the Olympic flag to the accompaniment of the Olympic anthem; the performance of the host nation's national anthem; the torch relay and lighting of the Olympic cauldron; and oaths taken on behalf of participating athletes and judges. While the basic content of these elements is dictated by Olympic Charter byelaws, in practice participating nations inflect these standard rituals with nationally specific meanings, thus domesticating these universalist moments. In the opening ceremonies examined here, all of the compulsory ritual elements were domesticated by the host nations to some degree. However, this trend is most clearly illustrated by two rituals: the performance of the host's national anthem and the lighting of the Olympic cauldron.

Not surprisingly the performance of the national anthem is an event deeply infused with national symbolism. In Nagano musicians in period costume performed the national anthem on traditional instruments in the style of ancient court music (*gagaku*), thus evoking the nation's deep cultural heritage. Notably, the lyrics of the national anthem were barely audible, and although most host nations choose this moment to display their national flag, the Japanese flag was conspicuously absent. Because of lingering associations between the national flag, the national anthem, and Japanese wartime aggression, the flag and anthem have been at the center of national and international debates.[6] Critics within Japan and abroad suggest that the continued use of these symbols reflects a more general failure of the Japanese government to accept responsibility for its wartime acts of aggression throughout Asia and the Pacific. It is not surprising that amidst such controversy, the presentation of the national anthem and flag was subdued.

In Sydney, by contrast, the singing of the national anthem was followed by 120 men and women on horseback parading Australian flags around the stadium. The riders wore Akubra hats and Driza-Bone coats in a salute to the Australian stockmen made famous in the nineteenth-century poetry of Banjo Paterson.[7] The theme music from the movie version of Paterson's epic poem *The Man from Snowy River* made explicit the link between Australian nationhood, symbolized in the flag, and a largely white, rural, and masculine national identity.

Lastly, the Salt Lake City performance of the US national anthem and the display of the US flag were replete with references to the nation's "war on terror" in the wake of the September 11, 2001, attacks on Washington, DC, and New York City.[8] The battered flag which flew on the World Trade Center on September 11 was brought into the stadium by US Olympians and members of the New York City Police and Fire Departments and the New York City Port Authority, those agencies most closely associated with the search and rescue efforts following the attacks. The Mormon Tabernacle Choir sang the national anthem as pictures of fluttering US flags were projected on stadium video screens. The segment was richly layered, evoking the divine through the use of the Choir; evoking the nation through its most potent symbol of nationhood, the flag; evoking the power of the state through the presence of the enforcers of law and order; and serving as homage to the victims of the September attacks.

Notwithstanding the power and majesty of other Olympic rituals, the entrance of the Olympic torch and the lighting of the Olympic cauldron have been the climax of Olympic opening ceremonies since Adolf Hitler's director of the 1936 Berlin Games introduced the ritual in its present form (Toohey and Veal 2000, 59). Following in the Berlin tradition, the Olympic torch is lit on Mount Olympus and then embarks on a relay tour to and through the next host nation. The torch relay, though a recent invention, symbolically links the current host nation to the revered civilization of ancient Greece, and the lighting of the cauldron at the end of the opening ceremony becomes an experience akin to religious ecstasy. The intensity of the moment is explained on two levels. On one level, the host nation becomes, at least temporarily, metonymic with ancient Greece, at the center of a civilization. On a more primal level, the ritual enacts a Promethean taming of the fire of the gods, humanity's mastery over environment and destiny.

In Nagano, Chris Moon, a British amputee landmine survivor, carried the torch into the stadium surrounded by Japanese children singing the theme song of the Games, *When Children Rule the World*. The message was one of international pacifism, consistent with Japan's Constitutionally mandated pacifism. The torch was then passed to both male and female Japanese Olympians, who presented it to Olympic medallist Itō Midori. Itō, dressed in robes and a headdress reminiscent of ancient imperial regalia, emerged from behind giant Japanese folding fans to light the cauldron amidst the last climactic phrases of Puccini's *Madama Butterfly*. In Puccini's Orientalist opera, the title character is the epitome of passive Japaneseness, suffering and sacrificing for her Western lover. In linking Itō with *Madama Butterfly*, traditional Japanese femininity became the vehicle for nonthreatening assertions of national pride.

In Sydney, the Games marking the centennial of women's participation in Olympic competition, the torch was carried around the stadium by six female Australian Olympians, and ultimately presented to Aboriginal Australian runner Cathy Freeman. Freeman waded into a shallow pool where she ignited the cauldron from within a cascade of water. The disk-shaped cauldron then ascended to the top of the stadium along the course of a waterfall several stories tall. The narrative of nation played out in these closing moments of the ceremony centered on both the timelessness of nature and progress through human endeavor: the blending of water and fire evoked the two overriding natural features of the Australian continent, the sea and the desert; and the dramatic ascent of the cauldron suggested the mastery of nature through advanced technology. In addition, the choice of Freeman as the bearer of nation in this dramatic scene can be read as a proud assertion of Australian egalitarianism and multiculturalism.

In Salt Lake City, the torch was borne around the stadium by pairs of current and former Olympians, both men and women. The torch was finally passed to Mike Eruzione, captain of the 1980 Olympic men's ice hockey team. Eruzione was then joined by his former teammates, and the men lit the cauldron as a team. The choice of the 1980 hockey team must be understood in relation to the events of September 11, 2001, and the military actions in which the US was engaged at the time of the Salt Lake Games. At the height of the Cold War, the 1980 US men's hockey team defeated the team from the USSR and went on to win the gold medal at the Lake Placid Games. The defeat of the Soviet powerhouse by the underdog US team was seen to portend the victory of the US over its Cold War enemies. In 2002, the appearance of the team at the climactic moment of the ceremony evoked these Cold War triumphs. The moment served as a symbolic assertion of American power, a promise to once again defeat its enemies in the so-called war on terror.

In sum, the host nations examined here incorporated the compulsory rituals of the opening ceremony into their own narratives of nation, refiguring these universalist moments as displays of national character, pride, power, and progress. Most strikingly, in the case of Salt Lake City, the avowedly apolitical compulsory rituals of the opening ceremony were transformed into endorsements of US military and police action against selected targets both within the nation and abroad.

Staging Japanese National Identity: The Nagano Interpretive Program

In addition to the mandatory ritual elements, Olympic opening ceremonies incorporate interpretive programs which typically showcase the host nation's culture, history, and achievements. At the Nagano Games, the interpretive program began with a symbolic calling together of participants. While the centuries-old bell at Zenkoji Shrine summoned local participants, the assembled audience watched live satellite links from Germany, Australia, the US, China, and South Africa where an international choir waited to perform Beethoven's *Ode to Joy*. These first few moments marked out the themes that ran throughout the interpretive segments of the ceremony: the importance of community, both local and global; Japanese cultural uniqueness; and the blending of tradition with cutting-edge technology.

Scholarly and popular discussions of Japaneseness both in Japan and in the West have long stressed collectivism as a key organizational principle of Japanese society. In particular, this group ethic features prominently in widely circulating explanations of Japan's rapid economic development in the postwar period. It is not surprising, therefore, that collective action was a central theme of Nagano's staging of Japaneseness. The most prominent dramatization of collectivism was in the raising of eight "sacred pillars" (*ombashira*) on the stadium floor, in the first of the main interpretive segments. In this segment, one thousand Japanese men and women in festival coats manually raised the enormous wooden pillars while singing and chanting to coordinate their actions. The performance exemplified not only harmonious group relations, but also harmony with nature and with the gods; for the pillars were raised at the north, south, east, and west entrances to the stadium, signifying nature as a balanced totality, and the pillars themselves, each hewn from a single tree, were said to host Shinto spirits.

The segment may be read as an allegory of Japan's rise to economic superpower status through collective action, sacrifice of individual needs to the needs of the group, and a strong work ethic, all within the context of traditional Confucian and Shinto values. Another segment of the opening ceremony celebrated the importance of Japan's membership in the *global* community. In the finale to the opening ceremony, Japanese conductor Seiji Ozawa directed choirs on five continents in a performance of *Ode to Joy* from Beethoven's Ninth Symphony. This coming together of performers from the five regions of the globe symbolized in the Olympic Rings was consistent not only with the universalism of the Olympic movement, but with the Japanese policy of internationalization (*kokusaika*) which has been at the forefront of much government, corporate, and social policy in Japan since the 1970s.[9]

At its heart, Japanese internationalization represents an attempt to increase the nation's involvement in the international exchange of commodities, ideas, and (to a certain extent) people. Ozawa himself epitomizes the new "global citizen" (*kokusaijin*) celebrated in the rhetoric of internationalization. Born in China to Japanese parents, Ozawa was educated in Tokyo, studied and conducted throughout Europe and North America, and became the longest serving music director of the Boston Symphony Orchestra. His presence in the finale of the Nagano opening ceremony was not only an assertion of national pride in the achievements of one native son, but also served specifically as a reminder that Japan is an active participant in global "high" culture and an enthusiastic member of an increasingly interconnected global community.

The cultural universalism of the finale stood in contrast to discourses of cultural uniqueness found in the other main interpretive segments of Nagano's opening ceremony. The raising of the *ombashira* described above, as well as the sumo ring-entering ritual, and the dance of the "guardian spirits" (*dōsojin*), evoked ancient customs, beliefs, and ways of life said to be unique to Japan.

The raising of the sacred pillars was followed by a ring-entering ritual by Japan's top-ranked sumo wrestlers. Sumo, the national sport of Japan, is said to have originated as a form of entertainment to placate the Shinto spirits and ensure a good harvest. The matches originally took place at Shinto shrines, and even today retain the trappings of Shinto. At the Nagano opening ceremony the place of sumo in national self-conceptions was emphasized by the fact that it was in the middle of the ring-entering ceremony that the Emperor and Empress entered the stadium. Once they took their seats, the Grand Champion performed a ritual stomping to drive out malevolent spirits and purify the venue. The segment drew on strong symbolic and historical connections between sumo, Shinto, the Emperor, and the nation. That is, Shinto is the indigenous religion of Japan, with beliefs and practices that are said to make the nation unique; and the Emperor himself is traditionally considered the high priest of Shinto and is said to be a direct descendant of the Sun Goddess, arch-protector of the nation. Thus on one level the sumo segment linked Japanese national identity with the virility and physical strength of the wrestlers, and on another level sumo served as a marker of Japan's cultural uniqueness and ancient traditions.

The guardian spirit (*dōsojin*) segment of the opening ceremony continued this discourse of national uniqueness. The *dōsojin* are Shinto spirits said to protect travellers as well as roads, borders, bridges, and other transitional zones. In the opening ceremony, dancers in *dōsojin* costumes were surrounded by children in rustic traditional cloaks. The children eventually cast off the cloaks to reveal bright sweaters woven in the colors of each participating nation's flag. The segment thus served both to assert Japan's cultural uniqueness by way of its indigenous religion, and to claim a place for the nation in the international community through the children's display of all the national colors of participating nations.

The Nagano interpretive program in its totality revealed the place of categories of gender and ethnicity in Japanese national self-conceptions. Both men and women featured in the performance, but in distinct roles. Through the use of sumo wrestlers, Seiji Ozawa, and the Emperor, masculinity was associated with physical strength, virtuosity, and both sacred and secular power. Conversely, the women featured in the performance, from the demure Empress to Itō Midori as "Madama Butterfly," exemplified passive and Orientalized femininity. In addition, the performance excluded Japan's sizeable ethnoracial minority groups,[10] whose distinctive customs and contributions were elided by an overarching theme of cultural and ethnoracial homogeneity.

Such gendered and racialized discourses of Japanese national identity are grounded in relations of dominance. Recent scholarship suggests that women in Japan face disadvantages relative to men, in the home, at school, and at work, and ethnoracial minorities face disadvantages in education, employment, and criminal justice relative to the majority group.[11] The staging of female subordination and ethnoracial homogeneity not only mirrors such disadvantage but serves to legitimize long-standing social hierarchies based on gender, race, and ethnicity.

At the same time, however, these gendered and racialized discourses of national identity challenge such social hierarchies in subtle ways. The penultimate torchbearer in the Nagano opening ceremony, women's marathon Olympian Hiromi Suzuki, was dressed in a costume that was half tracksuit and half kimono with one elegant trailing sleeve. Thus, Suzuki bore not only the torch, but markers of both traditional Japanese femininity and contemporary female athleticism. Additionally, during the sumo ring-entering ceremony, virile Japanese masculinity was embodied most notably not by a native son, but by Hawaiian-born sumo Grand Champion Akebono (Chad Rowan). Such elements, whether by design or not, disrupt the veneer of Orientalized femininity and ethnoracial homogeneity of the opening ceremony.

Staging Australian National Identity: The Sydney Interpretive Program

In contrast to the Nagano interpretive program, the Sydney program featured both men and women of a variety of ethnoracial backgrounds in a variety of social roles; however, such messages of diversity were staged against a backdrop of hegemonic white masculinity. In the opening segment of the interpretive program, the riders representing the "Man from Snowy River" evoked the nation's rural heritage. While both women and men and ethnoracial minorities as well as whites were among the 120 riders, the segment celebrated above all the hearty white stockmen and frontiersmen lauded in nineteenth- and early twentieth-century Australian literature. The sequence constructed archetypical Australianness as white and masculine, and the subsequent representations of Aboriginal Australians, nonwhite migrant Australians, and Australian women were to some degree constructed as deviations from that archetype.

The next two interpretive segments focused on the nation's natural environment and indigenous peoples. The manifest themes of the segments were the beauty and power of nature and the ancient connections between Aboriginal peoples and the land. However, underlying such messages were more subtle constructions of white-Australian dominance and containment both of nature and the indigenous people who inhabit it. The segments expose the Australian "white nation fantasy," the taken-for-granted notion that whites are the legitimate owners and rulers of the Australian nation, and therefore have both the right and the responsibility to monitor and control ethnoracial Others (Hage 1998).

Exemplifying such polysemic narratives, the *Deep Sea Dreaming* segment was structured as the dream of a young, white Australian girl swimming through a magical seascape of deepwater creatures. The girl who "swam" through the scene (suspended in the air by wires) was dwarfed by nature as it was staged on and above the stadium floor, but at the same time, she defied nature by moving freely and with ease through the "water." This defiance of nature was repeated in the next sequence, entitled *Awakening*. The sequence constructed nature as a hostile and threatening force. In this instance, fire-breathers and performers wielding flaming apparatus swept across the stadium floor to symbolize the bushfires to which the Australian landscape is prone. However, even such dangerous natural forces were readily tamed by the performers who manipulated the flames at will apparently without the aid of protective clothing or other technological devices.

It was also in this segment that indigenous Australians first appeared in the opening ceremony, and, in fact, took an active role in choreographing the sequence (Elder 2007, 35). Aboriginal performers in body paint and "traditional" costumes including grass skirts, loincloths, and breastplates, danced through symbolically purifying eucalyptus smoke, as the young white girl from the previous segment watched from above. The sequence was richly layered with both complementary and competing meanings. On one level, the scene symbolized reconciliation between indigenous peoples and white Australians and a national pride in cultural diversity. At the same time, the sequence established an ancient pedigree for an otherwise young nation, thus extending the discourse of national identity back through time immemorial.

On another level, the Aboriginal performance served as an advertisement for international tourism. In Australia as well as elsewhere, indigenous customs, ways of life, and arts and crafts are frequently commercialized for the consumption of tourists (Zeppel 1998). The performance at the opening ceremony may be read as a way to whet the appetites of potential visitors for such exotic fare. It is also significant that the onstage observer of this spectacle was a young white Australian. Her gaze was the proprietary gaze of white Australia, watching over and controlling the indigenous population in much the same way it monitors and tames the landscape. In fact, the segment constructed Aboriginal peoples as primordial, closer to nature than to the structures of contemporary nationhood.

The *Arrivals* sequence was likewise complexly layered. On its surface, the sequence dramatized the arrival of immigrants from the five regions of the globe symbolized in the Olympic rings, and the contributions these immigrants have made to the Australian nation. However, in the representational details, Australian conceptions of the national Self and the Other can be discerned.

Asia was represented in part by dancing women, dressed variously in theatrical Balinese dress, Japanese kimono, or cabaret-style belly-dancer costumes. Differences in clothing style and choreography notwithstanding, all of these women were positioned as exemplars of exoticized Oriental femininity. Additionally, performers representing Chinese festival dragons, sacred cows, and lotus flowers evoked the ancient religious and other cultural traditions of the region. Due to Australia's proximity to Asia, fascination with and fear of Asia has been a long-running theme in discussions of nationhood. From pre-Federation attempts to limit migration from Asia, to World War II rhetoric of the "Yellow Peril," to the stoking of anti-Asian sentiments by figures such as Geoffrey Blainey and Pauline Hanson in the 1980s and 1990s, widely circulating discourses of national identity have constructed an essentialized Asia as the exotic and menacing Other to the Australian national Self. Such discourses have centered principally on perceived cultural, and especially religious, differences of the kind neatly encapsulated in the opening ceremony.

Australia's complex relationship to Europe was likewise reflected in opening ceremony representations. Europe was represented by performers dressed as musical instruments, jesters, and ballet dancers, as well as dancers in costumes representing the solar system. Thus Europe was metonymically linked with the "high" culture of classical music and ballet, with courtly traditions, and with scientific and technological advances, such as those that have allowed for space exploration. From the earliest period of European colonization, the Australian colonies, and later the Federation, positioned themselves as outposts of British civilization. Opening ceremony representations reflected long-standing perceptions of Europe as the pinnacle of culture and learning, as well as Australian self-designation as essentially a European (specifically a British) society. The extent to which Australian national identity *should* be bound up with European/British institutions continues to be a hotly debated national issue, as demonstrated by the 1999 national referendum on breaking Constitutional ties with Britain.[12]

Representations of the Americas in the *Arrivals* sequence reflected Australia's ambivalent relationship with this region. The Americas were represented by three distinct character-types: Latin American salsa dancers; performers dressed as indigenous people in large feathered headdresses; and performers dressed in the red, white, and blue of the US flag, including a Statue of Liberty. On the one hand, the representations positioned the Americas as a source of pleasurable spectacle, of music, dance, and indigenous costume. On the other hand, the performance contained the only nation-specific references in the *Arrivals* sequence, in the form of the unmistakable motifs of the United States flag and the Statue of Liberty. The domination of such powerful national symbols over the regional identity of the Americas reflects continuing Australian concerns over the Americanization of Australian life (see Bell and Bell 1999). In contemporary discussions of Australian political, economic, and cultural affairs, the US looms large, sometimes in the form of a neocolonial bogeyman, sometimes as a model of success to be admired and emulated.

Finally, representations of Africa and Oceania were in many ways less complex and more monolithic than those of other regions of the globe. Africa was represented primarily by dancers in tribal-patterned cloaks and masks and simple garments apparently fashioned out of natural materials, such as grasses, barks, and animal skins. Such simplistic associations between Africa, nature, and the "primitive" reflect both imperialist attitudes inherited from Britain, and the reality of historically rather limited contact between Australia and the people and nations of Africa. Representations of Oceania, on the other hand, were slightly more multidimensional, reflecting Australia's location in the region. Oceania was represented primarily by three sets of characters: island natives in grass skirts; participants in modern water sports, with beach balls and inner tubes; and performers apparently representing contemporary manual laborers, dressed in blue jeans and T-shirts. Within such representations of regional identity, there was a clear distinction between the Australian national Self and Others. Australianness was associated with sport and leisure, with productive labor, and with modernity. Otherness was associated with the "native" and the premodern.

It is of particular interest that the *Arrivals* segment was situated between two segments that more explicitly celebrated white Euro-Australian masculinity. Before the *Arrivals* sequence discussed above, a segment entitled *Tin Symphony* reenacted two events in Australian history: the arrival of Captain James Cook in Australia and the last stand of nineteenth-century outlaw Ned Kelly. Directly following the *Arrivals* sequence, the *Eternity* segment dramatized the technological and economic development of the nation. Each segment provides further insight into gendered and racialized discourses of Australian national identity.

In 1770 navigator James Cook claimed eastern Australia for England on the grounds that the land was *terra nullius*, an uninhabited land. Cook's claim paved the way for English colonization of the continent along with the displacement and slaughter of indigenous people, and the subsequent social, political, and economic marginalization of their descendants. Not surprisingly, the brutal realities of colonization were not represented in the *Tin Symphony* segment. Rather, in this segment, Cook was shown arriving in Australia on a comically oversized bicycle, approaching the new land with a childlike innocence and wonder. In a familiar refrain of Australian narratives of nation, the history of oppression and genocide was obscured by constructions of Europeans as the bearers of civilization and progress to a land forgotten by time.

The second part of the *Tin Symphony* sequence was a portrayal of Ned Kelly's final confrontation with authorities. Kelly was a notorious "bushranger" who, despite robbing banks, killing police officers, and holding entire towns hostage, won a degree of support from struggling small landowners in rural Victoria.[13] Some small-scale farmers and graziers saw Kelly's actions as resistance against an establishment perceived to be corrupt. In his final showdown with authorities Kelly and his partners wore suits of armor fashioned from ploughshares. The confrontation, which ended in his arrest and execution, has been widely celebrated in Australian literature, art, and film, shaping Kelly into an iconoclastic folk hero who embodies traits central to dominant discourses of Australian identity: bravery, irreverence, innovation, determination and, arguably, white masculinity.

The last of the large choreographed segments of the interpretive program was structured as a celebration of the Australian worker. In the extended dance sequence, performers in the de facto workman's uniform of boots, shorts or jeans, and singlets and flannel shirts, danced on sheet metal squares and an iron superstructure representing the Sydney Harbor Bridge. While both women and men participated in the performance, Australia's "working man" was the key focus of the segment. From the middle of the nineteenth century, Australia promoted itself as a "working man's paradise" on the basis of relatively favorable employment conditions for the kinds of manual laborers celebrated in this segment. With late twentieth-century deindustrialization and the decline of unionism, Australia is less often hailed as a paradise for the working class today; nonetheless, images of the working man remain inextricably bound up with contemporary notions of Australianness.

The Sydney interpretive program as a whole constructed a predominantly white masculine discourse of Australian national identity. While female performers were present throughout the segments, the narratives presented were overwhelmingly tales of Australian manhood, of stockmen, explorers, outlaws, and steelworkers overcoming natural and social obstacles to forge a new nation and a uniquely Australian character. Likewise, Aboriginal Australians and performers representing nonwhite migrants to Australia were present in impressive numbers. However, qualitatively, these groups were essentialized and rendered peripheral to the narrative of nation. Indigenous Australians were positioned as part of nature and the primordial past, and carefully excised from the story of European colonization and development of the modern nation-state. As a further index of the marginality of Aboriginal Australians in official discourses of national identity, the ritual conducted by the indigenous Koori people at the opening ceremony to welcome spectators and athletes to their land was not included in the televised broadcast of the opening ceremony, nor in the official DVD of the event (Elder 2007, 36–37).

Additionally, immigrants, both white and nonwhite, were represented via stereotypes that reflect national preoccupations and priorities. Immigrants from Asia, Africa, and elsewhere in Oceania, in particular, were represented in ways that marked them as Australia's alters: backward, exotic, and premodern. Such representations of women and ethnoracial minorities both reflect the well-documented material disadvantages experienced by these groups in Australia and help naturalize the continued subordination of these groups. At the same time, however, the strong numerical representation of women and ethnoracial minorities among the cast of performers to some extent challenges the white masculine hegemony of the opening ceremony's narrative of nation.

Staging US National Identity:
The Salt Lake City Interpretive Program

The interpretive program of the Salt Lake City opening ceremony shared a number of similarities with the Sydney interpretive program. This narrative of US national identity explored the relationship between humanity and nature, incorporated indigenous peoples and immigrants of diverse backgrounds, presented a sanitized account of colonization, and celebrated both technology and cultural pluralism. The Salt Lake program differed from its counterparts in Sydney and Nagano, however, in two principle ways: it featured a woman from an ethnoracial minority group as an emblem of all Olympic athletes; and it invited more overtly political readings of its discourse of national identity.

A key theme running throughout the interpretive program was humanity's relationship to, and ultimate victory over, nature. This was exemplified particularly in the *Fire Within* segments around which the interpretive program was structured. In the first of these segments, the "Child of Light," a young white boy, struggled to make his way through a raging winter storm. A white man representing the "Fire Within" helped guide the boy to safety. The segment was a parable of humanity's (and America's) search for strength and meaning, and the triumph of human will in the face of adversity. In this sense, the story was timeless and universal. Nonetheless, the fact that white males personified both humanity/America (the child) and its will and drive (the fire), reveals the extent to which white male perspectives and experiences are still dominant in discourses of American identity.

However, the next of the interpretive segments more explicitly celebrated American ethnoracial diversity. In this sequence, performers from five Native American nations bestowed greetings and blessings on the Olympic participants and staged a drum circle dance. The Native American participants wore seemingly traditional costumes and representatives of each nation spoke in their indigenous languages. The segment shared marked similarities with the Sydney program. On its surface, it was a broad endorsement of American cultural pluralism: the languages, costumes, music, and dance of the indigenous performers were presented as pleasurable and apolitical multicultural spectacle, what Fish (1997) has called "boutique multiculturalism." At another level, this spectacle may be understood as both a way of promoting tourism to the western US and a way to establish a depth of history for a relatively young nation. Finally, as in the Sydney program, a young white child was featured as the onstage observer of the indigenous performance. There is a certain useful ambiguity in both the Sydney and Salt Lake representations. That is, it is unclear whether the indigenous performers are guiding and teaching their young white observers or performing for them. Such ambiguity is useful in the sense that it allows the audience to interpret the power relations between the colonizers and the colonized according to their own inclinations.

Also, strikingly similar to the Sydney program, the Salt Lake program staged a highly expurgated narrative of colonization. In the *Pioneers* sequence, the "Child of Light" and a single Native American man led diverse groups of settlers across the continent. Performers representing miners, trappers, farmers, cowboys, missionaries, and soldiers from a variety of immigrant backgrounds, marched side by side in the stadium, with no recognition of the historical tensions and even lethal conflicts between these groups. It is of course hardly surprising that historical realities such as slavery, genocide, and racially discriminatory immigration and labor practices are obscured in narratives of nation. Discourses of national identity are, after all, as much stories of what the nation *should* be as they are stories of what the nation was and is. The final scenes of the sequence neatly illustrated this point. In these scenes, settlers of all backgrounds joined together in a rousing dance. The sequence closed with a reenactment of the completion of the railroad that spanned the country from east to west. The diverse cast again danced together, any competing interests forgotten, and all united in a celebration of technological progress.

Ethnoracial diversity was further endorsed through the segment of the interpretive program that dramatized the development of an Olympic champion. In this segment, a number of girls and young women of Asian descent portrayed a young figure skater growing in strength, ability, and confidence. At last, Asian-American Olympic gold medalist Kristi Yamaguchi took to the ice as the embodiment of hard-won athletic excellence. The segment stands apart from other Olympic opening ceremony segments examined here in that, while a number of female athletes featured prominently in the three ceremonies, Yamaguchi was the only woman who explicitly represented the athletic achievements of both women and men. This is a reversal of the more typical pattern of the experiences and contributions of women and ethnoracial minority groups being subsumed in representations of males of the dominant ethnoracial group.

Finally, the gendered and racialized discourses of national identity in the Salt Lake opening ceremony must be understood in relation to the larger political, military, and other social conditions at the time of the Games. In February of 2002, the United States was still reeling politically, economically, and psychologically from the September 11, 2001, attacks on New York and Washington, DC. Just two weeks before the Salt Lake Games opened, President Bush, in his annual State of the Union address detailed increased military spending to battle terrorist organizations and the states that support them. This so-called war was being waged on multiple fronts with a variety of methods: with military troops in Afghanistan and elsewhere in the world; with increased surveillance of the US populace under the aegis of the newly created Office for Homeland Security; and, arguably, with mass-mediated messages designed to win world support for the actions of the US state. In this context, the Salt Lake Olympic opening ceremony became another front in the US war on terror.

This chapter has already addressed some of the more overtly political moments of the opening ceremony—the parading of the American flag that flew over the World Trade Center on the day of the September attacks; and the lighting of the cauldron by the 1980 men's hockey team, a reminder of US victories over its Cold War adversaries. There were additional references to the events of September 11 and US responses to them. First, before the formal start of the opening ceremony, a New York City police officer in full dress uniform performed *God Bless America*, a song that had been performed across the nation in the weeks following the September attacks in a demonstration of the strength and unity of America. The lyrics of the song suggest divine support of the nation, legitimizing collective national actions such as those undertaken in the war on terror. Next, both Salt Lake Organizing Committee Chairman Mitt Romney and IOC President Jacques Rogge explicitly referred to the September attacks in their opening speeches. Romney suggested in the wake of the attacks people around the world desired the kind of peace and respect for human rights, personal dreams, and personal achievements fostered by the Olympic Movement. Likewise Rogge, speaking on behalf of all the Olympic nations, promised the American public that, "We stand united with you in the promotion of our common ideals and hope for world peace." And last, President Bush chose to make his official opening declaration while sitting among US athletes, seemingly without bodyguards. The choice was significant in that it demonstrated national confidence and even defiance amidst widespread concerns that the Games might be the target of terrorist attacks.

For the most part these evocations of the US war on terror were dominated by images of white American masculinity.[14] The overriding masculinity of such discourses of national identity is explained in part by the nation's engagement in active combat at the time of the Olympic Games. In times of armed conflict, a nation's frontline military combatants are typically figured as the bearers and defenders of nationhood. Since these frontline US forces are overwhelmingly male, it is not surprising that masculinity was celebrated in the narratives of nation constructed in the Olympic opening ceremony. In addition, after September 11, 2001, US narratives of nation have focused consistently on the opposition between *us* (Judeo-Christian Americans) and *them* (Muslims or "Middle Eastern-looking people").[15] Therefore, the largely white, masculine images of the Salt Lake opening ceremony can be understood as reflections of national self-conceptions at the time of the Olympic Games. However, such representations also help sustain the more long-standing subordination of women and ethnoracial minorities in the United States. The continued underrepresentation of women and ethnoracial minorities in elected office and the persistent income gaps between white men and other categories of workers demonstrate that women and ethnoracial minorities still face substantial material disadvantages in the United States today.

Nonetheless, discourses of national identity contain spaces for contestation as they shift in response to changing social conditions. Against a backdrop of white American masculinity in the Salt Lake opening ceremony, the positioning of an Asian-American woman as a symbol of all Olympic athletes serves as a reminder of the increasing visibility of women and ethnoracial minorities across the American social landscape.

OLYMPIC OPENING CEREMONIES: WINNERS AND LOSERS

Discussions of winners and losers in relation to the Olympics generally focus on the competing athletes. However, with reference to the Olympic opening ceremonies analyzed here, there are three main "winners," that is, those who benefit from the narratives of nation constructed on the Olympic stage.

The first of these winners are capital interests: the manufacturers, service providers, broadcasters, advertising firms, and other for-profit enterprises that realize financial gains from constructing widely palatable gendered and racialized discourses of national identity in Olympic opening ceremonies. Some of these financial gains are direct, such as the advertising revenue a broadcaster realizes through sales of airtime during the opening ceremony. Some of these gains are less direct, but include increased sales made by Olympic Partner corporations through their association with sporting excellence and the Olympic Movement and increased demand for travel and tourism services due to public interest generated by opening ceremony representations.

The second of these winners are groups who are socially dominant on the basis of such characteristics as class, gender, race, ethnicity, national origin, or religious affiliation. Discourses of national identity which mirror relations of dominance potentially legitimize and help sustain long-standing hierarchies of power in each nation. However, the opening ceremonies described here in one sense challenge these hierarchies as well. The inclusion of women and ethnoracial minorities in opening ceremonies, even if it is largely tokenistic, can be seen as a reflection of an emerging ideal of equality and inclusiveness. The repetition of such ideals has the potential to contribute to positive social change.

The third and perhaps biggest winner is the state. The discourses of national identity staged at the Olympics serve the interests of the state in two principle ways: by increasing the host nation's international profile, and therefore potentially improving its bargaining position in international negotiations; and by contributing to social control in domestic affairs. For instance, Japanese ethnoracial homogeneity and cultural uniqueness were shown to be central themes in the Nagano opening ceremony. Such representations bolster state authority both domestically and internationally. On the domestic front, the rhetoric of homogeneity masks the presence of ethnoracial minority communities within the nation, and allows the state to avoid making the complex and costly reforms necessary to reduce the material disadvantages faced by these groups.

In addition, the rhetoric of ethnoracial homogeneity may serve to stifle domestic dissent; for if the nation is popularly conceptualized as an organic and unified whole which has evolved naturally through the millennia, the state itself can be understood as a natural and native institution of that highly integrated structure. The state is figured, then, not as a tool of the establishment or an oppressor of the masses, but the natural and legitimate extension of "the people." By this logic, resistance to state authority is dampened, as struggle against the state becomes as futile as a struggle against oneself. Likewise, the rhetoric of Japanese uniqueness has long been used by the Japanese state in international affairs, whether to justify its imperialist expansion in the mid-twentieth century, or to seek exemptions from free-trade agreements by arguing that certain imports (such as foreign rice or beef) do not suit the unique requirements of the Japanese.

State interests were likewise served by the constructions of national identity in the Sydney opening ceremony. Gender parity, reconciliation between white and Aboriginal Australians, and ethnoracial diversity were central themes of the ceremony. Such celebratory egalitarian discourses mask the continuing material disadvantages faced by women, indigenous peoples, and nonwhite migrants in Australia, allowing the state to avoid responsibility for the kinds of social reforms necessary for reducing such inequalities. Furthermore, positive representations of disadvantaged groups in discourses of national identity may serve to placate these groups. The inclusion of a substantial number of indigenous participants in the ceremony may be read in part as a response to continuing international pressure over the state's human rights record in regards to Aboriginal Australians. In April 2000, just months before the Sydney Olympics, the United Nations Committee on the Elimination of Racial Discrimination (CERD) outlined ongoing human rights concerns in Australia. These included the overrepresentation of indigenous Australians in the nation's prisons; a disproportionate number of Aboriginal deaths in police custody; the adoption of mandatory sentencing in parts of Australia which has resulted in higher incarceration rates for indigenous people; and the violation of the land rights of indigenous peoples (CERD 2000).

Finally, in the Salt Lake opening ceremony the interests of the state are most readily observable. As in Nagano and Sydney, selective and depoliticized representations of the nation's past and present serve to obscure both historical social injustices and patterns of institutionalized inequality in the US today. Furthermore, both the compulsory ritual elements and the interpretive program at Salt Lake made frequent references to the attacks of September 2001 and the state's responses to them. The opening ceremony thus served as a propaganda machine for the US state, to garner world support for its war on terror.

Regarding the "losers" in the game of Olympic ceremonials, as argued throughout this volume, discourses of national identity that symbolically marginalize women and ethnoracial minorities naturalize and therefore help sustain their continued subordination. In this sense, these subordinated groups are on the losing side of the gendered and racialized discourses of national identity analyzed here. However, such losses are by no means inevitable; all discourses of national identity, whether in their content or in their silences, generate critiques which may actually fuel social change. In addition, contestations may come in the form of Olympic participants themselves deviating from the ceremonial "script," as Tommy Smith and John Carlos did with their Black Power salutes at the 1968 Mexico City Games, or as Cathy Freeman did when she wrapped herself in an Aboriginal flag after a Commonwealth Games victory in 1994. Moreover, the audience itself has the power to contest gendered and racialized discourses of national identity by critiquing, protesting, and working to construct alternative narratives of nation.

7 Selling the Nation
Gender, Race, and National Identity in Television Advertisements

Advertisements sell more than products; they sell, among other things, values, ways of life, and conceptions of self and the Other.[1] Media theorists have long argued that advertisements serve to sell mass audiences such ideologies as capitalist consumerism, imperialism, racism, and patriarchy.[2] In addition, advertisements sell particular visions of the imagined community, by celebrating certain values, highlighting certain ways of life, and featuring casts with socially preferred characteristics. In the United States, for instance, advertisements create a universe in which nearly everyone is young, good-looking, able-bodied, heterosexual, and white.[3] Advertisements seek to persuade through their aestheticized articulation of social ideals and values. They provide the viewer with "reality as it should be—life and lives worth emulating" (Schudson 1984, 220); and in so doing, they provide models for identity formation, at the level of both the individual and the nation. Thus advertisements serve as a rich source of discourses of national identity.

This chapter examines discourses of national identity in the television advertisements of Australia and Japan. Traditional content analysis is one tool I use to explore representations of gender, race, and ethnicity in the ads. While such analysis helps reveal dynamics of power and identity in the two nations, one of my key contentions in this volume is that discourses of national identity are not simply foisted on the public by state, media, or intellectual elites. Rather, they are collectively constructed. In this chapter, therefore, I go beyond textual analysis to examine the interplay between text and audience. I interviewed almost two hundred people in Australia and Japan about their reactions to a sample of advertisements and the discourses of national identity they carry. Their comments reveal that while widely circulating, mass-mediated discourses of national identity are often embraced by the citizenry and viewed as true and authentic to some degree, such representations are also subject to critique, creative interpretation, and outright rejection.

THE TEXTS

I chose to analyze television advertisements rather than print or radio advertisements for a number of reasons. Television is perhaps the most pervasive and invasive of the mass media. Its multisensory messages demand the
audience's attention in a way that other broadcast and print media cannot. Furthermore, unlike these other media whose messages are increasingly
aimed at niche markets, television messages on free-to-air broadcasters are
directed toward a broader audience.[4] These messages, therefore, offer clues
as to which values, experiences, and ways of life are assumed to be shared
by the mass (usually national) target audience.

The sample here consists of all the advertisements appearing in a single
broadcast day on four regional free-to-air stations, two in Australia and two in
Japan.[5] Both the Australian and Japanese samples include one spring and one
summer broadcast day, approximately three months apart, and one broadcast day in a week leading up to a national holiday. This sampling yielded a
total of 373 Australian advertisements and 593 Japanese advertisements. The
sample was then narrowed to those advertisements which included at least
one foregrounded adult.[6] Advertisements containing only children, animated
characters, or characters whose gender could not be discerned were excluded,
as were station and movie promotions, the former because they present difficulties in terms of gender classifications, and the latter because they are more
akin to full-length television programs than to product advertisements.

The advertisements were then analyzed for four key dimensions of discourses
of national identity: the social relationships, values, and ethics of the national
community; the nation's material and symbolic culture; the nation's physical
environment; and its everyday leisure practices. In applying these analytical
categories to the sample of television advertisements, a simple one-to-one cor-
respondence between signs and their intended meanings was not assumed, for
advertisements are polysemic, with complex interrelations between the signs
employed. Rather the overall discursive effects of the advertisements, what
Goffman (1979) has termed the "gestalt," were considered more central to the
generation of meaning. Therefore each advertisement (rather than individual
signs within each advertisement) was treated as a unit of analysis. It should be
noted that advertisements can, and frequently do, make use of multiple appeals
to national identity. After applying the codes to the sample, 114 Australian
advertisements and 185 Japanese advertisements were judged to contain representations of national identity. It is these advertisements I will focus on here.

THE COMMUNITIES

In order to explore audience responses to these advertised discourses of
national identity, I selected two rural communities, "Plainsview" located in

the Australian island state of Tasmania and "Hirogawa" located in the Japanese island prefecture of Hokkaido.[7] These communities were chosen for their demographic, economic, and geographical similarities. Both Tasmania and Hokkaido have economies based primarily on agriculture, aquaculture, forestry, and tourism. Both are experiencing rural depopulation and lower levels of economic growth than their respective mainlands, and both are on the geographic, economic, and political margins of their nations (Table 7.1). Likewise, the two townships studied are similar in their population size relative to their respective state/prefectural populations, their proximity to the state/prefectural capital, and their local economic conditions (Table 7.2).

Just as regions with similar profiles were chosen, closely matched samples of focus group participants from Hokkaido and Tasmania were constructed (Table 7.3). As Hofstede (1998) has argued, because national populations

Table 7.1 Tasmania and Hokkaido: Selected Characteristics[8]

	Characteristics	Tasmania		Hokkaido	
Geography	Land area	68, 400 km²		83, 452 km²	
	Location	The southernmost state in Australia, Tasmania is located approximately 220 kilometers south of the mainland.		The northernmost prefecture in Japan, Hokkaido is located approximately 30 kilometers north of Honshu.	
Population	Population	474,000 people		5,699,000 people	
	Population as percentage of total national population	3%		5%	
	Age distribution of population	0–14 years	23%	0–14 years	15%
		15–64 years	65%	15–64 years	69%
		65+ years	12%	65+ years	16%
	Annual population growth	Tasmania −0.1% (1999–2000)	All Australia +1.2% (1999–2000)	Hokkaido −0.4% (1995–2000)	All Japan +1.1% (1995–2000)
Average Income	State/prefectural average per capita income as percentage of national average per capita income	88%		91%	

Table 7.2 Plainsview and Hirogawa: Selected Characteristics[9]

	Characteristics	Plainsview		Hirogawa	
Geography	Land area	5,620 km² encompassing six semi-independent townships		204 km² encompassing twenty-five semi-independent townships	
	Distance from state/prefectural capital	40 km		40 km	
Population	Population	12,176 people		15,634 people	
	Age distribution of population	0–14 years	26%	0–14 years	13%
		15–64 years	64%	15–64 years	65%
		65+ years	10%	65+ years	22%
Education	Number of schools by type	Primary	4	Primary	4
		High school	3	High school	3
		Other	1	Other	2
Labor	Leading employment sectors by percentage of total workforce employed[10]	Trade, service, transport, and communications (54%)		Trade, service, transport, and communications (50%)	
		Mining, construction, and manufacturing (23%)		Mining, construction, and manufacturing (28%)	
		Agriculture, forestry, and fishery (23%)		Agriculture, forestry, and fishery (22%)	

are so complex and diverse, population samples in cross-national studies can never be truly representative; therefore, in cross-national research it is most productive to compare groups in similar social locations. This allows both the differences and similarities between nations to come into sharper focus. In order to achieve closely matched samples, snowball sampling was used to recruit participants who met gender, occupation, and age specifications. Therefore both the Australian and Japanese samples consisted of men and women ranging in age from teenagers to octogenarians, in the following social categories: students, teachers, public servants, business owners, private sector employees, farmers, and retirees. Because few ethnoracial Others live in these two areas, the samples do not reflect the national ethnoracial diversity of Japan and Australia; however, the samples do reflect accurately the ethnoracial composition of the two communities studied.[11]

So, while this chapter discusses discourses of national identity, it must be stressed that the discourses examined here are those constructed in

Table 7.3 Demographic Characteristics of Research Participants*

Participant Characteristics	Japanese Participants	Australian Participants	Total Participants
High School Students	17	11	28
Male	11	5	
Female	6	6	
Teachers	17	4	21
Male	7	2	
Female	10	2	
Public Servants	23	12	35
Males born before 1945	6	0	
Males born after 1945	9	4	
Females born before 1945	0	0	
Females born after 1945	8	8	
Business Owners	12	11	23
Male	7	5	
Female	5	6	
Employees (Private Sector)	12	8	20
Male	7	5	
Female	5	3	
Farmers	21	21	42
Males born before 1945	5	5	
Males born after 1945	5	7	
Females born before 1945	5	4	
Females born after 1945	6	5	
Retired People	14	12	26
Male	8	6	
Female	6	6	
TOTAL	116	79	195*

*169 participants were interviewed in focus groups. The remaining twenty-six (roughly one person in each category) were interviewed individually.

particular (marginal) locations at particular points in time. As in the rest of this volume, the aim of this analysis is not to describe the most "accurate" or "authentic" discourses of Australianness and Japaneseness. Rather, the chapter examines the way national identity is gendered and racialized in two similar communities in Australia and Japan.

THE CONTENT ANALYSIS

Although Australian and Japanese advertisers used similar conventions to evoke a sense of national belonging, there were differences in the frequency with which these conventions were employed.[12] In the sample of Australian advertisements, Australianness was most often represented through images of leisure activities. This is consistent with state, scholarly, and popular discourses throughout the twentieth century which have constructed Australians as easygoing, leisure-loving people.[13] In the Japanese sample, Japaneseness was most often represented through images of social relations and social ethics, suggesting a widespread perception that Japanese social cohesiveness is a distinguishing national feature. This echoes state, scholarly, and popular discourses of Japanese uniqueness (the *Nihonjinron*) which emphasize collectivism, mutual obligation, interdependence, and ethnoracial homogeneity as definitive Japanese traits.[14] Clearly then, discourses of national identity in Australian and Japanese television advertisements are broadly consistent with widely circulating constructions of the imagined community in each nation. But to what degree are such discourses gendered and racialized? Who represents or symbolizes the nation?

Gendered Discourses of National Identity

When the advertisements were coded for the gender, race, and ethnicity of the carrier of national identity, it was found that men were more likely than women to be the carriers of Australianness, while women were more likely than men to be the carriers of Japaneseness.[15] What such broad comparisons do not reveal, however, is the nature of these representations. Women in the Japanese sample were about three times more likely than men to embody Japaneseness through domestic activities, with, for example, kimono-clad housewives teaching their daughters how to cook, or preparing meals for husbands returning from the office. Men, on the other hand, were about three times more likely to embody Japaneseness through their leisure activities, such as playing golf or *pachinko* (best described as a cross between pinball and a slot machine), learning *kendo*, or practicing *karate*. Furthermore, men embodying Japaneseness were almost twice as likely as women to be shown engaged in paid labor.

Men in the advertisements were also more likely than women (by a ratio of 3:2) to embody national identity in contemporary Japanese settings, while

women were more likely than men (by a ratio of 5:4) to embody Japaneseness in a traditional setting. So, while men were portrayed, for example, as
company executives, baseball players, and rock stars, women were more
typically portrayed as kimono-clad brides, geisha, or participants in tea
ceremony.

In sum, in the sample of Japanese advertisements, women were represented in ways that emphasized their unpaid domestic labor, their passivity,
and their subservience. The frequent positioning of women in traditional
and domestic settings rather than contemporary and public settings obscures
their active contributions to contemporary public life, where they constitute,
for instance, almost half of the paid labor force.

The Australian advertisements also showed marked gender differences
in the ways men and women embody national identity. Similar to trends
found in the Japanese sample, women in the Australian sample of advertisements were more than four times as likely as their male counterparts to
embody Australianness through their domestic roles. Women were shown at
home, for example, teaching young children to read, or preparing snacks for
their children returning home from school. Also like the Japanese sample,
Australian men were much more likely to demonstrate their Australianness
through their leisure activities than women, whom they outnumbered four
to one as they surfed, cycled, or shared a beer with their mates. They also
outnumbered women two to one in representations of paid labor, although
almost 70 percent of working-age women in Australia are engaged in paid
labor.

Unlike the Japanese sample, however, the Australian sample showed men
outnumbering women in representations of both contemporary culture (by
a ratio of 3:1) *and* traditional culture (by a striking ratio of 12:1). In contemporary settings, Australian men were shown in roles such as Rotarians,
cricket stars, and surf iron men, and in traditional settings they frequently
worked as farmers and stockmen. This notable dearth of women in images
of both traditional and contemporary Australian culture and the positioning
of women firmly within the domestic realm is consistent with the historical
underrepresentation of women in official narratives of nation.[16]

The national identities constructed in the television advertisements of
Australia and Japan are indisputably *gendered* national identities. However, it would be overly simplistic to suggest that Australian national identity is masculine while Japanese national identity is feminine. This false
dichotomy masks an important similarity between Australian and Japanese
mass-mediated discourses of national identity: both reflect and reinforce a
long-standing gender order in which women are constructed as largely domestic and passive, while men are constructed as largely public and active.

The analysis of general representational patterns here should not be
understood to deny the great diversity of images present in the advertisements. In both Australian and Japanese samples a small number of advertisements presented gender role reversals in which women were engaged in

paid labor or leisure while their male partners engaged in domestic tasks. An Australian advertisement in which a young man daydreamed about cooking dinner for his girlfriend, and a Japanese advertisement in which a man cleaned the toilet while his wife watched, are typical of this subset of advertisements. Such advertisements reflect and potentially contribute to changing gender roles in these two settings and subvert narratives of nation which position women as largely domestic and subservient. Such representations suggest that gendered discourses of national identity do not always mirror and maintain patriarchal relations, but can serve as counternarratives of nation, by challenging patriarchy, or at the very least reflecting tensions over shifting power relations.

Racialized Discourses of National Identity

Content analysis of the television advertisements reveals that constructions of Australianness and Japaneseness are not only gendered but also racialized. As scholars of Australia and Japan have noted, the notion of white national proprietorship in Australia and the notion of monoracialism in Japan have been central to discourses of national identity in these two settings.[17] Therefore, it is not surprising that of Australian television advertisements with at least one adult character (n=250), the vast majority (81 percent) of advertisements had only white characters; and of Japanese television advertisements with at least one adult character (n=466), the vast majority (83 percent) of advertisements featured only Japanese characters.

The terms "white" and "Japanese" here indicate only character types or roles. No assumptions have been made about the actual ethnoracial background of the actors, only about the apparent ethnicity of the characters they play. Furthermore, no claims are made about how closely television advertisements mirror the ethnoracial composition of the national populations of Australia and Japan. Because the categories of "white" in Australia and "Japanese" in Japan are fluid and relative, it is impossible to accurately calculate what percentages of the respective national populations belong to these groups. As Hage (1998) has suggested, in Australia "white" is not an either-or category; one person may be considered "more white" than another, just as one person may be considered "more Australian" than another, depending not only on their appearance, but their religion, the kind of language they speak, their style of dress, or the sports they play. Likewise, "Japanese" is a shifting category which includes, depending on the context, all Japanese citizens, noncitizens who are the descendants of expatriate Japanese (*nisei* and *sansei*), citizens or noncitizens who have only one Japanese parent (*haafu*), and/or some ethnoracial minorities in Japan (such as the *Ainu* or *Ryūkyū*). For the purposes of this content analysis, if the ethnoracial roles of the characters were not discernible (through such cues as physical features, clothing, and language use), the advertisement was excluded from analysis.

The percentage of advertisements with only white or Japanese characters is even higher when the sample of advertisements is narrowed to those with images of national identity. Of advertisements with representations of Australianness (n=114), 84 percent featured only white characters, while of advertisements with representations of Japaneseness (n=185), 94 percent featured only Japanese characters.

Furthermore, in the majority of advertisements featuring ethnoracial Others, these characters generally did not participate in the everyday settings, activities, or social relations most frequently associated with representations of Australianness and Japaneseness.[18] For example, relatively few Australian advertisements with ethnoracial minority characters showed these characters engaged in everyday work, domestic, or leisure settings; only 17 percent of these advertisements cast ethnoracial minorities as "ordinary" Australians, including bankers, family members, and holidaymakers, among others. Instead, the majority (63 percent) of the advertisements positioned ethnoracial Others as either spectacles—for example singers, dancers, actors, or professional athletes—or as relatively low-status service personnel, including cooks and hotel staff. Moreover, another 8 percent of these advertisements showed ethnoracial Others, usually in Third World nations, as recipients of Australian charitable assistance.

The representation of ethnoracial Others in the television advertisements of Japan is remarkably similar to the representation of ethnoracial Others in Australian advertisements. Few Japanese advertisements featuring ethnoracial minorities showed them in everyday work, domestic, or leisure settings in Japan. Instead, 34 percent of Japanese advertisements with ethnoracial minorities featured foreign celebrities, entertainers, or professional athletes; and another 9 percent of the advertisements showed relatively low-status foreign Others producing goods or providing services for Japanese consumption. Of the remaining advertisements with ethnoracial Others, 24 percent featured only foreigners in foreign settings, such as a group of whites dining at a Parisian restaurant, or a white British couple driving through the English countryside, images apparently designed to give the advertised products an air of exoticism.

TALKING BACK: AUDIENCE RESPONSES TO ADVERTISED DISCOURSES OF NATIONAL IDENTITY

The textual analysis here suggests that advertised images of Australianness and Japaneseness for the most part reproduce social hierarchies in which women and ethnoracial Others are subordinated and marginalized in these nations. However, discourses of national identity are not simply constructed in a top-down fashion by media elites. Because national identities are collectively constructed discourses, it is necessary to examine not only mass-mediated narratives of nation, but also audience perceptions of those discourses. When given the opportunity to talk back to the ads, research participants in Plainsview, Tasmania, and Hirogawa, Hokkaido, readily did so, suggesting that audiences do not just passively absorb media constructions of national identity, but to some degree engage with them, interpret them, and critique them.

Quantitative Measures of Audience Response

As a first step toward gauging audience responses to discourses of national identity in the television advertisements, a selection of advertisements was screened in Australian and Japanese focus groups and participants were asked to rate the advertisements on how Australian or Japanese they were.[19] Participants watched thirteen advertisements from their own countries. Advertisements were selected for the gender and ethnoracial background of the principal characters, and for the advertisement type—nostalgic, humorous, serious, and so on.[20] Participants rated the advertisements on a Likert scale of 1 (Not at all Australian/Japanese) to 5 (Very Australian/Japanese). The mean scores reveal that in both the Australian and Japanese samples, advertisements with nostalgic images were perceived by participants to be the most Australian or Japanese (Table 7.4).[21]

In the Australian survey results, the three advertisements with the highest mean scores for Australianness all consisted of predominantly nostalgic images. However, those nostalgic advertisements with some or all male characters were considered more Australian than those nostalgic advertisements with only female characters. This is part of a wider trend, in which most advertisements with only female characters were perceived to be less Australian than those advertisements with some or all male characters. The only exceptions to this trend were advertisements in which a male character was present but engaged in non-gender-stereotypical behavior (in this case, planning and cooking dinner for his girlfriend), or when ethnoracial minority characters were also present in an advertisement with a white male. These cases suggest that reversed gender roles and nonwhite characters diminish the Australianness established by the white male presence. Representations of leisure in the advertisements provide a telling example. As noted earlier, images of leisure practices are central to advertised discourses of Australian national identity. However, while advertisements featuring male characters engaged in leisure pursuits were abundant in the total advertisement sample, and were given relatively high marks for their Australianness, advertisements featuring female characters engaged in leisure were very scarce in the sample, and the advertisement shown to focus groups was rated second to the lowest for its Australianness.

In terms of ethnicity, the four advertisements considered most Australian (those advertisements which received a mean score of 4.0 or above), were peopled by only white characters, while three out of the four advertisements considered least Australian contained ethnoracial minority characters.

Table 7.4 Audience Response Survey: Mean Score of Perceived Australianness and Japaneseness[22]

Rank	Australian Advertisement Type with Gender and Ethnicity of Main Characters	Australianness Mean Score	Japanese Advertisement Type with Gender and Ethnicity of Main Characters	Japaneseness Mean Score
1	Nostalgic-serious: Male, Female, White	4.58	Nostalgic-serious: Male, Japanese	4.63
2	Nostalgic-serious: Male, White	4.50	Nostalgic-humorous: Male, Japanese	4.32
3	Nostalgic-humorous: Male, White	4.43	Humorous mix of old and new: Male, Japanese	4.26
4	Contemporary leisure: Male, White	4.09	Nostalgic-serious: Female, Japanese	4.23
5	Humorous mixture of old and new: Male, Female, White, Asian	3.64	Nostalgic-humorous: Female, Japanese	3.95
6	Contemporary leisure: Male, White	3.36	Contemporary leisure: Female, Japanese	3.75
7	Nostalgic-serious: Female, White	3.33	Humorous mix of old and new: Female, Japanese	3.74
8	Nostalgic-humorous: Female, White	3.32	Neutral: Male, Female, Japanese	3.38
9	Changing social roles: Male, Female, White	2.91	Changing social roles: Male, Female, Japanese	3.21
10	Multiculturalism: Male, Female, Asian	2.62	Changing social roles: Male, Female, Japanese	3.16
11	Neutral: Male, Female, White, Asian	2.55	Internationalization: Female, Japanese, White	3.04
12	Contemporary leisure: Female, White	2.07	Contemporary leisure: Male, Japanese	3.00
13	Multiculturalism: Female, Asian	1.55	Internationalization: Male, Japanese, White	2.15

Considering the pervasiveness of Australia's "white nation" discourses, it is not surprising that advertisements featuring ethnoracial Others were perceived to be less Australian than those featuring only whites. However, one advertisement featuring ethnoracial Others ranked in the top five most Australian advertisements. It is worthwhile analyzing this advertisement in greater detail.

In this advertisement for lamb, a white Australian father presides over the Sunday roast lamb meal, an event constructed as an Australian tradition. However, when he discovers that the main dish is Tandoori Lamb, he feigns displeasure at the exotic fare. Then, with a chime of sitar music, the camera pans back to reveal his grown white daughter, her Indian husband, and their children. The whole family laughs, and the slogan reads, "Lamb: The Multicultural Meal." The advertisement marks the Indian man and the biracial children as ethnoracial Others, yet admits them into the Australian family and its cherished Sunday ritual in an enactment of multiculturalism, a newly adopted national value. As one Plainsview resident succinctly put it, the ad was "really Australian—because of the multiculturalism."

The other three advertisements featuring ethnoracial Others ranked tenth, eleventh, and last in perceived Australianness. All featured Asian characters unaccompanied by whites. Without the presence of a white character to mark them as Australian, many viewers commented that the advertisements seemed foreign or "could have been anywhere." The presence of nonwhite characters alone was not enough to convey an image of multiculturalism to viewers. The Australian audience response surveys suggest that viewers conceptualized multiculturalism as the interaction between majority and minority groups.

The Japanese audience response survey results show that advertisements with nostalgic images consistently rated high on Japaneseness. In a trend similar to the Australian results, nostalgic advertisements with male principal characters were considered more Japanese than those with female characters. Such advertisements were rare, however. The majority of nostalgic advertisements featured women, almost always dressed in kimono and exemplifying a traditional passive and nurturing femininity. The kimono itself was identified as a strong marker of Japaneseness by Hirogawa viewers. As one viewer explained it, "Even though we are not dressed in kimono [these days] . . . when we see them we feel somehow relieved . . . deeply relaxed. When we see them we feel, 'Ah, this is Japan. This is where we are.'"

In terms of race and ethnicity, as noted earlier, relatively few advertisements featured ethnoracial Others; and of the advertisements shown to focus groups, the two featuring ethnoracial Others ranked eleventh and last in terms of their perceived Japaneseness. Interestingly, the principal characters of the advertisement rated least Japanese were, in fact, Japanese. The advertisement featured two teenaged boys dressed in American hip-hop fashion, rapping about the soft drink Sprite. However, the young Japanese men sang in Kansai dialect, which differs substantially from the dialect of Japanese spoken by the focus group participants. This combination of dialect, clothing style, and music style perhaps accounts for the intriguing fact that many Japanese viewers believed that these young men were singing in English. This may explain why the ad was judged the least Japanese advertisement in the sample.

Qualitative Measures of Australian Audience Response

In focus group discussions of the advertisements and in-depth interviews, I asked the residents of Plainsview to tell me what Australians were like, and to describe a typical Australian. Responses were consistent across gender, age, and occupational groups: the typical Australian is easygoing, friendly, sport-loving, self-deprecating, and often explicitly male. As Roger, a high school teacher, summarized the national character, it is ". . . the beer-drinking . . . sort of very gregarious type of character, or the outback type image or the sun-bronzed life-saver type of image . . . anti-authority . . . a sort of happy-go-lucky, she'll-be-right-mate, battler type image." Another teacher, Lisa, directly addressed such gendered imagery in her comments:

> Isn't it funny when someone says "Think about an Australian," you think of men? You think of the sort of typical ocker man. . . . So that's the first thing that just came into my head then. Just the sort of typical man with the singlet and the can of beer in one hand standing around the barbecue.[23]

While these two teachers went on to distance themselves from such imagery by noting that it is both clichéd and sexist, other participants seemed to embrace such discourses and make links with their own lives. After Brenda, a businessperson, remarked that the Crocodile Dundee character was "a fairly typical Australian," she added that she actually knew such people. "My dad is actually probably a bit of a Crocodile Dundee . . . he's the typical tough guy." Likewise, another businessperson, Brian, drew on explicitly gendered imagery in his description of the typical Australian: ". . . the man who works with his hands forty hours a day [sic] on farms and in factories, in the trades . . . the self-employed man in a small business." As the owner of a small business in the low-status salvage sector, Brian in a sense inserted himself into discourses of national identity. Likewise, Brenda, who disclosed that the small shop she ran with her sisters was barely profitable, made a claim on national identity by offering her father as an exemplar of Australianness. These two businesspeople may not have been wealthy or high-status members of their communities, but widely circulating (and gendered) discourses of national identity allowed them to position themselves near the symbolic center of the imagined community.

In a sense, all of the participants I interviewed were in marginal positions relative to the nation as a whole. They were residents of small, rural townships in island locations far from the hubs of national political, economic, and cultural life. Many participants explicitly addressed that sense of marginality. High school boys and girls both commented on Tasmania's perceived difference. As 16-year-old James noted, "Tasmania is sort of like their own little country . . . A lot of [mainland] people think that they are more civilized than Tasmanians." His classmates agreed.

> ANNE: Tasmania is kind of different to the rest of the states, to the rest of the country.
> MEG: Yes, we are different. We are considered not to be a part of Australia really, and that we have two heads . . .[24]
> ANNE: They say that because they reckon we're interbred.

Likewise, Dominic, a youth services worker, expressed concern about the defeatist attitudes of Tasmanian young people. They see Tasmania as "the armpit of the universe," he noted. A group of female public servants similarly observed that young people only feel they have "made it" in life if they leave Tasmania and succeed on the mainland.

Tasmania was behind the times, many participants observed: "ten years behind," "fifty years behind," "back in the 60s." One participant quipped that upon landing in Tasmania airline stewardesses should remind passengers to set their watches back twenty years. Interestingly however, many participants transformed their community's perceived marginality and backwardness into a source of pride. Because Tasmania is located so far from the nation's major urban centers, they argued, Plainsview had survived relatively unchanged for generations, and was therefore more traditional and more authentically Australian than places like Sydney or Melbourne. "I think in Tasmania really in lots of ways it's all that's good about Australia," Phillip, a schoolteacher, remarked. "You know, that warmth and friendliness and openness, the ability to laugh at yourself, the welcoming nature of the majority of the people, the openness to new ideas . . ." Two businesswomen echoed these sentiments.

> TRUDY: They say [coming here] is like coming back in time . . . It is so slow and laid-back. And people are friendlier.
> MARGARET: They haven't got time to stop and be friendly on the mainland anymore.

In a sense, then, residents of Plainsview used the trope of rural marginality to symbolically place themselves at the center of the national imagined community, to write themselves into discourses of national identity.

Participants commented extensively on Tasmania's lack of racial and ethnic diversity relative to mainland urban centers. Some, like Paula, a schoolteacher, lamented the lack of diversity and expressed a desire for a "more colorful mix" of children at her school. However, others expressed pride in being "the original type of White Australian," the "Anglo-Saxon descendants," "remnants of the Anglo-Saxon British." Most participants who addressed issues of race suggested that Plainsview and Tasmania more generally were very tolerant, open, and welcoming to people of all backgrounds largely *because* there were so few minorities. As Edward, a small business owner, observed, "Where there is a larger grouping [of minorities] they are seen to be more of a threat." The mainland, by contrast, was consistently characterized as a site of interracial tension and violence, a "nest of vipers." Several participants, including businesspeople, high school students, and farmers, recalled visits to the mainland when they felt like foreigners in their own country. There were "Vietnamese people . . . babbling in their own language"; "everyone was Asian"; and "you were lucky if you saw anybody that was speaking Australian."

One small business owner, Leanne, expressed anxieties about new arrivals to the nation altering its character:

> The thing is we are losing our national identity. We are losing our Australian identity . . . because of too much immigration of one type [Asian] . . . They want to conglomerate in their own little areas, and want to make their own little area their own country . . . They want us as Australians to change to their ways. Well, I don't accept that. I don't want to be Asianized.

She later suggested that Asians constitute "another species," and she recalled with apparent pride an incident in which she grabbed a "little Asian" man "by the scruff of the collar" and shouted obscenities at him for not allowing an elderly white woman to board a train ahead of him. Asians are racist, she asserted: "They have respect for their own elders, [but] they had no respect for an elderly white person."

Although Leanne's comments were among the most explicitly anti-immigrant and anti-Asian views expressed by Plainsview residents, many participants suggested that people of Asian descent, Muslims, "people with accents," and even Aboriginal Australians were not really regarded as "true-blue Aussies." As Anne, a high school student, noted, for example, "The Aboriginals are actually the native Australians, but no one thinks of them as actual—as an Australian person."

Qualitative Measures of Japanese Audience Response

In Hirogawa, research participants shared their notions of Japaneseness with me. As they elaborated on the typical traits of the Japanese, they were careful to point out that each of these characteristics has a downside.[25] Hirogawa residents suggested that the Japanese are group-oriented (but too easily influenced); they are reserved and considerate (but cannot express how they really feel); they are racially and culturally homogeneous (but also racially prejudiced); they live in harmony with other Japanese (but reject outsiders); they are hardworking (but are prone to overwork); and they are persevering and patient (but do not protest when they should).

These traits, they explained, have been inherited from ancient times (*zutto mukashi kara*) and are, in some sense, natural and inevitable. As Mr. Saisho, a retiree, commented on Japanese social harmony, "Since the olden days, the Japanese people have tried to work in harmony with others. Because there have been so many people living in a small land, they have avoided conflicts as much as they could." Or as groups of farmers, private sector employees, business owners, and teachers all remarked, because Japan has never had a significant number of foreign migrants, the Japanese do not know how to interact with outsiders. "We have a very old custom of not accepting foreigners," explained Mr. Kawabuchi, an older farmer.

Most national traits were said to apply to Japanese men and women equally: everybody does things "just because other people do them"; everybody "helps those who are falling down"; everybody is uncomfortable with (or "repulsed by") foreigners; everybody has "the same color skin, hair, and eyes." But two of the national traits described by participants were at least implicitly gendered, hard work and perseverance.

Both the positively valued trait of working hard and its downside, overworking to the detriment of homelife and health, were strongly associated in participant's comments with one national archetype: the *sarariman* (the salaried male worker). Ms. Higuchi, a woman who runs a small family business with her mother-in-law, noted,

> In Japan . . . it's good if you work hard. . . . I think this, and my husband thinks the same, that it's good for men to work. But they don't have much time when they come home, time to see their children and to spend in their homelife. . . . So these are sad times.

Ms. Higuchi suggested that this national (male) propensity toward overwork may account, in part, for the rise in school violence, the rise in violence committed by children against family members, and the decline in public morals more generally. Curiously, however, although Ms. Higuchi mentioned that she has devoted approximately nine hours a day for the last twenty years to the family business, as well as maintaining a sizeable field of vegetables for family consumption and working as a day laborer on her brother's farm, she insisted that she has "never worked." It is possible her claim to have never worked reflects a desire to be, or to be perceived as, an affluent stay-at-home wife who enjoys the so-called *san-shoku-hirune-tsuki* (the "three meals a day and an afternoon nap" lifestyle). Such a claim might also be seen as a strategy to distance herself from the kind of overwork she associated with social decline. However, what Ms. Higuchi's narrative clearly reveals is that while men's labor is understood as the work, hard work, or even overwork central to notions of Japanese national identity, women's labor, whether income-generating or not, is largely excluded from images of national working life.

It is primarily women, however, who are associated with another national characteristic noted by participants, perseverance or the ability to endure (*gaman*). Ms. Sasaki, a prominent young business owner, suggested early in our conversation that, "It is a Japanese trait that people just endure, not saying what they really want to say." While the gendering of this national trait is not clear from this statement, later in our discussion she added,

> I think men, in general, have decision-making ability; they can make re-sponsible decisions faster. On the other hand, women, in general, don't have this ability, but they can endure difficult things better instead. So society is structured so that men have the decision-making role and women endure difficult things continuously.

Such comments suggest that the perceived national trait of endurance or patience is, at least implicitly, gendered in the feminine. It seems to be associated, in particular, with the image of the long-suffering Japanese wife and mother, pervasive in mass-mediated texts, perhaps most famously in the popular television series *Oshin*.[26] Participants noted that the female embodiment of this national trait is a source of pride for many women. As Ms. Sasaki explained, women who can endure are "secretly very proud of themselves." However, women's apparent pride in their ability to endure can obscure the effects of such discourses. Discourses of women's endurance serve to naturalize the patriarchal social relations Ms. Sasaki described and seemingly accepted. So even as female participants used the notion of endurance to claim a place for themselves in visions of national identity, their vision reflected a social order that places them in a subordinate position.

Perhaps the clearest marker of Japaneseness in the minds of the residents of Hirogawa was race. People from all walks of life drew a clear line between "we Japanese" (*ware ware nihonjin*) and foreign Others (*gaijin* or *gaikoku-jin*). Foreign Others were often implicitly or explicitly racialized. Whites were usually referred to as Westerners (*seiyō no hito*) or Americans (*amerika-jin*) regardless of nationality. People of African descent were almost without exception identified as Blacks (*koku-jin*) regardless of nationality. And the term Asian (*ajia-jin*) was applied only to non-Japanese Asians, usually with some negative connotations. Many of the people I interviewed argued that the Japanese needed to develop greater understanding and acceptance of foreigners, but when asked whether foreigners could ever *become* Japanese, everyone agreed they could not. Such comments suggest that Japaneseness was conceived by Hirogawa residents not just as a category of national belonging but as a category of racial belonging.

As in Tasmania, participants in Hokkaido acknowledged their own mar-ginality within the nation. "We are like the foreigners of Japan," observed

Mr. Hashimoto, a private sector employee. The theme surfaced again in a conversation with young public servants. "I've heard that people from Hokkaido are looked down on in Honshu," Ms. Osawa offered. Ms. Hara, her colleague, agreed, but added that although mainlanders look down on them, people in Hokkaido are more close-knit and community spirited. Other participants commented on differences between Hokkaido and the mainland. Hokkaido lagged behind in its economy, they observed, but preserved traditional customs and values. Again, in a move similar to that observed among rural Australians, these rural Japanese participants acknowledged their geographic and sociopolitical marginality, and yet they inverted it by suggesting that, compared to cities, rural areas are more "traditional," more community-oriented, and in some ways more authentic examples of national values and ways of life.

CONTESTATIONS

The interview material examined here generally supports the findings of the content analysis. Both in the sample of advertisements and in interviews with residents of rural Australia and Japan, race and ethnicity, especially skin color and language, are powerful markers of national belonging. Narratives of nation in both Australia and Japan are also gendered. In Australia masculine traits and archetypes clearly dominate national imagery. In Japan, discourses of national identity are more subtly gendered, but in ways that reproduce the notion of men as active workers and proprietors of the nation and women as their passive, long-suffering wives and mothers.

Yet residents of Plainsview and Hirogawa also contested and critiqued widely circulating constructions of national identity, such as those in the advertisements. A few comments exemplify such critiques:

I think that our Australian image is warped, in a way. It's untrue. [Edward, business owner]

It's more of a media image than it is a true image. [Audrey, public servant]

The stereotypical Australian culture, I think, has never existed. . . . I haven't seen it. [Dominic, public servant]

There isn't a unique culture in Japan anyway. It was originally introduced from overseas in the olden days. [Ms. Hara, public servant]

I'm a little different from other Japanese, because I don't have that fantasy that Japan is a monoracial nation. [Ms. Honda, professor]

> In my opinion . . . the old-fashioned images are most Japanese . . . [but it's] an ideal form of Japan, or what we want Japan to be like. [Mr. Ando, business owner]

Such comments, and other more detailed critiques by participants in both nations, demonstrate that discourses of national identity are contentious; they are constantly in flux and are employed in complex ways by people as they make sense of their own locations within the national imagined community. It is worth noting that those in more marginal social positions—women, more recent arrivals to the community, or people with attitudes considered extreme by the larger community—were more likely than others to contest widely circulating discourses of national identity, and in some cases construct more inclusive counternarratives of nation.

So even while widely circulating discourses of national identity can serve to legitimate and sustain current social hierarchies based on gender, race, and ethnicity, people can and do construct alternative discourses of national identity which challenge these very hierarchies. Such counternarratives of nation are not merely transitory and fruitless protests. Because discourses of national identity are collectively constructed, such discursive interventions have the potential to reshape broader narratives of nation.

In closing, all too often scholars in the rarefied environment of academe forget to listen to the very people we purport to study. Unless we believe—and I do not—that national identities are either inborn traits or purely top-down constructions imposed on the powerless masses, we must take time to listen not only to what our fellow scholars have to say about national identity, but to what "ordinary" people make of such discourses. Due to the time and resources required for in-depth ethnographic work, it has not been possible for me to incorporate such material into the other case studies in this volume. However the results in this chapter serve as a reminder of the importance and value of such research to a fuller understanding of collectively constructed discourses of national identity.

8 Defining the Nation Through Its Other

Islamophobia in Post-9/11 Letters to the Editor

Few events generate more potent discourses of national identity than warfare.[1] Identifying and defining the enemy necessarily involves defining who we are as a nation. Warfare has the potential to unite previously divided groups in defense against an external Other, just as Colley (1992) suggests frequent warfare between Britain and France (especially 1689–1815) helped unite the English, Scots, and Welsh in national defense. It can also lead to the further marginalization of certain minority groups within the national community, as Japanese-Americans interned during World War II will testify. In times of armed conflict, the enemy is routinely demonized and dehumanized. No doubt conceptualizing our foes as devils or beasts makes it easier to commit acts of violence against them.

In the wake of the attacks on the World Trade Center and the Pentagon on September 11, 2001, US President George Bush declared a war on terror.[2] This "crusade," as he initially called it, was not a conventional war against specific nations, but a battle against "evildoers" in any nation who used terrorist tactics for political ends. Like conventional wars, however, the war on terror has prompted broad public discussion on the nature of the enemy, and by extension, on the nature of the national self.

This chapter examines discourses of national identity in the US, UK, and Australia in the twelve months following the 9/11 attacks. I analyze letters to the editor in the newspapers of each nation, looking for evidence of Islamophobia, the fear and disparagement of Muslims and Islam.[3] Undoubtedly because the 9/11 attackers were characterized as "Islamic extremists" linked with Middle Eastern terrorist groups, Muslims, Arabs, people of Middle Eastern descent, and Islam itself have been commonly identified as enemies in the war on terror. As we shall see, in the twelve months following the 9/11 attacks, letters to the editor in the US, UK, and Australia constructed discourses of national identity centered on a contrast between a civilized, humane Judeo-Christian national self and a violent, fanatical Muslim Other.

ANALYZING LETTERS TO THE EDITOR

Following the 9/11 attacks, newspapers both within the United States and around the world published countless letters to the editor containing expressions of grief, anger, and fear, attributions of blame and calls to action (Hogan 2006). Such letters are certainly of interest for insights they provide into public opinion on the attacks and the subsequent war on terror. Moreover, to scholars of national identity, these letters reveal widespread and largely taken-for-granted assumptions about the national self and the enemy Other.

It is crucial to acknowledge, however, that letters to the editor do not necessarily reflect the full range of opinions on a given issue. Because newspapers typically receive many more letters than they can publish, editors use their discretion in selecting a small number for publication.[4] This process inevitably filters out not only letters judged to be offensive, libelous, or factually incorrect, but those considered irrelevant to current concerns or too divergent from mainstream views. So despite the temptation to see letters to the editor as *vox populi*, a true reflection of public sentiment, we must read them as a form of "structured dialog" (Hall et al. 1978), the product of an articulation between letter writers and editorial staff.[5]

The possibility exists, therefore, that the patterns of Islamophobia described here reflect editors' biases more than the prejudice or xenophobia of their respective nations. Perhaps the only way to make such a determination would be to compare the views expressed in letters to the editor with broad-based national opinion polls on the same issues, an undertaking unfortunately well beyond the scope of this chapter. Leaving aside the issue of how accurately these letters represent public opinion, we can say with certainty that in the months following 9/11, letters to the editor in the three nations selected for analysis both reflected and contributed to a general climate of Islamophobia in those three nations.

The analysis here draws on the tools of traditional content analysis and the principles of Critical Discourse Analysis. While simple descriptive statistics are provided to highlight patterns in the representation of the national self and the Muslim/Arab Other, more detailed attention is given to qualitative analysis.[6] Although numbers can point the researcher in the right direction, only a careful qualitative reading of the content allows us to identify nuances of representation.

The sample consists of 802 letters to the editor taken from three national broadsheets, *The New York Times*, *The Times* of London, and *The Australian*, each of which serves as the de facto newspaper of public record for its respective nation.[7] As such, these newspapers are frequently cited as sources by other media outlets. Thus, as Page (1996, 17) points out, ideas featured in such quality broadsheets have the potential to profoundly shape public debates.

Because my primary interest was in representations of the perceived enemy in the war on terror (i.e., "terrorists"), the electronic archives of the letters pages of each paper were searched for references to "terror," "terrorism," and "terrorist(s)" in the period of September 11, 2001, to September 11, 2002. The search yielded 282 Australian letters, 499 British letters, and 267 American letters. Due to the large number of British letters, every second letter was included in the sample. It was clear from the outset that writers of the letters to the editor examined here associated virtually all terrorists and terrorist acts with Muslims and Islam: 94 percent of letters in the US, 96 percent in the UK, and 99 percent in Australia, linked "terrorism" with Islam.

What such numbers do not tell us, however, is the precise nature of these representations. For a more in-depth understanding of constructions of the enemy and the national self, I turned to a detailed analysis of negative and positive stereotyping. Building on research conducted by the Runnymede Trust (1997), I coded the sample of letters for both negative stereotypes of Muslims and Islam and their positive correlates, usually attributed to the Judeo-Christian West. These traits included the following: *unjustifiably violent* versus *peaceful* or using *just force*; *fanatical* versus *rational*; *barbaric* versus *civilized*; *oppressive* versus *free, just, and democratic*; *inhumane* versus *humane*; *hateful and intolerant* versus *tolerant*; and *godly* versus *evil*.

Quantitative Measures

The most striking trend in representations of the national self and the Muslim Other in US, UK, and Australian letters to the editor is that with very few exceptions, Muslims are negatively stereotyped while positive traits are attributed to the national self (Figures 8.1–8.3). In all three nations Muslims are characterized as markedly more violent and fanatical. Muslims are almost never characterized as rational, civilized, free and just, or tolerant. The US, UK, and Australia, on the other hand, are never portrayed as inhumane or evil, and have a near monopoly on the just use of force. Such representations reflect widespread and long-standing Islamophobia within these three nations.

Nonetheless, letter writers reveal an awareness that such prejudicial views run contrary to their own nation's avowed commitment to diversity, tolerance, and equality. In all three nations some letters to the editor acknowledge that many or most Muslims are peaceful and law-abiding, and that "ordinary" (non-Muslim) Americans, Britons, and Australians can be ignorant and bigoted. Such opinions were particularly pronounced in Australian letters after a spate of anti-Muslim, anti-Arab, and anti-immigrant crimes committed by what one author characterized as "bigoted morons," and in American letters after the Reverend Jerry Falwell publicly blamed feminists, gays and lesbians, and non-Christians, among others, for the violence of 9/11.[8] In addition, as the Bush, Blair, and Howard administrations

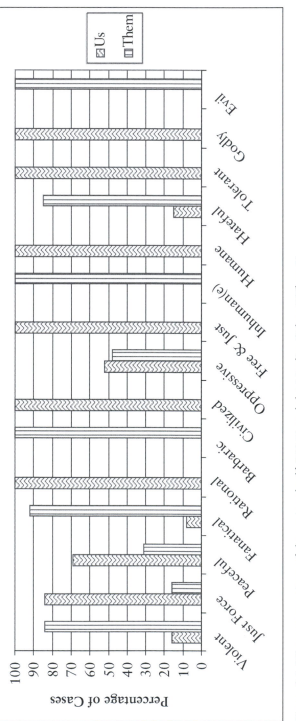

Figure 8.1 US representations of the national self ("Us") and the Muslim Other ("Them").

Figure 8.2 UK representations of the national self ("Us") and the Muslim Other ("Them").

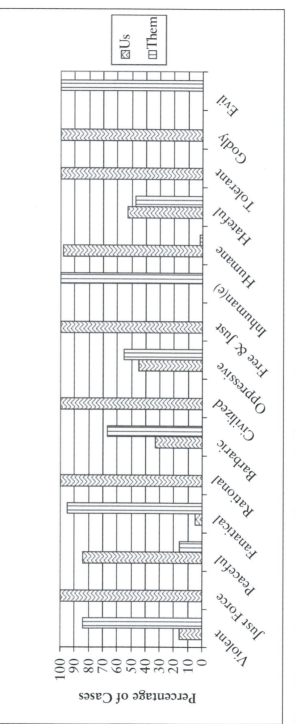

Figure 8.3 Australian representations of the national self ("Us") and the Muslim Other ("Them").

began instituting domestic anti-terror measures, some of which were widely perceived as significant curtailments of civil liberties and violations of the basic principals of justice and democracy, letter writers in all three nations expressed reservations that their states would become as oppressive and tyrannical as those of the 9/11 terrorists.

While there are no statistically significant differences between the nations in the Islamophobic stereotyping evidenced in post-9/11 letters to the editor, the degree of the negative stereotyping of the Muslim Other is made even clearer by aggregating all possible negative traits (Figure 8.4). In all three nations, the vast majority of unfavorable characteristics are attributed to Muslims.

Qualitative Analysis

While quantitative measures can chart the broad contours of Islamophobic stereotyping in the letters to the editor of all three nations, only detailed qualitative analysis can reveal the specific mechanisms by which discourses of national identity are inflected by categories of race, ethnicity, and gender. For the purposes of this analysis, we can identify five discursive tropes found in the letters to the editor: Simple Islamophobia, Enlightened Islamophobia, Auto-Orientalism, Anti-Orientalism, and Gendered Orientalism.

Simple Islamophobia

As Edward Said's classic work on Orientalism cogently argued, and as many subsequent studies have confirmed, Western discourses have long stereotyped the "Orient," particularly Muslims and the "Islamic World," as tyrannical, fanatical, bloodthirsty, and morally inferior to the Christian West.[9] Such representations are not only unjust and inaccurate, but, as Said points out, they have historically been used to justify the economic, cultural, and military domination of the Orient by Western powers.[10]

Such long-standing, uniformly negative representations can usefully be characterized as Simple Islamophobia. Certainly, such discourses are not "simple" in terms of their origins or their effects. Rather, I use the term "simple" because such views appear relatively untouched by any contemporary awareness of cultural relativism or multiculturalism. At its most extreme, Simple Islamophobia demonizes and dehumanizes Muslims. Indeed, a small subset of letters to the editor in all three nations characterize extremist Muslims as "inhuman," as "monsters," a "disease," a "plague," a "scourge," or simply "evil." More commonly, however, authors stop short of dehumanizing the Other while still repeating well-established negative stereotypes about Muslims and Islam. Excerpts 1 and 2 exemplify such letters. The author of the first letter writes in the context of heated public debates in Australia about whether the state should continue to admit asylum seekers from predominantly Muslim nations.

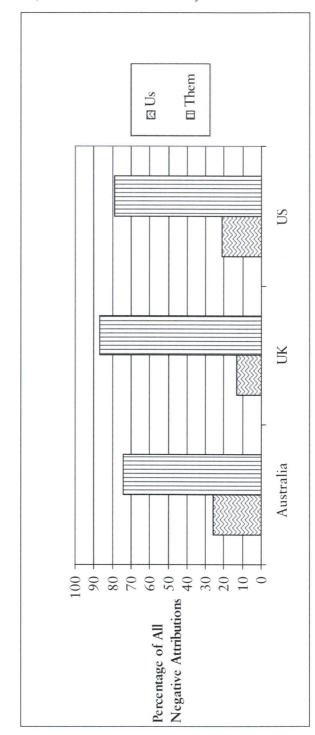

Figure 8.4 Negative traits attributed to "Us" and "Them."

Excerpt 1, *The Australian*:

> Lunatic, fanatical madmen don't care how they die in the name of the cause for it means, in their "religion," that they will reside in paradise forever.
>
> Risking their worthless lives in a leaky boat from Indonesia (or elsewhere) means nothing to their deranged minds. And sitting for a couple of years in a detention centre wouldn't deter them one iota from their evil ways—it would offer them opportunities to convert a captive audience. Some of those evil terrorists in New York had been there for years working away at being "ordinary" Americans.
>
> [T.N. Bankstown, NSW, 18 September 2001]

Not only does the letter characterize Muslims as "lunatic, fanatical madmen," as "worthless," "deranged," and "evil," but through the use of carefully placed quotation marks, Islam itself is derided as a pseudoreligion, a set of beliefs so unholy and repugnant to right-thinking individuals that it cannot be considered a viable faith. The letter furthermore portrays Muslims as a threat to Australia's national security. If Muslim refugees are allowed into the country, the writer suggests, they will bide their time, posing as "ordinary" Australians, quietly recruiting other murderous fanatics, until they are ready to attack.

The second letter is in response to a *New York Times* photograph.

Excerpt 2, *The New York Times*:

> When my 8-year-old saw your Feb. 26 front-page photo of Palestinian militants showing children his age how to use machine guns, he was puzzled. "Isn't that dangerous?" he asked. "Why are grown-ups showing kids how to do that?"
>
> Therein lies the problem. One could search throughout Israel and not find such a training program. That one side of the Mideast equation inculcates violence and hatred into its youngest minds, even at their own peril, is at the heart of the problem. These children are not being trained to use these guns for self-defense. They are being trained for terror. That Palestinians teach children that violence is preferable to coexistence seems to be one of the cruelest acts of this terrible conflict. For both sides. Peace will not come until children cease to be taught to hate.
>
> [S.M., Teaneck, New Jersey, 26 February 2002]

The author uses words rich in negative connotations to describe the Palestinian/Muslim Other: militant, inculcate, violence, hatred, peril, terror, cruelty. In addition, she utilizes what are reported to be the words of a child to construct the US and Israel (Judeo-Christian civilization) as innocent and peaceful, and Palestinians (the Muslim world) as sinister and violent. The use of the child's questions in the opening paragraph works on two levels.

First, it represents Palestinian actions as so illogical, unnatural, and contrary to American values that they "puzzled" the child. Furthermore, the child's questions imply that Palestinian "grown-ups" have less common sense and sheer humanity than the average American child.

In countless letters to the editor in all three nations, authors' lexical choices establish a binary relationship between the Western/Judeo-Christian self (Us) and the Arab/Muslim Other (Them). Pronominal choices often explicitly delineate Us from Them (see Seidel 1987 and Hage 1998), while descriptors serve to stereotype the two essentialized groups, as in Excerpt 3 (emphasis added).

Excerpt 3, *The Australian*:

> Whether *they* like it or not, the world including all Muslims will take a long hard look at Islam and how it is practiced after last week's horror.
>
> By definition, *they* exclude *themselves* from the world community. Islam is not just a religion, it dictates *their* whole life . . . And if, as *they* would have *us* believe, Islam is the savior of the people, why can't the affluent Muslim countries save the Muslim refugees?
>
> . . . In today's Muslim world, the only consistencies are the persecution of *their* own kind and others. Religions other than Islam didn't die out, but they adjusted to guarantee their survival. America and Australia, with secular law, practice a live-and-let-live philosophy. People are free to practice any religion or no religion if they so choose. Today's and history's Islam does not provide those options.
>
> *I* probably won't live long enough to see if Islam evolves. As *they* would have *us* believe, "Inshya Allah," *I* prefer to believe it is up to *them*.
>
> [G.G., Paddington, Queensland, 24 September 2001]

The use of pronouns in the letter leaves little doubt that the author does not include Muslims in the national imagined community. *They* set themselves apart from *us*. *They* persecute "*their* own kind" and commit acts of horror against *us*. Likewise, the author employs positively loaded language to describe the national self (community, guarantee, live-and-let-live philosophy, free, choose) and negatively loaded language to describe the Muslim Other (horror, exclude, dictate, persecution).

In addition to such lexical choices, the author introduces productive ambiguity in the last paragraph with the statement "I probably won't live long enough to see if Islam evolves." It is perhaps intentionally unclear whether the author is suggesting that s/he will not live "long enough" because s/he will be murdered by fanatical Muslims for voicing such views, or because Islam is incapable of anything more than snail-paced change.[11] Such ambiguity is productive in the sense that the author is able to construct Islam as violent and backward without actually asserting this directly.

Enlightened Islamophobia

In an analysis of the ways media representations shape understandings of race and racism in the United States, Jhally and Lewis (1992) utilize the concept of "enlightened racism." By this, they mean a new kind of racism based not so much on a belief in biologically inferior human subgroups, but rather on the belief that any disparities between racial groups in terms of income, education, health, and so on, are the result of certain dysfunctional cultural traits of minority groups. In other words, while it is no longer socially acceptable in the US to assert that certain groups lag behind due to their genetic inferiority, it has become commonplace to observe that these groups suffer from a kind of cultural inferiority.

We can usefully adapt the concept of enlightened racism here to discuss Enlightened Islamophobia. Specifically, these are discourses which acknowledge contemporary values based on cultural relativism, pluralism, tolerance, and equality, and which steer clear of references to biological differences between groups, but which nonetheless repeat negative stereotypes of the Muslim Other or reinforce the symbolic divide between Us and Them. Excerpts 4, 5, and 6 are cases in point.

Excerpt 4, *The New York Times*:

> Lynne Cheney and others miss the point when they assume that teaching about Islam is equivalent to excusing terrorism. Educators are trying to increase understanding of the culture of our Muslim neighbors, colleagues and students.
>
> [B.L., Tempe, AZ, 17 October 2001]

Excerpt 5, *The Times* of London:

> Once again Phillips points to our quandary in the West: how to reconcile individual Muslims we work with, live with, know and almost understand with terrorists and fanatics that some parts of Islam protect and promote.
>
> [G.E., London, 21 October 2001]

Excerpt 6, *The Australian*:

> . . . Seeing that the gulf dividing the Eastern Islamic world and the Western Christian world is at least as old as the Crusades, are we to expect that it can be bridged at will and all at once?
>
> People have a natural fear of the unfamiliar, but what they fear most from the present unregulated transmigration of Islamic peoples is that it would lead to the formation and perpetuation of large Islamic ghettos within the Australian community, with quite unforeseeable consequences for their future lives and for the lives of their children.

Everyone understands the deadly dangers of extreme forms of religious intolerance, irrespective of who practices it . . . The mass of public opinion would shift only when ordinary men and women could persuade themselves that the values held by the Muslim asylum-seekers were not fundamentally different from their own. This is unlikely to happen on a significant scale in the immediate aftermath of the New York catastrophe.

[M.P., Lower Mitcham, SA, 17 September 2001]

The author in Excerpt 4 writes in defense of American pluralism. She stresses the value of teaching and learning about Islam. Yet in subtle ways she reinforces the notion of essentialized differences between Muslims and the rest of *us*. She represents Muslims as having a single, monolithic "culture" that Americans can study, and she notes that Muslims are *our* neighbors and co-workers, but apparently they still are not *us*.

Similarly, the author of Excerpt 5 places Muslims among his neighbors and co-workers, but they are inscrutable Others, those *we* "know and *almost* understand." He then contrasts these everyday, presumably innocuous, Others with the violent and fanatical Islamic terrorist. So, even as he seems to be seeking a deeper understanding of those around him, he nonetheless categorizes Muslims into two broad types: inscrutable Others and threatening Others.

The author of Excerpt 6 likewise counts himself among those who recognize the value of religious tolerance. He even acknowledges a degree of diversity among "Islamic peoples." Nonetheless, he makes three closely interconnected points: that there is an ancient and seemingly inevitable "gulf" between Muslim and Christian civilizations; that Muslims are "fundamentally different" from the "ordinary men and women" of Australia; and that Australian fears of the Muslim Other are "natural." This supports his assertion that the nation should stop accepting Muslim refugees. In this appeal to Enlightened Islamophobia, denying entry to Muslim asylum seekers is for their own good, as they would be destined to live in "ghettos" and face possibly insurmountable difficulties. So denying refuge here becomes a humanitarian act, almost a moral obligation, consistent with contemporary notions of human rights and social justice.

These excerpts reveal a tendency, even among Americans, Britons, and Australians who embrace the principles of tolerance and diversity, to view the "Muslim world" as an undifferentiated whole, and to view Islam and Muslims as exotic or dangerous. Such views have been bolstered in recent years by best-selling tomes such as Samuel Huntington's (1996) *The Clash of Civilizations*.[12] Huntington and his defenders have largely ignored the substantial cultural, linguistic, political, and religious diversity among Muslims worldwide, and warned of inevitable conflicts between a Judeo-Christian West and its Muslim Other. They have also by and large failed to acknowledge the specific historical developments of the last three decades that have led to the rise of radical Islamicist movements.[13] Instead, Islam is portrayed as dangerous and regressive by its very nature.

In academic circles such arguments have been widely challenged as inaccurate, overly simplistic, and even racist. Nonetheless, high-profile best-selling authors such as Huntington no doubt lend a veneer of scholarly respectability to widely circulating stereotypes of Islam and its adherents as uniformly backward, violent, and irrational, and utterly different from *us*. What I am calling Enlightened Islamophobia is often subtle. Some may argue, in fact, that many of the sentiments in the letters here are not indicative of Islamophobia at all. The fact remains, however, that these forms of distancing and delineation are too common in the sample of letters to ignore. Such a prominent representational pattern seems to indicate underlying assumptions in the US, UK, and Australia about a natural divide between the Judeo-Christian national self and the Muslim Other.

Auto-Orientalism

A third discursive subtype in post-9/11 letters to the editor is what I will call Auto-Orientalism. The term Auto-Orientalism has been used by scholars of national identity in a variety of ways. In its broadest sense, it has been used to mean "self-discourse among orientals" (Lindstrom 1995, 35–36), or more specifically, a variety of nativist discourse which stresses an Eastern culture's uniqueness. However, I draw more closely on Said's description of Orientalism when I conceptualize Auto-Orientalism as negative self-stereotyping by Muslims and Arabs.

In one notable trend in the sample, Muslims and writers of Arab descent frequently defended their communities and their faith while simultaneously repeating well-established Islamophobic stereotypes. Excerpts 7 and 8 provide useful examples.

Excerpt 7, *The Times* of London:

> Less than 10% of the 2 million Muslims in Britain go to the mosques and to say "British Muslim support for terror" is an insult to our faith. We are grateful for the opportunity to adopt Britain as our home, but we are citizens as good as the most patriotic British. There is no other country more protective towards her minorities and more tolerant of all other religions than Britain . . .
>
> We may not like Britain for bombing starving, barefoot, nomadic tribes in Afghanistan, not because we are Muslims but because they are no match for our modern laser-guided weapons . . . We don't bomb Ireland for harbouring and America for funding IRA terrorists. Is the life of a Christian Anglo-Saxon terrorist more precious than a Muslim Arab terrorist?
>
> [A.S.D., London, 11 November 2001]

The Muslim author of this letter clearly includes Muslims in his notion of the national community: Britain is *our* home, he notes, and *we* are good and patriotic citizens. The author represents Britain as a tolerant, protective, and modern nation, while representing the people of Afghanistan as destitute, primitive tribesmen. Although the author calls for increased understanding of Muslims and Islam and equal treatment for Muslims and non-Muslims alike, he makes his point using the language and imagery of Islamophobia: the affluent, modern, enlightened West versus the primitive, bedraggled, tribal Muslim world.

In Excerpt 8, the writer identifies himself as a representative of the Islamic Council of Western Australia.

Excerpt 8, *The Australian*:

> Although the Muslim community at large has expressed its sorrow and unequivocal condemnation of the brutal attack on the US, the response we see from some Australian folks is very disappointing. Muslims have been witnessing harassment, attacks on schools, mosques and direct threats, especially towards Muslim ladies wearing the Islamic dress.
>
> Muslims residing in Australia are either skilled immigrants who have been contributing to the good of Australia, or those who have fled persecution and oppression from the tyrant rulers of the Middle East. Therefore we should not be expecting either of these groups to be backing terrorism, especially in the barbaric form we have seen in the US.
>
> It is unfair that Muslims in Australia pay for a crime they have never perpetrated nor supported. Ironically, Muslims have been subjected to a form of terrorism—which we should all be fighting. It is dangerous to import violence and hate to our Australian land, where the fabric of the population has always been multicultural and harmonious. Why should we incite violence and discrimination? . . . I am afraid that unless we restrain ourselves the only winner at the end of the day will be the evil.
> [M.I., Secretary of the Islamic Council, WA, 20 September 2001]

The author's overarching point here is that non-Muslim Australians need to refrain from discriminating against Muslim Australians. In making his case, he favorably characterizes Australian Muslims as skilled workers and members of a caring community, grieving with the rest of the world in the wake of the 9/11 attacks. Nonetheless, he also describes leaders in the Middle East as tyrannical, and the 9/11 attackers as barbaric. While it is true that tyrannical leaders may be found in the Middle East, just as they are found elsewhere in the world, and while the acts of the 9/11 attackers are generally acknowledged to have been particularly brutal, the language of Middle Eastern/Arab tyranny and barbarism is the language of Orientalism.

By contrast, the author asserts, Australia itself has "always been multicultural and harmonious," an assertion which, of course, ignores the mass extermination of indigenous Australians, mass expulsions of nonwhites from the early Federation, and the long-lived White Australia Policy. He suggests that only after the acts by Muslim extremists has the nation become intolerant. Curiously, although he implies that discrimination against Muslim Australians is a form of "terrorism," he exhorts readers not to "import violence and hate." The notion of "importing" social disorder is used most widely in Australia today by opponents of immigration, who argue that migrants bring their ancient prejudices and tribal loyalties with them only to play them out violently on Australian soil. So while the author is advocating tolerance, he does so using the language of intolerance.

The author then closes the letter with a warning that "the evil" will win the day if violence and discrimination escalate. Again, a careful reading suggests that the evil to which the author refers is anti-Muslim discrimination itself. However, in post-9/11 Australian discussions of terrorism, the term "evil" is almost always applied to (Islamic) terrorists and terrorism. So the letter at least implies that these terrorists will benefit from the persecution of their coreligionists.

So what is happening here? It seems unlikely that these writers hold anti-Muslim attitudes, since they identify strongly as members of their respective Muslim communities. And clearly when they use phrases like "our Australian land" or "Britain is our home," they include Muslims in their vision of the national community. I would argue then that this is not Auto-Orientalism in the sense of believing negative stereotypes about oneself and one's community. Rather it appears that the authors have used the Islamophobic imagery of the dominant culture (Muslims as primitive, barbaric, tyrannical, violent, evil) as a way of engaging in dialog with the non-Muslim majority. In a sense, by adopting Auto-Orientalist discourse, they are speaking the language of the majority to affect positive change for the minority.

Anti-Orientalism and Gendered Orientalism

Two discursive tropes remain: Anti-Orientalism and Gendered Orientalism. These last two are less prevalent in the sample of letters than those earlier, and Gendered Orientalism in particular, is very subtle. Yet both contribute to narratives of nation by helping to define the national self and the Other.

Anti-Orientalist (or anti-Islamophobic) discourses are conceptualized here as those discourses which characterize various ethnoracial and national groups, particularly Muslims, in nonstereotypical ways. Often such letters explicitly critique Islamophobic stereotypes, overgeneralizations about Islam and Muslims, and anti-Muslim discrimination, and appeal to either national or universal values, as in Excerpts 9 through 11.

Excerpt 9, *The New York Times*:

Thomas L. Friedman's generalization of what he terms "bin Ladenism" makes it seem as if it is a sentiment sweeping through the Middle

East like wildfire. In reality, Arab leaders, Arab civil society and the people in general have spoken out on numerous occasions condemning the heinous acts of terror perpetrated against America . . .

[H.E.N., Washington, D.C., 9 November 2001]

Excerpt 10, *The Times* of London:

Despite the fact that Muslim communities throughout the world have condemned the terrorist attacks and have joined in with the rest in mourning and praying for the families of the victims, they have been harassed and verbally abused. Using the word Islamic with words such as terrorist, extremists etc. paints the whole Muslim community and Islam as being terrorists and extremists. Would Israeli atrocities against innocent civilians be called Jewish terrorism?

[A.V., London, 16 September 2001]

Excerpt 11, *The Australian*:

Australian Muslims (including boat people) are no more responsible for the US terrorist plane crashes than I am for the Oklahoma City bombing. Victimisation must strongly be condemned by all of us if our claimed principles of tolerance and a fair go are to be anything more than rhetoric.

[J.M., Albany Creek, QLD, 14 September 2001]

Such Anti-Orientalist letters often appear designed principally to set the record straight about Muslims and Islam: not all Muslims support bin Laden; not all Muslims are terrorists; and ordinary Muslims are as different from the 9/11 attackers as ordinary Christians are from Oklahoma City bomber Timothy McVeigh.[14] In addition to challenging Islamophobic stereotypes, such letters often make broader appeals to national or even pannational (Arab/Muslim) identity. Such appeals are exemplified by references to "Arab civil society" in Excerpt 9 and to the much vaunted Australian ethics of "tolerance and a fair go" in Excerpt 11. Such letters therefore serve not only to humanize and universalize the Other, but to help define and celebrate the national self by reminding readers of what are assumed to be shared national values.

Finally, recent feminist scholarship has noted the many ways Orientalist discourses have been and continue to be gendered.[15] Western political, academic, artistic, and popular discourses have commonly positioned Oriental women as passive, subordinate, eroticized objects of male desire and power, while representing Oriental men as either effete cowards or brutish tyrants. In contrast, the West has celebrated its own perceived masculine agency and all the traits associated with it: strength, rationality, courage, and the just use of force, among others. Gendered imagery has thus been used to emphasize essentialized differences between Occident and Orient. Representations in the letters to the editor examined here are to some extent consistent with such well-established Orientalist stereotypes.

Perhaps most striking in terms of gendered representations is the overwhelming dominance of male voices and deeds in the letters. Of the 740 named individuals mentioned in the letters, 702 of them, or 95 percent of all those named, were men. These men, as politicians, intellectuals, military leaders, experts, and of course "terrorists," were sometimes praised and sometimes lambasted, but uniformly portrayed as people who shaped national and world affairs. By contrast, the few women named in the letters (4 percent of individuals in Britain, and 6 percent in the US and Australia) were almost without exception positioned on the margins of current affairs. Some letters dismissed the named women as uninformed, cowardly, or ineffectual. And when women such as Mary Robinson, Cherie Blair, and Susan Sontag spoke out in defense of human rights or attempted to explore the roots of terrorism in conditions of inequality and oppression, they were accused of abetting the enemy and undermining the global war on terror.

By far the most common representation of women, both named and unnamed, was as victims: a mother killed in the 9/11 attacks, a pregnant friend killed by a Palestinian suicide bomber, a human rights worker attacked, a vulnerable daughter studying in Israel. Both Muslim and non-Muslim women were portrayed as weak and vulnerable. However, while at least some non-Muslim women were individuated—mainly politicians and intellectuals—not a single Muslim woman was named in the entire sample of letters. Instead, Muslim women were portrayed as an undifferentiated mass, brutalized and silenced by tyrannical (usually Muslim) men.

By contrast, the language employed in the letters makes it clear that men are active agents fighting for either good or evil. Authors write of country-*men*, service*men*, *brothers*, *fathers*, and *grandfathers* defending the nation against mad*men*, tribes*men*, megalomaniacal strong*men*, and a *brother*hood of fanatical Arab terrorists. Thus both terrorism and counterterrorism are represented as male activities, with women positioned as the passive victims or beneficiaries of those actions.

CONSEQUENCES OF POST-9/11 ISLAMOPHOBIA

One key assertion of this volume is that discourses of national identity matter. That is, they affect our lives in material ways by not only reflecting but also contributing to the privileging or marginalization of certain groups. There is perhaps no clearer recent illustration of this point than the case of Islamophobic discourses in the post-9/11 period.

Representations of the violent, fanatical Muslim/Arab man have pervaded the mass media in the US, the UK, and Australia since the 9/11 attacks, not only in letters to the editor such as those examined here, but in movies, television dramas, political cartoons, radio talk shows, and broadcast news, among others.[16] Such representations have without a doubt both mirrored and shaped a social climate in which Muslims and people of Middle Eastern descent have increasingly become the objects of hostility, fear, and discrimination. While it is not possible to provide a comprehensive discussion of post-9/11 anti-Muslim discrimination here, certain trends and events provide insight into the consequences of Islamophobia in the US, UK, and Australia since September of 2001.

In the US, for example, Kaushal et al. (2007) report a significant drop in the wages of Arab and Muslim men since the attacks of 9/11, and Cavendish and Disha (2007) chart a dramatic rise in anti-Muslim and anti-Arab hate crimes since the attacks. During the same period, provisions of the USA PATRIOT Act have officially endorsed the use of racial profiling in defense of national security, resulting in the routine heightened scrutiny of men of Arab descent, a significant number of whom have been subjected to state detention and even deportation. Also reflecting broader concerns over both national security and the perceived degradation of the American way of life, the post-9/11 period has been marked by the rise of a very vocal anti-immigration movement, the development of vigilante border control groups, and the passage of legislation to construct a massive wall along portions of the US border. Fear of the Muslim enemy Other has thus translated into more widespread xenophobia.

Similarly, during the same period Britain has seen a rise in crimes against Muslims, heightened monitoring and detention of Muslims, and public calls for immigration reform. Between September 11, 2001, and the end of 2006, almost 1,200 people were arrested under the Terrorism Act, the majority of whom were Muslims (Home Office 2007; Institute of Race Relations 2004). The state has carried out a number of massive anti-terrorism "sweeps" of predominantly Muslim neighborhoods. And after fifty-two commuters and four apparent suicide bombers died in the July 2005 London Underground attacks, anti-terrorism authorities reaffirmed a "shoot to kill" order for suspected bombers, and announced that thousands of British Muslims were under surveillance. Later that month, a Brazilian electrician, Charles de Menezes was shot dead by police who mistook him for a Muslim suicide bomber. An inquiry into the incident subsequently determined that Britain's top counterterrorism officer, Andy Hayman, had "misled" the public about crucial details in the case (BBC 2007). Meanwhile, right-wing political groups such as the British National Party have capitalized on the rising tide of Islamophobia by fielding a record number of candidates in local elections, running primarily on an anti-Muslim platform.

As in Britain and the US, in the post-9/11 period Australia witnessed an increase in the number of anti-Muslim and anti-Arab hate crimes, the adoption of restrictive anti-immigration and anti-terrorism laws, and acrimonious debates over asylum seekers from the Middle East (see the Human Rights and Equal Opportunity Commission 2004; Poynting and Mason 2006; and Elder 2007). Tensions between the Australian Muslim/Middle Eastern community and white majority Australians culminated in the Cronulla riots of December 2005 in which a crowd of several thousand (mainly white) Australians gathered to protest perceived infractions by Lebanese youths. The protest turned violent when two men of Middle Eastern descent were surrounded and beaten, sparking several days of sporadic attacks on both sides of the conflict. State responses to the riots were split. Some national leaders downplayed the social significance of the events. Prime Minister Howard characterized the violence as "domestic discord" and unlawful "nonsense" and Opposition leader Kim Beazley reassured the nation that Australian multiculturalism was still "alive and well."[17] Local officials, however, treated the violence as racially motivated crime indicative of ethnoracial tensions heightened after the attacks of 9/11 and the 12 October 2002 Bali nightclub bombing that killed eighty-eight Australians.

The patterns of post-9/11 Islamophobia in the US, UK, and Australia are remarkably similar: a rise in violence against Muslims and those perceived to be of Arab/Middle Eastern descent; intensified calls to limit immigration; increased use of racial profiling against Muslims/Arabs, sometimes resulting in unjust arrest, injury, and in the de Menezes case even death; detention and/or deportation of Muslims and Arabs deemed to be a threat to national security; and intensive Othering of Muslims/Arabs through the mass media of each of the nations examined here.

Certainly it would be overly simplistic to argue that Islamophobic discourses of national identity such as those found in letters to the editor or other media texts, somehow *cause* hate crimes, anti-immigrant sentiment, or repressive state practices. However it would be likewise naïve to assert that media texts play no role in creating a climate in which discrimination against Muslims and people of Middle Eastern descent is normalized, even valorized. Symbolic violence, the use of words and images to denigrate and dehumanize Muslims/Arabs, makes actual material violence against them seem (to some) justified, even necessary.

Of course the most dramatic examples of this are the US-led military invasions of Afghanistan in 2001 and Iraq in 2003 and the subsequent occupations of those nations. In making a case for war, President Bush drew heavily on long-standing Orientalist binaries: good versus evil; peaceful versus violent; rational versus fanatical; free versus oppressive; Us versus Them.[18] And despite significant public opposition in Britain and Australia, Prime Ministers Blair and Howard enthusiastically embraced and contributed to these military actions.[19] The case of Islamophobic discourses of national identity in the post-9/11 context serves as a reminder that far from being innocent or inconsequential, constructions of the national self and its Others can be implicated in bloodshed. While it is true that we collectively construct "imagined communities" the outcomes of those national imaginings are very real and potentially deadly.

9 Defending the Nation
Gender, Race, and National Identity in Press Coverage of Private Jessica Lynch

Warfare has both pragmatic and symbolic dimensions. At the practical level, war typically centers on the control of land, wealth, populations, or political processes. At the symbolic level, however, war can be understood as the ritual assertion of collective (often national) identity. As noted in the previous chapter, warfare often generates potent narratives of the national self and its enemy Others.

This chapter examines gendered and racialized discourses of national identity in American, British, and Australian press coverage of events during the 2003 invasion of Iraq. Specifically, the chapter contrasts coverage given to US Army Private Jessica Lynch with coverage given to other members of her unit who were captured or killed when their supply convoy came under fire. Central to the analysis are the ways the soldiers' gendered and racialized bodies serve as markers of national identity, the ways discourses of national identity both sustain and challenge relations of dominance, and the ways narratives of nation are perpetuated and reshaped by national and international media dynamics.

CAPTIVES

On 20 March 2003 the US military, supported principally by troops from the UK and Australia, launched an aerial invasion of Iraq. On 23 March, as ground troops advanced on Baghdad, the US Army's 507th Maintenance Company became separated from their supply convoy and came under attack near Nassiriya. Nine of the unit's members were killed, including Private First Class (Pfc.) Lori Piestewa, Private Brandon Sloan, and Specialist James Kiehl. Six more soldiers were detained by Iraqi authorities. Five, including Specialist Shoshana Johnson, Pfc. Patrick Miller, and Specialist Edgar Hernandez, were shown being interrogated on Al-Jazeera Television, but were later released unharmed. The sixth, Pfc. Jessica Lynch, went missing in action, but was rescued on 1 April by US Special Forces in a highly publicized midnight raid on a Nassiriya hospital.

In the days and weeks following the skirmish at Nassiriya, the members of the 507th were not the only ones held captive. The American public, supplied with saturation media coverage of the unfolding events, were captivated by the story of the missing and captured soldiers, as interviews with tearful family members, military spokespeople, and experts on prisoners of war filled the airwaves and the press. Special attention was given to fears and speculation about the kinds of violence the female captives might face. While coverage was somewhat more subdued in Britain and Australia, it still prompted ample public commentary.

While the international press provided coverage of all of the 507th soldiers captured or killed during the ambush, coverage varied both quantitatively and qualitatively with the gender, race, and ethnicity of the soldiers. A disproportionate amount of the coverage was given to just one soldier, Pfc. Jessica Lynch, a petite blond teenager with girl-next-door good looks.

ANALYZING PRESS COVERAGE

The Lynch story was such a national and international sensation that it has attracted considerable scholarly attention.[1] Most of this scholarship, although thought provoking, is largely impressionistic, based on in-depth readings of a few significant texts, events, and images. By contrast, this chapter systematically samples and analyzes press coverage of Jessica Lynch and other members of her unit, for discourses of gendered and racialized national identity. In addition, the previous work on the topic of Lynch almost without exception treats the Lynch story as a national (American) phenomenon. This chapter takes a broader view by considering differences, similarities, and possible cross-fertilization of press coverage in three of the nations involved in the invasion of Iraq.

To this end, a content analysis was conducted on 427 newspaper articles in the six months following the incident at Nassiriya in ten national newspapers: *USA Today, The New York Times, The Washington Post,* and *The Wall Street Journal* in the US; *The Independent, The Times* of London, and *The Guardian* in the UK; and *The Sydney Morning Herald, The Australian,* and *The Age* in Australia. The data set includes all articles in which the name of at least one of the seven Army 507th soldiers listed earlier appeared. Each article was treated as a unit of analysis and was coded for both reference type (the length and detail of the coverage) and qualitative descriptions of the soldiers (including references to their gender, race, or ethnicity, and aspects of their appearance, social statuses, and personality traits).

The content analysis was structured to test three central hypotheses. The first hypothesis was that female soldiers would receive more coverage (both in numbers of articles and level of detail) than male soldiers, but that the coverage would be highly gender stereotypical. This prediction was based on the fact that while increasing numbers of women are entering the military, warfare is still symbolically gendered in the masculine.[2] It was considered likely, therefore, that female soldiers on the front line would have novelty value and attract more media coverage. However, at the same time, it was predicted that any potential threats posed to masculinity by the presence of women soldiers would be neutralized by conventional representations of passive femininity and assertive masculinity.

The second hypothesis was that white soldiers would receive more coverage than soldiers of color, as measured both by number of articles and level of detail. This prediction was based on both the historical dominance of whites in the national narratives of the US, UK, and Australia and the continuing material disadvantages of most ethnoracial minority groups in these nations. Press coverage which rendered soldiers of color less visible, less fully individuated people than white soldiers would both reflect long-standing ethnoracial inequalities in these nations and help maintain such inequalities by legitimizing the continued dominance of whites over ethnoracial minorities.

The third hypothesis was that coverage of the soldiers would be less stereotypically gendered and racialized in certain subsets of the data. Specifically, it was predicted that the UK and Australian press coverage would be less stereotypically gendered and racialized than US coverage. This hypothesis was premised on the notion that because the US was more heavily invested in the invasion of Iraq, US press coverage would be more likely than coverage elsewhere to feature the kind of conservative gender and ethnoracial hierarchies that reaffirm the authority of the largely white, male rulers and leaders of the nation. Likewise, it was predicted that different types of newspapers would represent gender, race, and ethnicity in ways that catered to the views and interests of their different readerships.

GENDERED AND RACIALIZED DISCOURSES OF NATIONAL IDENTITY

Both the first and second hypotheses are supported by the evidence (Table 9.1). That is, in press references to the soldiers of the 507th, females outnumber males by more than six to one and white soldiers outnumber soldiers of color by more than three to one. Most strikingly, Pfc. Lynch garners the overwhelming majority of the press coverage, being singled out in 85 percent of the articles.

Besides differences in the quantity of coverage, there are differences in the quality of coverage. The coverage was categorized into three main types: cases in which the soldier was *mentioned* (up to two lines of text), *individuated* (three to ten lines, with some personal details or quotations included), or *featured* (more than ten lines, with personal details or quotations included). As seen in Table 9.2, most articles simply mention the soldiers. Between 50

Table 9.1 Press Coverage of 507th Soldiers*

Soldier	Gender	Race/Ethnicity	Status on 23 March 2003	Number of Articles	Percentage of Total Articles
Jessica Lynch	Female	White	MIA**	364	85
Shoshana Johnson	Female	Black	POW	51	12
Lori Piestewa	Female	Native American	KIA	41	10
Patrick Miller	Male	White	POW	20	5
Edgar Hernandez	Male	Hispanic	POW	22	5
Brandon Sloan	Male	Black	KIA	10	2
James Kiehl	Male	White	KIA	8	2

*While the data set contains 427 articles, some articles refer to more than one of the seven soldiers. Therefore, the "# of articles" totals more than 427, and the "% of total articles" totals more than 100%.
**Soldiers' status includes missing in action (MIA), prisoner of war (POW), killed in action (KIA).

and 96 percent of references to the soldiers are brief mentions. However, the trends already noted hold true here as well: female soldiers are more likely to be *featured* than male soldiers, and white soldiers are more likely to be *featured* than soldiers of color. Again, Lynch stands out here, with by far the greatest number of feature articles.

Table 9.2 Coverage Type for 507th Soldiers

Soldier	Sex	Race/Ethnicity	Mentioned	Individuated	Featured
Lynch (N=364)	Female	White	222	55	87
Johnson (N=51)	Female	Black	34	9	8
Piestewa (N=41)	Female	Native American	28	5	8
Miller (N=20)	Male	White	13	6	1
Hernandez (N=22)	Male	Hispanic	21	1	—
Sloan (N=10)	Male	Black	7	3	—
Kiehl (N=8)	Male	White	4	1	3

The prominence of Lynch in the media coverage is explained by three main factors: the timing of her rescue, the sensational staging of her rescue, and Lynch's personal characteristics—particularly her age, race, gender, and appearance. In regards to the timing of the rescue, Lynch's retrieval served as a potent morale booster for the administrations, troops, and publics of the US, UK, and Australia in the midst of mounting criticisms of the invasion of Iraq. The invasion, after all, had dubious credibility in terms of international law, lacked UN support, and (despite President Bush's frequent references to the Coalition of the Willing) attracted only limited support among other nations around the world. The apparent failure to ensure the safety of a non-combat support unit only further undermined confidence in the endeavor.

It was in this context that Lynch's rescue provided a vehicle for narratives of American heroism and self-sacrifice, and allowed White House and military press engines to recast the invasion as an altruistic undertaking by America and its closest allies. With the footage of a weakly smiling Lynch wrapped in the American flag, there was at last a marketable image to match the mission's code name, Operation Iraqi Freedom.

The dramatic circumstances of the rescue further contributed to media and public interest in Lynch. The footage of the rescue, filmed with night-vision cameras by the Special Operations team conducting the raid, featured American soldiers storming the hospital in a spray of gunfire, kicking down doors, and finally rushing their injured comrade to a waiting helicopter. It was a moment of military triumph right out of Hollywood, smacking of Baudrillardian hyperreality in a graphic demonstration of life imitating art. Baudrillard's (1995) analysis of the Gulf War describes the "virtual" nature of contemporary warfare, where the battle between images becomes at least as important as, and (depending on one's position in the conflict) *more* important than, battles between bodies and armaments. While the degree to which the US military scripted this event for maximum PR effect has yet to be established, certainly Lynch's rescue represented a victory for the Bush administration on the ideological battlefield of public opinion.

In addition to the timing and circumstances of the rescue, Lynch's personal characteristics captured media and public interest in the US by appealing to America's national self-conceptions. In the context of the invasion of Iraq, the Jessica Lynch story received so much play in the US media, in part, because it fit so perfectly with dominant discourses of American national identity. In other words, it constructed a pleasing and self-affirming story about the nation.

Amidst heavy criticism of the seemingly imperialist turn in American policy, Lynch appeared, youthful and vital, the picture of innocence, a soldier with noble ideals. And this is how America has long seen itself, particularly in relation to its military actions: as a young, robust nation, acting not out of cynical self-interest, but out of altruism—protecting the weak, freeing the captive, replacing tyranny and chaos with justice and order, fighting only "good" wars. As many media commentators noted, after her rescue Jessica

Lynch became the "face of the war," at least in the US. And that "face" showed the nation at its best.

Likewise in the UK and Australia, where the administrations of Prime Ministers Blair and Howard had been facing widespread criticism for their decision to participate in the invasion, the Lynch story became an Allied success story. The story seemed to reaffirm the justness and nobility of the unpopular campaign.

At the same time, the Lynch story contributed to American, British, and Australian discourses of national identity in another way: it both reflected, and to some degree eased, two of the major tensions that have dominated these societies for the last forty years, tensions over hierarchies of gender and race. Since the rise of the civil rights and women's movements in the 1960s and 1970s, political, economic, and cultural changes have increasingly challenged white men's long-standing dominance of the public life of these nations. The Jessica Lynch story, as constructed in the media, both acknowledged and to some degree defused this crisis in the national gender and racial orders by naturalizing traditional gender and racial hierarchies.

The press coverage of the 507th reproduced such hierarchies in the ways it positioned soldiers as either active agents or passive victims. References to each soldier were coded for references to their independent and dependent traits. Instances of the soldier acting upon others or the world (for instance, leading, protecting, fighting, or demonstrating heroism) were coded as *independent*, while instances of the soldier being acted upon by others (for instance, being rescued, protected, wounded, or victimized) were coded as *dependent*. Not surprisingly, all of the soldiers were more likely to be represented as dependent rather than independent, regardless of their gender or ethnoracial background (Figure 9.1). This is explained by the fact that all of the soldiers included in the study had been either captured or killed in action.

However, two trends emerge from the data. First, while the soldier's gender did not strongly influence the likelihood of being represented as independent, female soldiers were significantly more likely than males to have their dependent traits stressed in press coverage. Second, while the soldier's ethnoracial background did not have a substantial influence on representations of dependent traits, white soldiers were twice as likely as soldiers of color to be represented as independent. Such representations reproduce long-standing gender and ethnoracial hierarchies in the US, the UK, and Australia by constructing women and people of color as passive and subordinate while presenting men and whites as active and autonomous.

Coverage of Lynch, in particular, reveals the power of deeply ingrained gender stereotypes. When Lynch was first rescued, the press constructed her as a heroic warrior. A frequently quoted *Washington Post* article reported that Lynch fought fiercely, firing on enemy soldiers until her ammunition was spent (Schmidt and Loeb 2003). Very quickly, however, this construction of the female Rambo was disputed, and what emerged instead was the

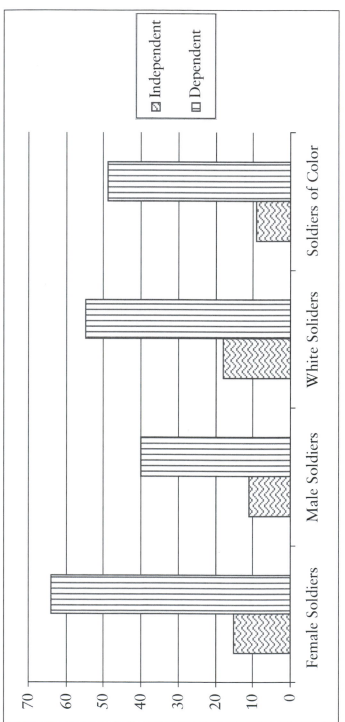

Figure 9.1 References to independent and dependent traits by gender and race of soldiers.

image of Lynch as a frightened, helpless, childlike victim. The press virtually stopped discussing her actions, and instead focused on her appearance, her fragility, her emotional state, and what had been done *to* her—her capture, her rescue, and her treatment in the hands both of enemies and comrades. Later coverage described her as ". . . the petite, blond 19-year-old who'd been named Miss Congeniality in the county fair beauty pageant and play-fully wore combat boots beneath her senior prom dress" (Jones 2003). So Lynch went from being portrayed as an active subject, a battlefield hero, to a passive object and a media spectacle.

Such a shift in the representation of Lynch reveals a tension within dis-courses of national identity in the US, the UK, and Australia. The initial construction of Lynch as warrior served as a reminder that women in all three nations are now in the military, working alongside male soldiers in this symbolically most masculine of jobs. It is likely that such a narrative was so eagerly promoted in these nations because it reconfirmed a common point of pride in the US, the UK, and Australia—the idea that they are pro-gressive nations, nations that value equality of opportunity for all people. Press coverage throughout the six months following the capture of Lynch stressed the inroads women had made into the previously all-male domain of the military. This construction of the Allies as equal opportunity nations furthermore served to differentiate them from the target of their violence. For instance, the press offered frequent reminders of how poorly women were treated in Iraq and throughout the region. Such arguments are nothing new, of course. Throughout the most intensive period of Western imperial-ism, colonial powers differentiated themselves from subaltern populations by labeling indigenous gender practices (everything from veiling to matrilin-eal descent) barbaric.

So the Lynch story first discursively constructed the Anglophone Allies as moral and progressive nations. But then, before Lynch's heroism could become a serious challenge to patriarchy, the representations of Lynch shifted to conform to gender stereotypes. In this way, the crisis in the gender order was eased by both acknowledging that increasing numbers of women were soldiers, and neutralizing any potential threat to masculinity and patriarchy by portraying female soldiers as essentially delicate, emotional, and in need of male protection and rescue. Ultimately then, the Lynch story sustained rather than challenged the patriarchal social order of the three Allied nations by simply reiterating the clichéd stereotype of the damsel in distress.

A later incident in Iraq would further demonstrate the use of gender stereotyping in press coverage of female soldiers. In 2004, when the story of prisoner abuse by US soldiers at Abu Ghraib prison first came to light, media attention focused keenly on one soldier. Specialist Lynndie England, like Lynch, was a petite young woman. One widely circulated image from the scandal was that of a smiling Lynndie England giving a thumbs-up sign as she stood before a group of naked prisoners who had been forced to form a human pyramid. As the story developed, it was revealed that England had been sexually involved with another soldier, Specialist Charles Graner, and was allegedly pregnant with his child. Some in the media suggested that Graner had manipulated England into participating in the abuse. So while Jessica Lynch had been the face of innocence and England became the face of scandalous sadism, both young women were portrayed as lacking agency. Both were said to have been controlled by others. Both were pawns caught up in what was essentially a struggle between men.

The Lynch story further both mirrored and helped sustain continued white dominance in the US, the UK, and Australia. On the surface, press coverage of the racially and ethnically diverse group of soldiers captured or killed when the Army's 507th met resistance in Nassiriya celebrated the pluralist ideal currently fashionable in these three nations. However, out of this group of seven white, black, Hispanic, and Native American soldiers, three of whom lost their lives and three of whom endured captivity weeks longer than Lynch, it was Lynch who garnered the vast majority of the media attention, and it is Lynch who has reaped the greatest rewards.

On the basis of her celebrity, Lynch received numerous gifts and offers including automobiles, extensive house renovations, an offer of a full scholarship to the university of her choice, a US$1 million book contract (shared with her coauthor), and lucrative film, television, and other media offers. She was also awarded an Army discharge on a disability pension of 80 percent. By contrast, Shoshana Johnson, the female Panamanian-American soldier who sustained serious injuries in the Nassiriya skirmish and was shown in captivity on Al-Jazeera Television, received little media attention and no discernible financial gain, and was retired from the Army on a 30 percent disability pension. So despite its superficial celebration of racial and ethnic equality, the Jessica Lynch story, and its material effects, in the end positioned whites as the leaders and the standouts. A white soldier was lauded, while the role of soldiers of color was downplayed.

CROSS-NATIONAL COMPARISONS

With the first two hypotheses confirmed by the data here, the third hypothesis remains to be tested. Data from the content analysis were analyzed to identify any statistically significant differences in representations between the US, UK, and Australia, and between different types of newspapers.

The first and most obvious difference between the nations was the sheer quantity of the coverage: 221 articles in the US, 129 in the UK, and 77 in Australia. While press coverage outside the US was predictably less intense than in the soldiers' home country, the combined press and broadcast coverage of the story prompted editorials in Britain and Australia complaining about the disproportionate attention given to one missing soldier.

Although it was predicted that British and Australian press coverage would be less stereotypically gendered and racialized than US coverage, there were almost no statistically significant differences between coverage in the three countries. In terms of gender stereotypical representations, for instance, art and media scholars have long observed that in texts ranging from high art to popular culture, men are routinely positioned as active subjects while women are portrayed as passive objects with their bodies, their physical appearance, stressed over their actions. As Berger (1972, 45) famously observed, "Men act and women appear." In all three nations, the press coverage of the soldiers of the Army 507th was consistent with such conventions of gender representation. In each nation, up to 14 percent of articles with references to a female soldier stressed some aspect of her appearance. By contrast, only one article in the entire data set made reference to the appearance of a male soldier.

Likewise, there were few statistically significant differences between the countries in representations of the race or ethnicity of the soldiers. In all three nations it was the norm to mention the soldiers' race or ethnicity only in cases where they belonged to minority groups. For instance, while it was common for Lori Piestewa to be identified as a Native American or Shoshana Johnson as black or Panamanian-born, James Kiehl and Patrick Miller were never identified as white. In all three nations, it appears that whiteness is the expected norm for members of the national community, and race is only worth mentioning if it deviates from this national norm.

One difference between the nations did emerge in representations of race, however. The British papers were significantly more likely to refer to Shoshana Johnson's race, usually identified as "black."[3] However, this detail was most often presented in the course of critiquing perceived racial inequalities in the US. While critiques of apparent racial inequalities in the treatment of the soldiers were rare in the US coverage, a number of British editorials explicitly raised issues of race and racism. As one editorial in *The Independent* remarked,

> Cynics might assume that American forces went the extra mile to save Private Lynch precisely because she was such an iconic young figure . . . so typical of the American ideal. . . . It is also recognizable that America does have a hierarchy of life, with pretty blondes at the top, black Americans and Native Americans further down and the rest of the world trailing hopelessly. Which might help explain the unseemly rush to war. (Orr 2003)

None of the US articles in the data set made this link between racial disparities in media attention to the soldiers and racist sentiments underpinning the invasion of Iraq, an essentialized Muslim/Arab Other. In this instance, at least, it appears that news outlets in the UK were more willing than those in the US to challenge widely circulating discourses of American national identity. After all, news organizations outside the US were unlikely to alienate their audiences, and thus lose revenue, by assailing America's national mythology. In fact, critiques of American racism in the UK press could be seen as affirmations of Britain's own commitment to racial equality.

MEDIA DYNAMICS

It is commonly asserted that the political or ideological orientation of newspaper owners and editors shapes the presentation of the news.[4] Analysis of the ways coverage of the Army 507th varied by the ideological orientation of the newspapers examined is complicated by lack of agreement among scholars and media organizations regarding the categorization of newspapers by ideology. While newspapers are routinely categorized as "liberal," "conservative," or "centrist," some scholars have argued that due to contemporary global media economics, including media consolidation and the growing reliance on wire services for coverage, such distinctions are of limited analytical value. To examine potential differences in representation between the newspapers and to test the usefulness of ideological orientation as an analytical category, the papers in the data set were first categorized by broad ideological orientation. *The Wall Street Journal*, *The New York Times*, *The Times* of London, and *The Australian* were classified as conservative; *The Washington Post*, *The Guardian*, and *The Age* as progressive; and *USA Today*, *The Independent*, and the *Sydney Morning Herald* as centrist. Using this classificatory scheme, press coverage was analyzed for gender and ethnoracial stereotypes. There were no statistically significant differences between the three types of papers in representations of gender or race. So in this analysis at least, a newspaper's ideological bent does not seem to affect gender or ethnoracial stereotyping.

However, when papers were separated into popular/populist papers versus serious/elitist publications, one statistically significant difference emerged.[5] Serious/elitist papers were more likely than popular/populist papers to present Pfc. Lynch as dependent. It may be that newspapers with a more elite readership have a greater investment in maintaining long-standing social hierarchies, such as the patriarchal gender order.

Perhaps more compelling than any differences between nations and categories of newspapers were the similarities between them, similarities that point to the growing global integration of the mass media. The uniformity of press constructions of Lynch is striking. Three excerpts serve to illustrate the homogeneity of the depictions.

The Washington Post, 3 April 2003

> Pfc. Jessica Lynch, rescued Tuesday from an Iraqi hospital, fought fiercely and shot several enemy soldiers after Iraqi soldiers ambushed the Army's 507th Ordinance Maintenance Company, firing her weapon until she ran out of ammunition, US officials said yesterday.

Lynch, a 19-year-old supply clerk, continued firing at the Iraqis even after she sustained multiple gunshot wounds and watched several other soldiers in her unit die around her in fighting March 23, one official said . . . "She was fighting to the death," the official said. "She did not want to be taken alive." (Schmidt and Loeb 2003)

The Australian, 4 April 2003

Jessica Lynch, the US solider seized from an Iraqi hospital in a dramatic rescue by special forces [*sic*], fought off enemy troops before her capture, shooting several before her ammunition ran out.

Private Lynch "continued firing at the Iraqis even after she sustained multiple gunshot wounds and watched several other soldiers in her unit die around her in fighting," according to a report in *The Washington Post*.

The 19-year-old supply clerk rescued on Wednesday morning from a hospital in southern Iraq "fought fiercely and shot several enemy soldiers . . . firing her weapon until she ran out of ammunition," according to the report, which cited a US official . . . "She was fighting to the death," the official said. "She did not want to be taken alive." (*The Australian* 2003)

The Times of London, 4 April 2003

Jessica Lynch, the slight support clerk with a passion for softball, basketball and teaching, plucked out of nine days of captivity by US Special Forces in a daring midnight gunfight, was depicted yesterday as a gun-toting battlefield hero. "She was fighting to the death," a US official told *The Washington Post*. "She did not want to be taken alive."

Quite where she found the strength to shoot back while her comrades lay dead or dying around her and she bled, apparently, from multiple bullet wounds, remains a mystery . . . One thing is certain: Private Lynch has won a place in history as a gritty, all-American hero, to rival the likes of Bonnie and Clyde. (Monaghan 2003)

Clearly the writers for *The Times* and *The Australian* drew heavily on the initial report by *The Washington Post*.[6] Although *The Times* reporter adds her own flourishes, curiously comparing Lynch to the outlaws Bonnie and Clyde, the three excerpts vary little in content or style. The similarities reveal a reality of media sourcing today: media outlets, faced with growing competition and consolidation, increasingly rely on a limited range of both official state sources and other media organizations for their information. Thus, although the claims of Lynch "fighting to the death" and firing until she ran out of ammunition were ultimately shown to be false, they were widely repeated as fact by news outlets around the world. The globalization of the mass media, it would seem, contributes to the global dissemination of gendered and racialized discourses of national identity.

It is worth noting that in the case of the Iraq invasion, the US, UK, and Australia shared military objectives. This is undoubtedly one of the reasons that British and Australian press coverage of wartime events so closely mirrored US representations in terms of gender, race, and ethnicity, albeit with a slightly greater tendency toward critique. As I have argued throughout this volume, however, discourses of national identity are collective constructions. They are constructed not only by those within the national community, but through a process of dynamic transnational negotiations of meaning.

Consider, for instance, the ways US coverage of the Lynch story was reframed by critiques in the British media. Most notably, in May of 2003 the BBC's *Correspondent* program aired an exposé of the Lynch rescue, alleging that the event was "one of the most stunning pieces of news management ever conceived" (BBC *Correspondent* 2003). Arguably, this report played an important part in the symbolic transformation of Lynch from warrior to victim, a victim not only of Iraqi violence (as US sources had previously alleged), but of manipulation by the US state propaganda machine.[7] By early June, *The Washington Post* had admitted inaccuracies in its coverage of the Lynch story and published several pieces questioning official representations of Lynch and her rescue. Some of these pieces referred specifically to the BBC documentary.[8] Shifting representations of Lynch serve as a reminder that discourses of national identity are not constructed in a kind of national vacuum, but also shaped and reshaped by the global flows of words, images, and ideas.

DISCOURSE MATTERS

We saw in the previous chapter that racialized discourses of national identity can be associated with grave material realities—discrimination, hate crimes, warfare. So, what are the larger implications of the Lynch story? Let us first consider the gendered aspects of the story. In order to understand the gender representations discussed here, it is necessary to go back to the beginning of the US-led war on terror in the aftermath of the September 11, 2001, attacks on the US. A number of scholars have argued that the 9/11 attacks precipitated a national crisis in masculinity, for the acts not only violated American security and sovereignty, but symbolically emasculated the nation.[9] First, the World Trade Center, phallic monument to the glory of American economic dominance, was felled ignominiously. Next, the Pentagon, bastion of American heterosexual masculinity, was brutally penetrated by a hostile force. Then, in the skies over Pennsylvania a group of American men lost the battle for control of their hijacked aircraft.[10] Significantly, as these events unfolded the US President and Vice President, symbolic patriarchs of the national family, were driven into hiding, seemingly rendered impotent by the assault. Thus, the nation suffered not only a devastating loss of life and property on 9/11, but a blow to the images of masculine agency that underpin American national self-conceptions.

A remedy for this national emasculation was found in military action. At the most basic level, the military invasions of Afghanistan and Iraq can be seen as pragmatic attempts to eliminate forces considered hostile to the US. At another level, however, such state-sanctioned violence can be understood as a reassertion of masculinity. As Ehrenreich has argued, cross-culturally and historically, warfare has been seen as a proving ground for masculinity. She writes that "men make war in part because war makes them men" (Ehrenreich 1997, 131). The ritual bloodletting of the Afghan and Iraq invasions not only served as retribution for and defense against the real or imagined deeds of the enemy but as a restoration of American manhood, the kind of "regeneration through violence" described by Slotkin (1973, 1992).

As Jeffords (1989) has argued in a cogent analysis of post–Vietnam War America, symbolic emasculation at the national level can result in the "remasculinization" of society, an increased tendency to privilege men and the masculine while denigrating women and supposedly feminine characteristics and activities. Initial evidence indicates such a turn toward the masculine, in the US at least, since the 9/11 attacks: from the lionization of New York City police*men* and fire*men* in the days immediately after the attacks, to the increased public focus on male military leaders, technical experts, and political authorities (Faludi 2007a). State rhetoric since the attacks has likewise been marked by hypermasculine bravado, most notably in President Bush's use of such Wild West language as "wanted dead or alive."

Gender stereotypes in the press coverage of the Army 507th only bolstered this masculinization of public discourses by constructing female soldiers as weak, passive, dependent, and in need of male protection, and male soldiers as not only strong, decisive protectors of their frail female comrades, but as guardians of the homeland and defenders of the innocent women and children of other nations. After the initial failure to capture Osama Bin Laden in the assault on Afghanistan, for instance, the attacks were reframed by the White House as an attempt to liberate Afghan women from the oppressive rule of the Taliban (Tickner 2002).

Certainly from a feminist perspective, this revival of the long-standing image of men as protectors and women as those in need of protection is undesirable because it denies women's full and equal participation in public life (see Stiehm 1982). Such gender representations do not merely pose threats to the autonomy of women, however; they threaten the very foundations of democracy. They do so by serving to naturalize and strengthen paternalistic, often authoritarian, rule. That is, the trope of masculine protection is extended beyond the imagined frailty of women and children and applied to society as a whole. The symbolic patriarchs of the nation, our political leaders, are positioned as having both the right and the responsibility to protect members of the national family from hostile outsiders, from each other, and even from themselves (cf. Young 2003). Such paternalistic authoritarianism is clearly evidenced in the 2001 USA PATRIOT Act, which entitles the state to conduct arbitrary searches and seizures, to monitor private communications and records, to detain individuals without charge or due process, and to shield the Executive Branch from legislative, judicial, and public scrutiny. Similar security reforms have likewise been instituted in the UK and Australia since the 9/11 attacks.[11]

This logic of paternalism has an ethnoracial dimension as well. That is, the state assumes the right to increasingly monitor and control all subordinate groups, whether women and children, ethnoracial minority groups within the nation, or racialized Others outside the nation. The invasions of both Afghanistan and Iraq, for instance, were framed as wars of "liberation," attempts by civilized, rational Western/Judeo-Christian states to bring order and justice to unruly Arab/Muslim societies (as seen in the previous chapter). Ethnoracial stereotyping in the press coverage examined here again naturalizes and legitimates continued white Western dominance at both the national and the global level, by constructing ethnoracial Others as groups requiring surveillance, guidance, and control.

It is clear then that the gender and ethnoracial representations in the press coverage analyzed in this chapter have far-reaching social implications. Not only are such patterns indicative of existing inequalities based on gender, race, and ethnicity in the three nations examined here, but they help maintain these inequalities while contributing to a growing imbalance of power between state elites and ordinary citizens.

In sum, press coverage of the US Army 507th soldiers in the US, the UK, and Australia on the surface celebrates the fashionable ideal of gender and racial equality, and builds on the notion that these are free, fair, moral, and progressive nations. British critiques of American racism notwithstanding, UK and Australian coverage closely mirrors US celebrations of Lynch. Analysis reveals clichéd gender stereotyping and the privileging of contributions of white soldiers over those of soldiers of color. Ultimately then, press coverage examined here simply strengthens white masculinist visions of national identity in the US, the UK, and Australia, and helps maintain a system based on patriarchy and white dominance. Thus, gendered and racialized war stories such as those examined here may not only contribute to the subordination of women and ethnoracial minorities, but also undermine the democratic process itself.

10 Touring the Nation
Gender, Race, and Nation in Travel Brochures

While travel brochures belong to the realm of disposable culture seldom subjected to critical analysis by scholars of national identity, tourism promotional materials construct both aestheticized and commercialized narratives of nation. Brochures for domestic travel feature the spaces, faces, and activities commonly used to exemplify the national community, and brochures for international travel help define the national self through contrasts with Others—other people, other places, and other ways of life. At the same time, travel brochures present images of ideal worlds and ideal selves to which the consumer is assumed to aspire. In so doing, the brochures both mirror and reproduce a whole range of taken-for-granted notions—notions about the nature of pleasure and desire, ideas about authenticity and artifice, understandings of history and culture, ideas about the noteworthiness of sites, and assumptions about things such as gender, class, and race. This chapter focuses on discourses of national identity in the travel brochures of the US, the UK, Australia, and Japan and the ways they are gendered and racialized.

THE APPROACH

As argued earlier, while states certainly invest heavily in shaping discourses of national identity through such things as grand spectacles and public monuments, some of the most powerful discourses of national belonging can be found in quotidian texts and practices. Discourses of national identity featured in such cultural forms as newspaper sports pages, household product packaging, or promotional pamphlets such as those examined here are all the more powerful because they bear seemingly natural, normal, and politically innocent collective views.

My analysis of travel brochures is grounded in the scholarly literatures on tourism and advertising. As O'Barr's (1994) study of representations of Otherness in advertising demonstrates, images of exoticized, eroticized, and infantilized foreign Others have long been used in travel advertising to promote foreign destinations. Representations of smiling and receptive "natives" are undoubtedly designed to assuage any fears travelers might have about venturing into unfamiliar territory. However this is more than simply a feel-good advertising convention, for the repetition of such messages both reflects and reproduces existing power hierarchies based on factors such as race, gender, and national origin.

Likewise, Urry's (1990) work on the "tourist gaze" can be extended to the positioning of Others as tourist spectacles. Travel brochure representations can be understood as assertions of both difference and dominance. The tourist gaze is characterized by three primary components: difference, pleasure, and power. In other words, objects of the tourist gaze must be sufficiently removed from the ordinary and everyday to be considered different; this difference must be perceived as pleasurable to experience; and tourists must maintain sufficient power over the objects of their gaze (Other people and Other places) to sustain that pleasure.

One common way of maintaining mastery over the tourist spectacle is through photography. Photographic representation, whether in tourist snapshots or in travel brochures, is in a sense an assertion of power. If surveillance is power, as Foucault suggests, then photography is an act of power maintenance and a photograph is the material evidence of that power.[1] Just as tourist snapshots can be seen as a way of managing difference and desire in contexts of contact with the Other, so travel brochures and their representation of exotic Others can be seen as a way of managing the complex mixture of fear and fascination in encounters with Other people and places.

But tourism is not only about seeing, it is about being seen. As Urry observes, a common selling point used to promote tourist destinations is that they attract the best sort of people—people of a certain class, age, or race; people with particular values or views; people the tourist will want to meet and who will validate the tourist's own sense of self. When travel brochures feature not exotic Others but seemingly "typical" travelers, those travelers are positioned as ideal selves. The implicit message is not only "This is who I could meet in this setting," but also "This is who I could *be*." Such representations shed light on who is considered to belong to the nation and the relative statuses of groups within various imagined communities.

With an eye toward examining constructions of national identity in travel brochures, between 2003 and 2006 I collected 429 travel brochures from around the capital cities of the four nations in the study.[2] The brochures were then coded for the advertised destination, the characteristics of all human figures represented on the brochure covers, and the primary marketing appeals (or "selling points") of each brochure. Of these, 262 brochures featured images of people. These are the brochures that concern us here. This is not a statistically representative sample of the many thousands of travel brochures available from travel agencies and kiosks throughout these capital cities, and therefore I make no claims to the statistical significance of the patterns described here. Instead, I suggest that a fairly typical sample of texts collected without theoretical filters can provide insight into widespread representational practices and the ideologies that underpin them. For this reason, I will provide only basic descriptive statistics here as indicators of the relative frequency of certain representations. More time will be given to detailed qualitative readings of a smaller number of brochures.

For the purposes of this content analysis, the ethnoracial attributions of featured characters were judged on a combination of appearance and role.[3] For instance, in a Japanese brochure for travel to South Korea, if a woman of Asian appearance were shown dressed in Korean-style clothing or serving Korean food, she would be judged to be portraying a Korean national. However, if she were shown dressed in Japanese-style clothing and checking into a Seoul hotel, she would be coded as "Japanese." When characters' ethnoracial role, gender, or age could not be discerned, these characteristics were coded as "unknown" and the individuals were excluded from the analysis.

QUANTITATIVE MEASURES

When the brochures are analyzed for the presence of ethnoracial majority and minority characters, it is clear that in all four countries domestic travel brochures portray the national community as quite racially homogeneous (Table 10.1).

In Japan, not a single non-Japanese character appears in the domestic brochures. In the British and Australian domestic brochures, minority ethnoracial groups are rarely pictured, and minority characters are never shown unless accompanied by a member of the majority group. It is almost as if nonmajority characters need to be chaperoned by those constructed as the

Table 10.1 Brochures with Majority and Minority Characters*

	Domestic Brochures (N=103)		International Brochures (N=159)	
Nation	Majority Character Present (%)	Minority Character Present (%)	Majority Character Present (%)	Minority Character Present (%)
US	93	23	85	15
UK	100	6	91	32
AUS	100	10	43	70
JAPAN	100	—	44	67

*Because some brochures contained both majority and minority characters, country totals equal more than 100%.

natural and normal proprietors of the nation, white Britons and Australians. Even in the US sample, which contains the most ethnoracial diversity, whites still appear in 93 percent of the brochures, establishing them as the clearly dominant majority.

Minority characters more often appear in brochures for international travel. In fact, they outnumber representations of ethnoracial majority populations in the case of Australian and Japanese brochures. However, quantitative measures tell only part of the story here. More important than sheer numbers of minority characters featured in the brochures is the nature of these representations. Which groups of people are selected for inclusion? How are they positioned? In particular, are they portrayed as active subjects or as passive objects of the majority group's tourist gaze? These are some of the questions I will attempt to answer through qualitative analysis.

CONSTRUCTIONS OF A RACIALIZED NATIONAL SELF

In all four of the nations here, domestic travel brochures portray the national community as racially and ethnically homogeneous, and almost uniformly young, heterosexual, and able-bodied.[4] Even in quite racially and ethnically diverse nations such as Australia and the US, travel brochure representations are heavily dominated by the ethnoracial majority.

Australia

As noted in Chapter 2, when Australia achieved Federation in 1901, *The Bulletin*, a leading newspaper of the day, carried on its masthead the slogan "Australia for the White Man," and one of the first acts of the newly constituted Parliament was to pass legislation restricting immigration by nonwhites. But changing attitudes and changing geopolitical realities in the post–World War II era have brought significant racial and ethnic diversity to the nation. While those of Anglo-Celtic origin are still in the majority, it is projected that by 2025, 38 percent of the Australian population will be from non-Anglo-Celtic backgrounds.[5]

Nonetheless, of the Australian domestic travel brochures, only two included nonwhites, and in both cases, these were indigenous Australians positioned not as active subjects, but as tourist commodities, spectacles for the presumed white Australian visitor. In one brochure for the Northern Territory, an area with a strong Aboriginal presence, an indigenous man in traditional body paint dances with boomerangs held high. In another for the same region, three local Aboriginal children are shown playing merrily in front of a colorful mural. In both cases, indigenous Australians are constructed as internal Others, exotic and archaic ethnoracial minorities, physically located within the nation, yet marked as culturally different. Rather than being portrayed as full and equal participants in the national community, they are positioned as part of the scenery, just another pleasurable spectacle to be captured in a white tourist's snapshot.

By contrast, the vast majority of the Australian domestic brochures feature young white men and women both as active consumers and as representatives of the national community. They are situated within families, groups of friends, and heterosexual romantic partnerships. They are shopping, eating, playing. They are constructed as average Australians exploring their own nation. And in each and every brochure in the sample these "average Australians" are white.

Such representations are consistent with the "white nation fantasy" mentioned earlier, the assumption within Australia that whites are the rightful proprietors of the nation (Hage 1998). Whites built the modern nation, so whites rule the modern nation, and whites have the power to include or exclude, tolerate or marginalize nonwhite populations as they see fit. In recent decades, nonwhite populations have been reasonably well tolerated by the majority population of Australia, and their foods, festivals, and arts have been embraced with enthusiasm. It is not surprising, therefore, to see indigenous Australians positioned as spectacles. However, the recent rise of anti-immigrant, anti-Asian, and anti-Muslim sentiments is evidence that when minority groups in Australia become too plentiful, too vocal, or otherwise too conspicuous, majority Australians often take steps to disempower, marginalize, or even eject them.

Japan

Compared with the other nations under consideration here, Japan is more culturally and ethnically homogeneous, and cultural and ethnoracial diversity is neither widely celebrated nor particularly well tolerated. It is not surprising, therefore, that minority characters do not appear in brochures for domestic travel. Instead of commodifying internal Others by making them colorful spectacles for the majority (as in Australia), the Japanese brochures simply leave them out. No traces of *Ryūkyū* or *Ainu* indigenous peoples are found even in brochures for Okinawa and Hokkaido, the respective homelands of these groups. There is also no trace of stigmatized groups such as ethnic Koreans and ethnic Chinese, *Burakumin*, or migrant laborers from Asia and South America.[6]

In fact, one notable feature of the Japanese domestic travel brochures is that relatively few of them include any people at all. Only about one-third of the brochures feature people, as compared to a range of 78 to 91 percent of brochures in the other three nations. Instead, there is a clear emphasis on nature in the Japanese brochures. This includes familiar images of natural landmarks such as Mt. Fuji and Lake Hakone, as well as images of what we might call cultured nature—an avenue lined with blossoming cherry trees, a carefully tended ornamental garden, or arrays of seasonal dishes. Underlying such images are discourses of national identity and national exceptionalism.

Japanese narratives of nation have long stressed the special relationship the Japanese have with nature.[7] Japan's indigenous religion, Shinto,
is an animistic religion that identifies spiritual entities and forces residing
throughout the natural world. And it is commonly asserted by proponents
of the *Nihonjinron* that the Japanese are deeply attuned to nature, and have
a unique capacity to recognize the potency of nature and effectively exploit
and even perfect it. Domestic travel brochures evoke such notions of the
national character when they construct nature as the focal point of domestic
tourism.

Another conspicuous feature of the Japanese domestic brochures is the
dearth of male characters. While women and men appear in almost equal
numbers in the domestic brochures of the other three nations, in the Japanese brochures women outnumber men by more than three to one. This
makes sense given the fact that young single women, with their relatively
high disposable incomes and lack of family responsibilities, are the most
avid consumers of domestic tourism services in the nation today. The young
women featured in the brochures are typically shown engaging in cultural
tourism, by sampling regional crafts, cuisine, shrines, and cultured nature.[8]
Again, such representations (and such tourist practices) make sense given
the history of domestic tourism in Japan. During the feudal period domestic
travel was limited by legal restrictions imposed by rival regional authorities,
and most commoners were only allowed to travel for the purposes of religious pilgrimage. Even today in Japan, there is a strong tendency to frame
tourism in terms of its educational or even spiritual benefits.

Overall then, relatively few men and no minority characters appear in
Japanese domestic brochures. However, concepts of Otherness are still
employed in domestic brochures. One brochure for travel to Hokkaido,
Japan's northernmost island prefecture, presents close-up photographs of a
young Japanese woman with very pale skin and vaguely Western facial features. The ad copy reads "Pure Winter Hokkaido. Beautiful White = Hokkaido." The concept of "whiteness" operates on several levels here. Certainly,
the brochure evokes the white winter landscape of this famously snowy
prefecture. In addition, the woman in the photos, with her fair complexion
rendered even lighter through photographic overexposure, is constructed as
beautifully "white." Through the use of "whiteness," she becomes the symbol of the destination. Close-ups of her lips and eyes equate the allure and
receptivity of the woman with that of the destination itself.

It must also be noted, however, that in the national imagination Hokkaido is an almost-foreign destination. Originally inhabited by the *Ainu*
people, Hokkaido only experienced intensive colonization by "mainland"
(Honshu) Japanese from the late nineteenth century. After 150 years, the
prefecture still has the lowest population density of any prefecture in Japan.
Its relatively sparse population, harsh winters, rugged wilderness, and geographical distance from the nation's centers of cultural, political, and economic authority contribute to the widespread perception that Hokkaido

differs significantly from the rest of Japan. Government policy both reflects and undoubtedly reinforces such perceptions, for unlike other prefectures, Hokkaido is managed in part by the national government under the auspices of the Hokkaido Development Agency.[9] In this way, Hokkaido is set apart from the rest of the nation and rendered almost foreign.

Arguably, since the arrival of Westerners in the Meiji Era (mid-nineteenth century), Japan's most significant foreign Other has been the West, exemplified in the national imagination by white Europeans and North Americans. Such associations contribute to the construction of Hokkaido as "white" space in this brochure.[10] The brochure expressed its sentiment in the form of an equation, "Beautiful White=Hokkaido." Likewise, we can reason that if Hokkaido=Foreign and Foreign=White, then Hokkaido=White. As Kelsky (2001) and others have noted, white foreigners are widely used in Japanese advertising today to give products an air of exotic beauty, modernity, authority, and desire. In this case we see an almost-white (but reassuringly Japanese) woman as the embodiment of an almost-foreign (but reassuringly Japanese) destination. And, by implication, the woman herself, or someone like her, becomes a tourist commodity. As the small caption at the bottom of the brochure states, "Just one short flight to beautiful whiteness." Just one short flight to this lovely, receptive woman, this lovely, receptive land.

The UK

In the UK sample, only one domestic travel brochure includes a nonwhite character, one man in a group of budget backpackers. The brochure carries explanations in several different languages, clearly targeting the international youth tourist market. It would appear then that while this minority man is clearly a tourist, he is positioned as a foreign visitor rather than a British tourist. So, despite Britain's growing nonwhite population, in the UK sample of domestic travel brochures all British tourists are white.

Such representations are consistent with assumptions exposed by Paul Gilroy in *There Ain't No Black in the Union Jack* (1987). Gilroy demonstrates that British discourses of national identity are racialized to such an extent that the categories "British" and "black" are effectively mutually exclusive. Since the first large group of nonwhite immigrants arrived in Britain in 1948, nonwhite ("black") immigration has been constructed as a social problem. Some opponents of nonwhite immigration have claimed that "blacks" bring crime, violence, immorality, and disease to the nation and pollute its racial stock. Less explicitly racist critics of nonwhite immigration, on the other hand, express concerns over conflicting values and cultural practices leading to interracial tension and social disintegration.[11]

According to the 2001 Home Office Census, Britain's population is 92 percent white, with small but visible "black," Asian, and Chinese populations, particularly prominent in metropolitan areas such as London where up to 40 percent of residents belong to minority groups.[12] Since the 11

September 2001 attacks in the United States, Britain's entry into the wars in Afghanistan and Iraq, and the 7 July 2005 London Underground bombings, Britain's Muslim population has been particularly prominent in the mass media. Yet despite the realities of British ethnoracial diversity, or perhaps even *because* of it, in the idealized world of tourist advertising, nonwhite Britons are invisible.

Instead, most domestic British brochures feature young white men and women visiting grand monuments to the country's venerable history and culture, principally its castles and manor houses.[13] There are two interrelated issues here. The first is that in the brochures only whites are positioned as British tourists, as active participants in the national community. The second is that most of the tourist sites featured in the brochures celebrate the nation's white, ruling class history. As Hewison (1987) and others have observed, British "heritage tourism" privileges the experiences of elites and obscures the realities of class, gender, and racial inequality.[14]

As a final point on British representations of the national self, as noted earlier, touristic pleasure lies not only in gazing at spectacles, but in being gazed upon. From the early days of mass tourism, tour promoters assured customers that only the right kind of people traveled to their destinations (Urry 1990). Arguably tourists today, like early mass tourists, travel both to see and to be seen by the "right" people. In the British domestic brochures the "right" people are clearly white people.

The US

Of the nations in this study, the US is the most racially and ethnically diverse. According to the 2001 US Census, 33 percent of the nation's population identifies as nonwhite. To some degree the sample of US travel brochures reflects this diversity. Of the US domestic brochures, 23 percent feature at least one nonwhite character, significantly more than in any other nation, but still small compared with the 93 percent of brochures that contain white characters. Again, what is more interesting than the sheer numbers here are the qualitative differences between representations of whites and nonwhites.

While some of the US domestic brochures position nonwhites as tourists and "average" Americans, ethnoracial minorities are also constructed as tourist spectacles in ways that whites are not. In one such example, a smiling young Hawaiian woman, a flower garland in her hair, invites mainland tourists to the islands, her beauty and accessibility serving as a reminder of the beauty and accessibility of the destination. By contrast, in the few cases where whites themselves are spectacles, they are either reenacting historical events or are representatives from the glamorous world of show business and entertainment. In other words, while nonwhites are positioned as internal Others, archaic, exotic, and culturally distinct from the national community, whites are more often positioned as key actors in important historical events and contemporary public affairs. Furthermore, the US domestic brochures more than any other nation promote travel within family groups. However, while many brochures feature white characters in the mixed-gender and mixed-age groups indicative of families, only one brochure features a non-white family group.

The messages here are subtle but powerful: America is a nation of families, and the "normal" family is white. America is world renowned for its show business glamor, and whites are the stars of the show. America is a land with a proud history to which only whites have contributed. While it is true that US domestic brochures include nonwhites in the national community and even sometimes position them as active consumers, the institutions, the history, and the culture of the nation are clearly constructed as white domains.

In fact, a case could be made that the presence of a significant number of ethnoracial minorities in the US brochures reveals more about "inclusivity" as a commercial imperative than about the material power and status of minority groups in the US today. Using representational conventions popularized by the United Colors of Benetton advertising campaigns of the 1980s and 1990s, promotional materials ranging from public service announcements to medical pamphlets and commercial ads now routinely feature self-consciously "diverse" groups: two whites, two blacks, one Latino, one Asian, and so on. Commenting on the Benetton strategy, Giroux writes that "In this context, difference is stripped of all social and political antagonisms and becomes a commercial symbol for what is youthfully chic, hip and fashionable" (1994, 19). Likewise, in the case of the US travel brochures, ethnoracial diversity serves as shorthand for certain American values: equality, opportunity, freedom, and multicultural tolerance. Such representations reaffirm the greatness of the nation, while depoliticizing and obscuring ongoing tensions and inequalities based on race and ethnicity.

CONSTRUCTION OF RACIALIZED NATIONAL OTHERS

So the travel brochures of all nations in the sample construct racialized national selves. With the exception of the US, virtually no ethnoracial minorities are included in representations of the national community itself. And in all nations, including the US, where minorities are included they are discursively Othered, by either positioning them as tourist spectacles or excluding them from the activities and groups that are central to representations of national life.

However, the racialization of Others is even clearer in the sample of international travel brochures in which human figures personify locations and cultures. The foreign Other has long been positioned as a tourist spectacle in travel advertising: the hula dancer, the dark-skinned "native" in tribal dress, a gaily attired mariachi musician. Such figures both symbolize destinations

and are offered as tourist commodities themselves. The unspoken promise is that the paying tourist will at least witness such spectacles, and perhaps even come to possess the exotic Other, either in the form of souvenir
snapshots, or more literally through intimate encounters. This is a common
representational trope in all of the nations under consideration here, with
19 percent of British brochures, 38 percent of US brochures, 44 percent of
Japanese brochures, and 62 percent of Australian brochures employing such
representations.

The British brochures for international travel feature, among others, photographs of an African woman in traditional dress carrying an infant on her
back; an African elder in his "native" costume; Buddhist monks filing out of
a temple somewhere in Asia; and Moroccan camel drivers in flowing robes.
The Japanese international brochures likewise feature Balinese and Spanish
dancers, Korean schoolgirls, and white American and Australian children.
And US international brochures offer smiling "native" children, folk dancers, and European palace guards. The general tendency, then, is to portray
national Others as nonthreatening by infantilizing, feminizing, or exoticiz-
ing them, and by portraying them as quaintly archaic.

The Australian international travel brochures employ this trope most frequently, at 62 percent of international brochures. As in the other nations,
women, children, and the elderly are the preferred representatives of more
exotic destinations. For Japan, a demure geisha and a young boy dressed
for a festival; for Vietnam and Thailand, small children playing on the steps
of a temple; for package tours through Asia, elderly men and women with
benign and welcoming smiles; for Tahiti, a young woman holding flowered
leis up in invitation. The use of women, children, and the elderly seems
intended to assuage fears of the Other and reassure Australian tourists of
their dominance over the Other. "Natives" are portrayed as picturesquely
poor and backward, physically small and weak, or sexually receptive. So
yes, Australian tourists will be in a foreign land, surrounded by "natives";
but they will still be in control by virtue of their wealth, their modernity, and
their white/Western/masculine subject position. One possible explanation
for the prevalence of such representations in Australia is the nation's somewhat anomalous position in the global order. As a Western nation located
in the Asian-Pacific region, it has always experienced a degree of anxiety
about the racialized Others that surround it. Perhaps in part because of the
geographical proximity of Asia, Australian brochures stress the cultural distance between the nation and its closest neighbors.

GENDERED DISCOURSES OF NATIONAL IDENTITY

Foreign Others are not always defined by their racial difference, however.
One particular Australian brochure for travel to New Caledonia illustrates
the way national differences can be constructed through categories of gender

and sexuality. The brochure features a curvaceous young woman in a blue, white, and red swimsuit that evokes the French flag. She is emerging from a tropical lagoon with one hand running through her hair and one hand caressing her own neck. The ad copy reads "A little piece of France . . . right on your doorstep." In this case, the woman herself symbolizes the destination. Dressed in the national flag, she *becomes* the French dependency of New Caledonia. Her pose makes both the woman and the destination appear desirable, inviting, and attainable. The ad copy reinforces this message with its double entendre: New Caledonia offers a "little piece of France" just as the woman herself is, in a common vulgarity, a desirable "little piece." The tourist gaze here is the male gaze, with Australian tourists positioned as the desiring and dominating Western male.

Given that women, particularly "native" women have consistently been positioned as commodities in tourist advertising, it would be reasonable to expect that more women than men would be constructed as tourist spectacles in the brochures. That was not the case: roughly equal numbers of men and women in both domestic and international brochures were depicted as spectacles for tourist consumption. There were qualitative differences, however. Only women were eroticized (depicted as sexual objects) and only women were infantilized (depicted in childish poses or engaged in childish pursuits). By contrast, when men were positioned as tourist spectacles, they were much more likely to be shown engaging in work: a blacksmith in period costume, a palace guard, and a gondolier, among others. Certainly these men were depicted as quaint, anachronistic, picturesque, but their labor gives them an agency generally lacking in depictions of women as spectacles.

IMPLICATIONS

Discourses of national identity in the travel brochures of the US, UK, Australia, and Japan are indisputably gendered and racialized. Most obviously women are infantilized and exoticized, foreign Others are essentialized, and internal Others are marginalized in representations of the national community. This is worthy of scholarly attention because such representations not only reflect existing inequalities within and between nations, but also perpetuate and amplify such inequalities by shaping the subjectivities of both majority and minority groups.

There are additional considerations here, however. The global tourism market is almost incalculably vast. US residents alone spend in excess of $556 billion per year on travel and tourism.[15] Such prodigious economic activity has the potential to spark substantial changes in global and local social relations, physical environments, ways of life, and even national identities.

At the global level, it is easy to see the inequalities built into the international tourist trade. While few citizens of poor nations can afford to travel the world, increasing numbers of tourists from wealthy nations, in their quest for the exotic and authentic, are venturing into areas of the world where poverty is rife, often spending most of their time in walled resorts and other carefully stage-managed tourist venues that insulate them from the economic and social realities of these destinations.[16] Although the development of tourism infrastructure undoubtedly creates new jobs and brings foreign currency into developing nations, the material effects of international tourism are by no means uniformly positive.

It could be argued, in fact, that relations between wealthy foreign tourists and impoverished service providers are inherently exploitative, particularly since many high-end hotels and resorts in developing nations are owned by foreign investors to whom most profits accrue. Women are at particular risk of exploitation in the international tourism market. A high proportion of tourism service jobs are filled by women, not only because they can often be hired at lower wages and in less secure positions than men, but also because tourism or "hospitality" work is commonly considered women's work, a natural extension of their caregiving and pleasure-giving roles as mothers and wives.

This exploitation is at its most extreme in the world of sex tourism. Although accurate numbers are understandably difficult to find, it is estimated that in Thailand alone there are approximately two hundred thousand sex workers, catering to a primarily foreign clientele (Singh and Hart 2007). The internet has made information on sex industry services more readily available and global economic inequalities resulting in favorable currency exchange rates for those in the developed world have made sex tourism more affordable and more easily accessible. While sex tourism around the world certainly creates jobs, it often does so at the cost of the health, security, and sometimes liberty of sex workers. Sex workers are at increased risk for HIV/AIDS and other sexually transmitted diseases, are more vulnerable to violence and arrest, and in the case of sex trafficking may be trapped indefinitely as slaves or indentured servants in the sex trade.[17]

Even as people's lives and livelihoods are transformed by the dynamics of global tourism, the physical environments in which they live are radically changing. As rice paddies become golf courses, mangrove swamps become beach resorts, and forests, grasslands, and reefs are turned into photo safari parks, pollution and resource depletion take their toll on the natural environment. And while international tourists glean the benefits of such developments, it is largely locals who suffer the undesirable side effects. In one dramatic illustration of this point, scientists have argued that one of the reasons the Indian Ocean tsunami of December 2004 was so devastating was that wetlands which normally serve as natural barriers to coastal surges had been destroyed to build tourist resorts (Danielsen et al. 2005).

Representations that position foreigners as essentialized, sometimes eroticized, and usually subordinate Others help justify certain exploitative practices of international tourism. Affluent tourists who spend more money for one night in a five-star resort hotel than most locals make in a year can salve their consciences with the notion that they are providing simple, happy "natives" with a livelihood. Just as white Europeans in the colonial era sought to better the "natives" through a combination of Christianity and Western culture, international tourism is often framed as a way of improving the lives of those who serve affluent tourists.

Finally, even national identities can be reshaped through the dynamics of tourism. As ways of life, social relations, and the physical spaces that are a strong source of group identity are transformed through tourism, local and national self-conceptions can undergo changes. As a nation of farmers becomes a nation of waiters, gardeners, and hotel maids, understandings of the character of the national community may shift. As once sacred forms of art are commodified as handicrafts for tourist consumption, both the art forms and the meanings behind them may shift. And as tourists seek the exotic and authentic, subordinate groups may quite consciously cultivate "exotic" practices or launch competing claims of authenticity and primacy.

Even domestic tourism has the potential to shape discourses of national identity. Cultural and heritage tourism, in particular, focus national attention on certain regions, events, groups of people, and "traditions" in ways that come to inflect discourses of national identity.[18] In the 1970s and 1980s, for instance, at the height of Japan's economic boom, two national advertising campaigns were launched to boost domestic tourism. The campaigns featured images most city dwellers would have regarded as exotic—agrarian landscapes, remote mountain villages, a lonely stretch of coastline, and so on. The campaigns both reflected and contributed to a general nostalgia for "old Japan" in the midst of rapid social changes. Commercial enterprises and local and regional authorities readily embraced the trend, developing festivals based on local "traditions," organizing folk crafts tours, offering workshops with practitioners of "ancient" arts, and developing their own nostalgic promotional materials. This trend toward nostalgic domestic tourism continues today, and is inextricably linked to national discourses of Japanese uniqueness (the *Nihonjinron*).[19]

In sum then, the travel brochures in the four nations examined here clearly reflect and reproduce gendered and racialized discourses of national identity. Travel brochures are just one small part of the tourism economy, a sector that trades in constructions of difference. Both the discourses and practices of tourism potentially contribute to the maintenance of long-standing social hierarchies within and between nations. However, they also have the potential to contribute to social change, including changes in hierarchies of power and shifts in discourses of national identity.

11 Remembering the Nation
Gendered and Racialized National Identity in National Museums and Living History Venues

Just as our understandings of the past shape our understandings of the present, constructions of the nation's history, its origins, and its trials and triumphs shape current imaginings of the nation. While the nation's history is constructed in everything from school textbooks to historical novels, parades and folk ballads, it is arguably museums and living history venues that provide some of the most authoritative and seemingly authentic visions of history.

Above all, those institutions designated "national" museums serve as the official arbiters of the nation's historical memory, and visitors perceive such museums as the most reliable and objective source of information about the past.[1] National museums collect artefacts and display them in ways that illustrate key moments in the nation's history and the defining traits of the nation and its people. Their primary purpose is to represent the nation both to itself and to international visitors. Thus, these museums are an important source of authorized discourses of national identity.[2]

Quite different but complimentary sources of national narratives are so-called living history venues. The label "living history" is used by institutions and organizations that endeavor to explore the past through hands-on activities. Visitors to a recreated pioneer homestead or Viking village might be given the opportunity to don period clothing, eat period food, work with period tools, or engage in period leisure activities, all within what are promoted as historically accurate settings. Like museums, living history venues create powerful visions of the nation's "heritage."[3] Unlike museums, however, living history venues are generally staffed by historical "interpreters" in period costume who serve not only to guide visitors through the site, but to engage visitors in a game of historical make-believe through a variety of role-playing activities. These interpreters are usually the principal source of information at living history venues. Compared with museums, there are relatively few interpretive signs, presumably because they would disrupt the illusion of stepping back in time.

Another distinguishing feature of living history venues is their emphasis on pleasure. As opposed to national museums where visitors are expected to move quietly and reverentially through the galleries, living history venues often encourage guests to join in loud and vigorous activities. However, it would be naïve to think that because the emphasis here is on fun, deeper messages about history and national belonging are absent. In fact, visitors may embrace such messages more enthusiastically precisely because they are experienced in the context of play.

Not only do living history venues and national museums present historical information differently, they also typically occupy quite different physical spaces. While national museums are usually housed in the grand buildings of capital cities, living history venues are often located on sprawling indoor–outdoor sites in more marginal areas, such as struggling rural or rust-belt regions. While some living history venues are located in and around national capitals, scholars have documented a recent trend for historical theme parks, living history venues, and other forms of heritage tourism to be undertaken in areas of economic decline.[4]

Certainly, the development of heritage tourism in economically troubled areas is aimed at increasing jobs and revenue and sometimes combating perceived social disintegration. But I argue that it serves another purpose as well. Rural or former industrial regions experiencing depopulation, high unemployment, and perhaps increasing crime and general social and material decay, are often intensely aware that they are viewed by the rest of the nation as undesirable places, places excluded from the national imaginary. Recreating significant moments in the nation's history at living history venues allows people in these marginal locations to write themselves back into discourses of national identity.

In this final case study, I analyze gendered and racialized narratives of nation in the national museums and living history sites of the US, UK, Australia, and Japan. While the national museums analyzed here are located in and around capital cities, I selected living history sites far from the political, economic, and cultural centers of their respective nations. These sites were chosen, in part, to test the degree to which discourses of national identity constructed in core national locations differ from narratives of nation constructed in more peripheral areas.

The national museums include the Smithsonian National Museum of American History in Washington, DC, the National Portrait Gallery in London, the National Museum of Australia in Canberra, and the National Museum of Japanese History on the outskirts of Tokyo. While these museums vary considerably in both their collections and their curatorial approaches, each in its own way provides visitors with an overview of the nation's history and collective identity.

Of the living history sites chosen for analysis, in the United States I selected Lincoln's New Salem in the small rural community of Petersburg, Illinois. The site is promoted as a reconstruction of New Salem, the village where Abraham Lincoln resided between 1831 and 1837. In the UK, I selected the Black Country Living Museum in the borough of Dudley in the deindustrializing West Midlands. The site celebrates the history of the coal-mining and ironworks region known as the "Black Country" for its once sooty skies and scorched landscapes. This "living museum" focuses on life in the eighteenth century through the early twentieth century. In Australia, I chose Sovereign Hill in Ballarat, Victoria, created in the style of an 1850s Victorian gold rush town. And in Japan, I selected Edo Wonderland in Noboribetsu, Hokkaido, which recreates an unnamed village from Japan's Edo Era (1600–1867).[5]

None of these living history sites is the best known or most heavily trafficked of historical tourist sites in its respective nation. As a measure of these venues' marginality, when making arrangements to travel to these sites, contacts in each of the four nations invariably asked, "Why do you want to go *there* to study national identity?" Such comments reveal that in addition to being geographically distant from national centers of power, each of the living history locations studied here occupies a marginal position in the national imaginary.

I spent between twenty and forty hours at each of the museums and living history sites documenting the presentation of gender, race, and ethnicity in the following: the content of exhibits; the organization of space within and around the sites; the promotion of exhibits through signage, banners, guidebooks, and other materials; special features such as live performances, films, lectures, and guided walks; and the activities and comments of visitors and guides. Both basic descriptive statistics and detailed qualitative readings are provided here, the former as indicators of overall representational trends, the latter as a means to developing a fuller and more detailed account of the narratives of nation constructed in these locations.

At the outset, let me stress that my intent is not to rate or rank the institutions examined here on issues such as historical accuracy or gender and ethnoracial inclusivity. Nor is my intent to attribute blame to curators and staff for any apparent biases or omissions. I would also not presume to dictate to museum professionals how they should address any issues of bias and balance. After all, even curators who are dedicated to providing accurate and sensitive coverage of minority groups and controversial issues may face substantial opposition from powerful donors, boards of directors, and the state (Levin 2007, 13). Rather, my intent is to reveal the extent and nature of gendered and racialized discourses of national identity at these venues, and to consider the ways such discourses reflect and help sustain or challenge social inequalities.

GENDER, RACE, AND NATION IN NATIONAL MUSEUMS

As forms of entertainment and sources of information have proliferated over recent decades, national museums across the world have found themselves struggling to retain their audiences and their profiles as premier arbiters of national history and culture. They increasingly face pressures to be both authoritative and entertaining, and to address (or even redress) long-standing social inequalities through inclusive curatorial practices.

Not surprisingly then, there were certain commonalities in the four national museums examined here. For instance, in all of the museums there were clearly attempts to include the stories of women and ethnoracial minorities. And while the emphasis in each museum was on celebrating the nation, its glories, its heroes, its hardships, there were also occasional critiques. Certain displays or interpretive materials in each museum challenged visitors to rethink taken-for-granted notions about the nation, and exhorted audiences to consider the perspectives of groups whose voices are usually silenced. Nonetheless, as this discussion will show, women and ethnoracial minorities were often subtly or even quite dramatically marginalized in constructions of national history and identity.

Smithsonian National Museum of American History

At the Smithsonian National Museum of American History (SNMAH), I analyzed three of the largest exhibits at the time of my visit: The Price of Freedom: Americans at War; Separate Is Not Equal: Brown V Board of Education; and Communities in a Changing Nation: The Promise of Nineteenth-Century America. I first analyzed the gender, race, and ethnicity of all of the individuals named or pictured in the three exhibits. The exhibits were predominantly white and male. Of the 1,336 individuals recorded, 66 percent were white and a full 80 percent were male.[6] This constitutes a dramatic underrepresentation of women and a slight overrepresentation of ethnoracial minorities relative to these group's numbers in the overall US population today (see Table 11.1).

But numbers alone cannot reveal the more subtle ways women and ethnoracial Others are marginalized in these narratives of the nation's history. Looking first at the largest of these exhibits, The Price of Freedom: Americans

Table 11.1 Percentage of Ethnoracial Majority and Minority Individuals in National Museum Exhibits Compared to Respective National Populations*

Museum/Nation	Majority Represented (%)	Minority Represented (%)	Estimated % of Minorities in National Population[26]
NPG/UK	95	4	9
NMJH/Japan	94	5	1–4
NMA/Australia	73	28	30
SNMAH/US	66	33	25

*Due to rounding, percentages do not equal 100%.

at War, the banner hanging at the entrance of the exhibit suggested that this vision of America was an inclusive one. It featured images of both male and female soldiers from a variety of ethnoracial backgrounds. And throughout the exhibit, despite the overwhelming numerical dominance of white males (81 percent white, 80 percent male), there was clearly an effort to include the stories of women and ethnoracial minorities. But the ways these groups were incorporated into the narrative of nation often (no doubt unintentionally) only reinforced their marginality.

One display on Civil War camp life exemplified this tendency. This display addressed much of the miscellany that did not fit elsewhere in the sizeable Civil War section: medical and cooking equipment, uniforms, musical instruments, and notably, both female nurses and Native American allies. These materials were located in a relatively small, dimly lit alcove that most visitors bypassed on their way to more eye-catching displays. The placards in the section offered only brief details, and consequently most visitors moved quickly through the alcove, pausing only momentarily to gaze into the cases. The marginality of women and Native Americans in narratives of nation was, in this instance, neatly captured by their placement on the shadowy margins of the display.

The coverage of a more recent conflict, the Vietnam War, demonstrated the complex intersection between gender, race, and national identity. Out of more than three hundred named individuals featured in The Price of Freedom, only three (or less than 1 percent) were nonwhite women. One of these women, a woman of Vietnamese descent, had been rescued by US Army medics when she was a newborn in the war-torn countryside of her homeland. Having lost her biological parents in the war, she was adopted by white American parents, baptized in the Catholic Church, and given an Anglo-American name. "They said we killed babies," one soldier included in the display remarked, but this story seemed to refute that perception.

Certainly, the infant rescue story seems designed to assuage any concerns or guilt visitors might have about the injustice of American actions in Vietnam, particularly the killing of innocent civilians. The story of a rescued Vietnamese girl might even be seen as a way of counterbalancing one of the most enduring images of the war for many Americans, Nick Ut's 1972 Pulitzer Prize winning photo of a young Vietnamese girl running naked down the road after being burned in a napalm attack. As Dickinson et al. (2005, 88) have observed, "Museums have the potential to cleanse, absolve or relieve visitors of painful, conflictual histories."

In terms of discourses of national identity, however, it is crucial to ask why this particular woman's story was included. I suggest that it is not just because this story reflects favorably upon the US military and portrays America as the world's savior, but because this woman serves as a marker of America's avowed multicultural ethic in the most nonthreatening form imaginable—a fully domesticated Other, an Anglicized, Christianized infant girl.

While The Price of Freedom constructed a definitively white and masculine narrative of nation, other exhibits within the museum focused more consciously on minority populations. Field to Factory: Afro-American Migration 1915–1940, First Ladies: Political Role, Public Image, and ¡Azúcar! The Life and Music of Celia Cruz focused primarily on African Americans, women, and Hispanic Americans respectively. Likewise, it is not surprising that in Separate Is Not Equal: Brown V Board of Education, an exhibit marking the fiftieth anniversary of the historic school desegregation ruling, representations of people of color outnumbered those of whites. Slightly more than half of those named or pictured were from minority ethnoracial groups. Those featured included prominent public leaders, artists, scholars, and ordinary people who experienced segregation and desegregation.

The interpretive materials of the exhibit and teams of well-rehearsed tour guides provided detailed discussion of both the institutional processes and individual prejudices that sustained racial segregation. Figures such as W. E. B. Du Bois, Thurgood Marshall, and Langston Hughes were represented as enlightened and courageous heroes battling, as Marshall put it, "to save this country's soul, white or black, whether they like it or not." However, the more prominent place afforded to people of color in this narrative of nation was not matched by more gender equitable representations. Of the three major exhibits analyzed here, Separate Is Not Equal was the most male dominated, with men accounting for 86 percent of those named or pictured.

Compared to The Price of Freedom and Separate Is Not Equal, the exhibit Communities in a Changing Nation: The Promise of Nineteenth-Century America gave a greater voice to women and a variety of ethnoracial minority populations. In fact, representations of ethnoracial minorities slightly outnumbered those of majority whites, and women were less dramatically underrepresented than in the other two major exhibits. But again, we must consider not only the numbers, but the subtleties of these representations.

The section Jewish Immigrants: The Promise of a New Life, for instance, provided extensive coverage of the lives of Jewish Americans in the nineteenth century. However, one focal point of the section, a mural-sized reproduction of Charles Ulrich's (1884) painting *In the Land of Promise, Castle Garden*, calls for a careful reading. The work depicts a presumably Jewish immigrant woman in an arrival depot nursing an infant, her breast fully exposed. At least one man in the background seems to leer at her as she gazes plaintively in the direction of the viewer.

On one level, the painting is a sympathetic portrayal of the trials faced by so many nineteenth-century immigrants who were crowded into screening facilities such as Castle Garden and Ellis Island. However, it is worth noting that this is also quite a sensual portrait of an immigrant woman, fleshy and fair, vulnerable and exposed not only to the gaze of the men around her but to the gaze of the museumgoer. If the painting hung in a museum replete with nudes, the sensuality of the portrait might not stand out. However, with a few notable exceptions such the Vargas "pinup girls" featured in a nostalgic display of World War II popular culture, the museum appeared to eschew body displays. This immigrant woman's partial nudity can therefore be seen as an index of her marginal status, based on her class, ethnicity, and gender.

Sandwiched between large sections devoted to European immigrants and African Americans, Communities in a Changing Nation offered a small explanatory note about another minority group, Native Americans:

> Americans have come from almost everywhere. The earliest immigrants established hundreds of nations, each with a distinctive Indian language and culture. About 700,000 Europeans moved to America before 1800. Some 400,000 Africans were brought over as slaves.

This text represents Native Americans as simply one of many immigrant groups. There is no acknowledgement of them as the indigenous inhabitants of the land. There is some sense of their cultural diversity, but not of their numbers nor the depth of their histories. And there is no hint of the displacement and genocide they experienced at the hands of European colonizers. Underpinning this narrative is what might be called the "We are all immigrants" trope. In the US, as in other racially and ethnically diverse nations, this trope is often employed in antiracist rhetoric, the message being, "Don't criticize immigrants, because we're all immigrants; we're all the same." However, in one sense such statements simply reinforce inequalities by obscuring different experiences of oppression and privilege, and, in the case of native inhabitants, denying both their prior claims to the land and their experiences of exile and extermination.

The final section of Communities in a Changing Nation focused on "African Americans in Slavery and Freedom." The focal point of the section was a full-sized recreation of a slave cabin complete with two slave girl mannequins. Although the child figures did not move, a recorded soundtrack brought visitors their voices as they talked, laughed, sang, and reflected on their harsh circumstances and the loss of loved ones who were "sold on." Although the section also included adults, most notably a display on African-American soldiers and nurses in the Civil War, the children's cabin was undeniably its centerpiece. In a pattern also seen in the travel brochures of the previous chapter, by positioning children as representatives of the group, internal Others here were rendered nonthreatening and sympathetic, but ultimately powerless.

Finally, one small display in this section on African Americans must be included in any discussion of constructions of the nation's history. The display told the story of a freed slave woman who eventually sold herself back into slavery because she was "overwhelmed" by discrimination and the separation from the rest of the African American community. It is curious that such a rare occurrence was included in this quite general overview of African Americans' experiences. The story seems to imply that at least some African Americans preferred slavery to freedom, and that they were most comfortable operating within its well-defined boundaries. Dickinson's (2005) observation about museums serving to "absolve" visitors of their guilty histories may best explain the inclusion of this particular story within the museum's narrative of nation.[7]

The National Portrait Gallery

At the close of the twentieth century, Britain's Millennium Commission was asked to fund the construction of what would be called History House, a national museum of British history. Proponents argued that in a rapidly globalizing world, Britons needed to be encouraged to remember and celebrate their distinctive national traits, experiences, and accomplishments, and no other national museum did this.[8] When I visited London in 2004, History House still had not been built, and arguably there was still no national museum dedicated specifically to the nation's history and identity. In a sense, however, the National Portrait Gallery (NPG), serves much the same purpose, dedicated as it is to highlighting "the men and women who have made and are making British history and culture" (NPG 2001, 8). Although the NPG is the only art museum to be included in this study, the Gallery's stated mission is "about history, not about art" (NPG 2008). This emphasis on the nation's history makes it a rich source of narratives of nation.

Of course all museums must operate, to some extent, within the constraints of their own collections. It will come as no surprise that those who bequeath enduring portraits of themselves to history are typically wealthy or famous—captains of industry, politicians, military leaders, nobles, intellectuals, artists. Neither is it surprising that the great majority of individuals featured in the collections of Britain's NPG are men, the historically dominant sex. Based on analysis of an electronic database of the Gallery's holdings, 73 percent of its portraits feature male subjects.[9]

Since the Gallery can only display a small fraction of its holdings at any given time, it would be theoretically possible to create displays that featured men and women in roughly equal numbers, although this would undoubtedly leave the institution open to charges of perverting national history in the service of political correctness. Site visits to the Gallery reveal no basis for such charges, however. In the exhibits analyzed in detail, 75 percent of portraits hung in the Gallery featured male subjects. In addition, only 4 percent of individuals represented were of nonwhite/non-European background, virtually all from the 1960s or later. If the NPG constructs a vision of the national imagined community, the community imagined is primarily white and male.[10]

Moreover, textual materials in the Gallery seldom reflected critically on matters of race or gender. In one example, Francis Hayman's portrait of military commander and colonial governor Robert Clive features a Bengali leader bowing to Clive at the 1757 Battle of Plassey, a crucial victory in Britain's assertion of colonial authority over the Indian subcontinent. The colors are vibrant, the details sumptuous, the lighting dramatic. And because the artist had never visited the region he portrayed, his representations of colonials in feathered turbans, jewels, and flowing golden robes reflect the Orientalist fantasies of the day. This dazzling portrait is an example of what we might call aestheticized racism, the representation of racialized power relations as things of beauty, to be gazed upon with admiration, desire, and national pride.

Yet the text accompanying the painting did not offer critical comment on issues of Orientalism or colonialism, nor even on the martial power the work glorifies. Under the heading "Britain Becomes a World Power," it read:

> By the end of the eighteenth century, thanks to her sea power and to trade, Britain had overtaken the old colonial powers including France and Spain, in America, the West Indies and India, and had made great new discoveries in the Pacific.

This text offers a simple celebration of British Imperialism. Colonialism is not dominance but a kind of friendly competition between European powers. State-sanctioned bloodshed is shielded by the euphemism of "sea power," and lands expropriated from indigenous inhabitants become "great new discoveries."

Representations of gender were likewise seldom submitted to critical analysis. Rather, interpretive materials largely reinforced long-standing gender stereotypes and hierarchies of power. The inscription accompanying a portrait of Emma, Lady Hamilton, was typical in this respect.

> Emma, Lady Hamilton (1765–1815): The daughter of a Cheshire blacksmith, Emma achieved celebrity through her beauty, personal vitality and skills as a performer. She is principally remembered as the artist George Romney's "muse" and for her love affair with Nelson.

Here the subject in the portrait is defined almost entirely through her relations with men: her father, her lover, and the artist she inspired. Although the text alludes to her skills, we are reminded that her historical significance lies primarily in her roles as model and mistress.[11]

Even in exhibits of late eighteenth-century portraits which showed a larger number of women not simply as the adjuncts of famous men, but as accomplished individuals in their own right, interpretive materials often pulled the viewer's focus away from those accomplishments and toward the women's sexual and family roles and their traditionally feminine attributes. The hall entitled Art, Invention and Thought: The Romantics provides a case in point.

The hall featured portraits of prominent writers, scientists, and artists of the Romantic period, each accompanied by an interpretive sign. Of the twenty-seven subjects in the room, including such luminaries as John Keats, Samuel Taylor Coleridge, and Jane Austen, only four were women.[12] And while the interpretive material on only one man mentioned his marital status, the notes on all of the women mentioned their marital or family status. Furthermore, while the men in the room were described with terms such as "radical," "inspired," "brilliant," "reckless," "progressive," and "innovative," the women and their works were described as "precocious," "deeply influenced" by others, and full of "refinement and charm."

To some degree the underrepresentation and stereotypical representation of women and ethnoracial minorities in national museums is an inevitable outcome of centuries of oppression. It may be unrealistic for contemporary museumgoers to hope for detailed and nuanced portrayals of marginalized groups from points in history when they had little visibility and little say over their own destinies, property, bodies, or images. However, in the NPG even displays of late twentieth-century portraits reproduced the white male dominance typical of earlier periods.

At first glance, the long narrow hall covering Britain from 1960–1990 appeared to epitomize the contemporary ethics of multicultural diversity and gender equality. Seven large portraits hung at the entrance of the hall. Two of the seven subjects were women and two were ethnoracial minority men. However, on closer inspection of the representations in this section, 83 percent of featured subjects were men, and 95 percent were white, underrepresenting both women and ethnoracial minorities compared with their numbers in the national population today (see Table 11.1). Only in the hall covering Britain Since 1990 was this underrepresentation of the two groups reduced. Of the portraits from this period, women were the subjects of 34 percent of the portraits, and ethnoracial minorities constituted 17 percent of those featured.

Museums of all kinds can of course reach beyond their own collections with temporary visiting exhibits. During the period of my site visits to the NPG, the museum was hosting the exhibition We Are the People, a collection of postcard portraits of ordinary Britons from the first half of the twentieth century. As interpretive materials explained, while historically only the wealthy could afford to preserve their images for posterity, by the turn of the twentieth century, new photographic technology had democratized portraiture, bringing it within the means of most Britons. In the period of roughly 1900–1935, the curator suggests, most ordinary Britons had preserved their likenesses in the kind of cheap and readily accessible portrait postcards featured in the exhibition (Phillips 2004).

The curator's stated goal was "to create an alternative National Portrait Gallery" and give "pictorial enfranchisement to those who constituted the nation, bore its children, did its jobs, fought its battles and made it work" (Phillips 2004, 21–22). In stark contrast to the Gallery's focus on the well-heeled and well-known, We Are the People constructed a narrative of nation grounded in the everyday experiences of ordinary people. It is perhaps not surprising then that the representations were in some ways more egalitarian than in the Gallery as a whole.

Men and women were represented in roughly equal numbers in the exhibition.[13] Qualitatively, however, the representations were fairly conventionally gendered, whether through the choices of photographers and the individuals who posed for the pictures, or through curatorial choices. It must be noted that the exhibition included only a carefully selected fraction of the curator's collection of fifty thousand portrait postcards (Phillips 2004, 21). Men dominated in representations of sport and the military, for instance, while only girls and women were featured in sections on clothing fashions and hairstyles. More men were shown winning prizes, while more women were shown quietly reading.[14] In these ways, the exhibition sustained the image of active, heroic masculinity and passive femininity.

Such gender ideals certainly dominated thinking in Britain in the first decades of the twentieth century. So the question here is not whether such representations are historically accurate. Rather, the question is whether the repetition of such gender stereotypes in an exhibition that purports to be a "visual census" of the nation (Phillips 2004, 21) helps naturalize long-standing gender binaries and hierarchies by suggesting a continuity between the past and the present. I would argue that it does.

Of particular interest in a study of national identity, however, are those portraits in which the subject more explicitly embodies the nation and its Others. For example, women in the postcard portraits frequently posed as Britannia with her Centurion's helmet, trident, and shield, at times presiding over people dressed as her colonial subjects in turbans, feathers, or tartans. These images employed the conventions of allegorical paintings in which female figures personify the nation. As such, the portraits are not only representations of the subjects themselves, but of their commitments to country, monarchy, and empire and their imaginings of the national community and its Others.

The collection also included portraits of costumed children, images which arguably tell us less about the children's tastes than about the values, identities, and fantasies of their parents, who most likely chose and paid for the photographs. Young children dressed as little brides and grooms or little nurses and soldiers, hint at parents' aspirations for their offspring. However, children were also dressed as racial or national others: girls posed demurely in kimono or vaguely Turkish-looking robes and veils; one boy in blackface makeup posed as a spear-carrying native, while other children donned buckskins and feathered headdresses.

Rather than revealing the aspirations of parents, such images hint at popular notions about colonial Others as "half devil and half child."[15] Colonials were assumed to be as helpless and naïve as children, yet also dangerous and wild. Such portraits both presumed and conveyed the superiority of mature

British civilization and neutralized the threat of colonial Others by infantilizing them. At the same time, posing children as quaint "savages" and Oriental maidens portrayed imperialism as a benign and innocent project. Again, while the portraits no doubt accurately capture popular sentiments in early twentieth-century Britain, exhibiting such images without commentary that encourages critical reflection arguably naturalizes the racist underpinnings of the imperial project.

Although the postcard exhibition featured numerous individuals posing as ethnoracial Others for patriotic, artistic, or humorous effect, only two out of almost fifteen hundred individuals featured in the exhibit appeared to be of nonwhite/non-European backgrounds, and both of these were men. Not a single nonwhite woman was featured in the exhibit. Again, the dearth of nonwhite subjects here could be due to curatorial choices, to the choices of photographers or nonwhite residents in Britain in the early decades of the twentieth century, or to some combination of those factors. But whatever the cause, the effect is the same. Although the title of the exhibition, We Are the People, seems to promise a true portrait of "the people," an authentic snapshot of the national community as a whole, that community is almost exclusively white, just as in it is in the Gallery as a whole.

National Museum of Australia

The National Museum of Australia (NMA) opened in March 2001 amidst controversy and discord. Its primary goal, seemingly simple enough, was to "tell the Australian story," that is, the story of Australia's land, people, and history (NMA 2003, 13). However, at the end of a planning process spanning more than twenty years, the Museum seemed to have as many detractors as supporters.[16] Controversies over the Museum filled newspaper editorial pages, centering on both the content of exhibits and the Museum building itself.

The first of these controversies was over the design of the building. Rather than creating a ponderous edifice of marble and classical columns, the architects designed a building of glass and metal with brightly painted and highly textured surfaces and unexpected angles.[17] The intent seems to have been to create an accessible, slightly whimsical, and distinctly anti-elitist structure within which to tell the story of a young and dynamic nation. While many in the architectural community praised the design, detractors labeled it "theme park Australia," a "confection of cheap cladding and plasterboard," a "spurious sideshow" of postmodern in-jokes masquerading as a temple to the common Australian (Stead 2004). The construction of the museum was further marred by tragedy when a young spectator was killed by flying debris during the demolition phase of the project, an event now marked by a small memorial to the child.

If controversies over the Museum's design and construction dominated public debate before the institution's opening, subsequent criticism has focused more consistently on the content of its exhibits. While defenders of the Museum claim that it provides a rich and balanced telling of the nation, critics have lambasted it as "a monument to horrendous political correctness."[18]

As is clear from even a brief stroll through the galleries, the Museum has certainly attempted to provide equal time, space, and voice to all Australians. Nowhere is this clearer than in the Eternity gallery, promoted as "a glimpse into Australia's past, present and future through the lives, emotions and experiences of its people." At the time of my site visits, it featured the portraits and stories of men and women with varied personal histories: the male subjects included, among others, a white hippie artist, an Indigenous cricketer, and an Afghan-Australian cameleer; the women, an Aboriginal teacher, a white race car driver, and a Vietnamese-Australian law student. Young and old were included, famous and "ordinary" people, gay men, disabled women, those who challenge traditional norms and those who exemplify traditional values.

In terms of ethnicity and social and gender roles, these representations were quite diverse. Nonetheless, in merely quantitative terms, men slightly outnumbered women and white Australians outnumbered nonwhite Australians by more than ten to one, a dramatic underrepresentation of ethnoracial minorities compared with their numbers in the overall population of the nation today (see Table 11.1). In qualitative terms, despite the apparent ethnoracial inclusivity and progressive gender ideology, the short biographies that accompanied each of the portraits typically celebrated the perspectives and institutions of a patriarchal white Australian society. For instance, while the military, football, and cricket received multiple references here, controversial issues of discrimination and inequality were largely ignored.

In one example, a description of Isabella Lynot, "Aunty Bella," a woman of mixed indigenous and European ancestry, explained that she had been removed from her indigenous family by the state and educated on a mission in the Kimberly region. While this would seem a logical point at which to discuss the issue of the long-running state policy of indigenous child removals, instead the biography noted that Lynot chose to stay on the mission for the rest of her life, being a teacher and surrogate mother for the indigenous girls who were brought there. "She lived for her Kimberly girls, the Church and her faith." This celebratory story of Christian faith and self-sacrifice seems to absolve Anglo-Australians of any guilt they might feel over the so-called Stolen Generations of indigenous children forcibly taken from their families in an attempt to "civilize" them.

In terms of overall patterns of representation in the main galleries of the museum, representations of white males vastly outnumbered those of women or people of color.[19] Nonetheless, of all the national museums analyzed here, the NMA cultivated the most explicitly critical perspective, what Frost (2005) calls "edgier interpretation." This perspective is "edgier" in the traditional sense of being new and discomfiting, but also in the sense of bringing to light the stories of those on the "edges" or margins of society.

Perhaps the most explicitly critical galleries in the museum were those devoted to immigration and to Aboriginal and Torres Strait Islander Peoples. Horizons: The People of Australia Since 1788 contained celebratory stories of persecuted, downtrodden, and unhappy people from around the world making their ways to Australia, a land of "trust . . . freedom . . . peace . . . prosperity and opportunities . . . the promised land." However, these celebratory stories were balanced by an explicitly critical discussion of immigration policies. As one interpretive sign noted,

> Governments have shaped Australia's population in different ways at different times. They have guarded against various dangers, real or perceived—"racial pollution," "moral contamination," illegal weapons and disease. Tools for government regulation have included immigration restrictions, censorship and quarantine.

Other interpretive materials in this section dealt with the issue of the detention of migrants during the two world wars, the denial of citizenship to Indigenous Australians, the White Australia Policy, and state-sponsored assimilation programs. Such a critical stance continued with a discussion of the policy of *terra nullius*. As noted earlier, under the eighteenth-century concept of *terra nullius* (empty land), a sovereign nation had the right to claim as its own any unoccupied territory it discovered. Despite the obvious presence of indigenous peoples in Australia, British colonial authorities declared the land uninhabited, an issue raised in the display titled Terra Nullius: The Lie of the Land.

This heading introduces a useful ambiguity, for the "lie of the land" can mean both the topography of Australia and the falsehood that the land was unoccupied. However, despite this suggestive title, the interpretive materials here did not suggest that the British actively "lied," but rather that they considered the land "empty" because they misunderstood the indigenous Australian cultures. So despite the critical edge here, at the core is an essentially apologist claim. Likewise, nearby hung a grossly distorted portrait of an indigenous man painted by a European artist. The interpretive sign noted that "Many early European sketches and paintings of Aboriginal people look strange and distorted to modern eyes. Artists were trying to make sense of something new and unfamiliar." Again, this explanation frames racist representations as instances of an innocent lack of understanding.

A critical perspective was further cultivated in the sizeable gallery called First Australians: Gallery of Aboriginal and Torres Strait Islander Peoples. The gallery is a defined physical space, set apart from other galleries both architecturally and through lighting and sound, and is located at the far end of the museum. At the time of my study, visitors entered the gallery through a darkened corridor with amplified sounds of indigenous voices and musical instruments. Although video screens in the corridor showed images of indigenous Australians and their artwork, the space seemed designed more as a transitional space than as an exhibit in its own right, and most visitors moved through it quickly.

Patterns of visitor use also marked this space as different from the rest of the museum. During the period of my observation (spanning five days), the First Australians gallery was typically less populated and quieter than other areas of the museum. During one sixty-minute observation period, in fact, only three other visitors entered the gallery although the rest of the museum was crowded. Likewise, the only example of defaced museum property I saw was in this gallery. Beneath a quote by an indigenous person exhorting visitors to remember that indigenous people "have been here from the beginning of time," the name of the speaker and the date of the statement had been partially scratched out. It is worth noting that among many of indigenous peoples in Australia, it is taboo to use the name of a deceased person. It is possible that the name and date were partially erased by a member of the Aboriginal community for this reason. This taboo might also partially explain the lack of named Aboriginal persons in displays throughout the museum.

In terms of gender representations, the museum's discourses of national identity were clearly male dominated, with men accounting for 79 percent of all people shown or named. In some sections of the museum, this was even more dramatic. For instance in Snapshots of Glory, a temporary display of photographs from Rugby World Cup competitions, 95 percent of the photos featured only men, and all of those identified by name were men.

In addition to such quantitative differences there were significant qualitative differences in gender representations. At the very heart of the museum—the center gallery of the main floor—was Nation: Symbols of Australia, a gallery dedicated to "some of the defining moments in Australian history since 1788" (NMA 2001, 19). The most striking feature of the gallery was *The Spirit of the Digger: A National Icon*, a large statue of a World War I soldier, reminiscent of many war memorials built around the country in the wake of the war. Several displays here repeated the notion that Australia only really became a nation through its participation in World War I: "Australian history began on April 25th, 1915, on the way to the firing line;" or "Gallipoli Peninsula—here Australia became a nation." While there were brief references to women and "blacks" who have served in the armed forces, representations of the "Digger" were almost exclusively white and male.[20] With no mention of the two thousand Australian women who served as nurses to the Anzac forces, women in the section were identified simply as "wives, mothers and sisters" of the celebrated Anzacs. The message is clear: if World War I made Australia a nation, the white male Anzac made Australia a nation.

A second focal point of the Nation gallery was a scale model of a 1950s suburban kitchen, where it was noted that to many Australians, the suburban family is a symbol of the "Australian way of life." In this and adjoining displays, women were represented largely as happy homemakers, but a degree of feminist critique was injected here with the inclusion of Louise Johnson's short film *The End of the Line*. The narrative featured a woman who cuts down her Hills Hoist clothes line (a ubiquitous feature of Australian suburbia) as a protest against her domestic role.

Such critiques notwithstanding, charges that the Museum distorts Australian history in the service of "political correctness" appear unfounded. Those concerned about diluting Australia's history and identity can rest assured that in its national museum, discourses of national identity are still decidedly focused on the experiences and perspectives of white men.

National Museum of Japanese History

With millennia of history to document, there is no shortage of museums in Japan. In 2001, the "big three" national museums at Tokyo, Kyoto, and Nara merged administratively to create a single National Museum of Japan. Each National Museum complex serves as a veritable vault of national treasures, with gallery after gallery of precious paintings, scrolls, ceramics, lacquerware, textiles, swords, and ritual objects, often displayed behind thick glass and monitored by uniformed guards.

By contrast, the National Museum of Japanese History (NMJH), opened in 1983, displays fewer national treasures, and instead endeavors to provide a cohesive narrative of Japanese history and culture through interactive exhibits (NMJH 2002, 4).[21] Also, quite unlike the institutions of the newly consolidated National Museum, it attempts to strike a balance between the experiences of elites and commoners. Peddlers and peasants find a place here among lords and emperors; fishnets and waterwheels are displayed as prominently as gilded screens. Consequently, the Museum presents a complex and multifaceted exploration of Japanese national self-conceptions.

As in the other nations examined here, the discourses of national identity constructed in this Japanese national museum carry meanings about both gender and race. In some ways these representations are consistent with the widely circulating discourses of national identity discussed throughout this volume. In other ways, however, the representations seem to challenge taken-for-granted notions about Japanese society, history, and culture.

Representations of race and ethnicity are a case in point. Consistent with popular notions of Japan's racial and ethnic homogeneity, the Museum included relatively few representations of non-Japanese. Only 5 percent of featured individuals were identifiably non-Japanese, a number in proportion with the number of ethnoracial minorities in Japan today (Table 11.1).[22] Those who were included were drawn from four main groups and periods: visitors from China in premodern Japan; Europeans and North Americans from the Meiji Era onward; the colonized indigenous *Ainu* people of Hokkaido; and resident Koreans living through the aftermath of the Great Kantō

Earthquake. More important than sheer numbers of minorities, however, are the ways they are positioned and portrayed.

Significantly, both in the English-language and Japanese-language interpretive materials, there was a distinctly critical edge to the discussion of the *Ainu* and ethnic Koreans. In the gallery on the settlement of Hokkaido one interpretive sign explained that,

> The *Ainu* people were stripped of their traditional ways of living, prohibited from using the *Ainu* language, forced to engage in farming, and compelled to move to other places. In this way, the development of Hokkaido was carried out based on restricting the rights of the native people.

While the explanation used the passive voice, thereby sidestepping the issue of just who was coercing the *Ainu* in this way, the message was clearly that the *Ainu* were ill-treated. One alcove in the gallery was, in fact, dedicated to the topic of anti-*Ainu* discrimination in its many forms. The discussion was detailed and frank, noting for instance that the *Ainu* were driven onto the poorest land, subjected to racial epithets, forced to adopt Japanese ways of life, and killed by diseases brought from the South. Conspicuously absent, however, was any discussion of the *Ainu* in contemporary Japan, their ongoing struggles for self-determination and legal recognition as an indigenous people.[23] Rather, any problems faced by the *Ainu* seem to be firmly located in the distant past.

Likewise anti-Korean discrimination was addressed frankly, but only within one historical context, the aftermath of the Great Kantō Earthquake, the massive 1923 quake which claimed an estimated one hundred thousand lives. Interpretive signs explained that in the wake of the disaster, Koreans were "victimized" due to unfounded rumors that they were poisoning wells in the area. While the scope of this victimization was not clear from the signs, visitors who took the time to seek out more detailed information from an interactive computer and video display could learn that an estimated 6,618 ethnic Koreans and another four hundred to six hundred ethnic Chinese were murdered in the aftermath of the quake. This display is remarkable in that a monumental national tragedy was used not as a vehicle for celebrating such national traits as fortitude, bravery, or solidarity, as tragic events are often used in Japan and elsewhere, but as a way of discussing and critiquing virulent and lethal Japanese xenophobia.

Nonetheless, conspicuously absent was any reference to continued discrimination against ethnic Koreans or ethnic Chinese, many of whom are currently excluded from full participation in public life by their status as alien residents.[24] Absent also were references to Japan's growing migrant communities, drawn particularly from Asia and South America; and the *Ryūkyū* people of Okinawa and the *Burakumin*, Japan's "untouchables," were each mentioned only briefly. The *Ryūkyū* Islands appeared as part of a larger discussion of life in fishing villages, but there was no discussion of the Japanese invasion and annexation of the once independent kingdom. And the *Burakumin* were only indirectly mentioned in the Meiji Era Civilization and Enlightenment gallery, with a note that because discrimination "has always been a problem in Japan" the Meiji government abolished the outcaste categories of *eta* and *hinin*. As with the section on the *Ainu*, the implication was that discrimination against such groups is a thing of the past.

In terms of gender representations, compared to national museums in the other nations under consideration here, the NMJH had a less marked gender imbalance (Table 11.2). This can be explained, in part, by the Museum's greater emphasis on unnamed commoners. Compared to the other national museums analyzed, it devoted relatively little space to famous historical figures. Less than 7 percent of representations throughout the museum were of named individuals. With less attention accorded to prominent leaders of the state, the military, science, the arts, religion, and industry, there was more room for the voices, experiences, and images of women.

Beyond sheer numbers, however, it is crucial to examine nuances of gender representation in the Museum. A diorama from Japan's Paleolithic period, and several displays focusing on working women, illustrate broader patterns of gender representation throughout the museum.

Gender representations in the diorama of a Paleolithic (Jomon Era) settlement were consistent with long-standing images of Paleolithic peoples in museums and educational materials in many nations today. As Ehrenberg (1989) has noted, contemporary interpretations of prehistory are profoundly shaped by current gender stereotypes and hierarchies. In the Jomon display, women were shown occupied primarily in food gathering, cooking, and childminding, while men were engaged in hunting and toolmaking. Few explanatory signs were provided, leaving visitors to rely primarily on lived experiences and gender stereotypes for their interpretation of prehistoric social roles. Whether or not the gender roles portrayed in the diorama are accurate, the implied continuity between past and present arguably lends Japan's contemporary gender order an air of naturalness and inevitability.

Table 11.2 Percentage of Men and Women Featured in National Museum Exhibits*

Museum	Men	Women
National Museum of American History	79	20
National Museum of Australia	79	22
National Portrait Gallery (London)	75	24
National Museum of Japanese History	62	37

*Due to rounding, percentages do not equal 100%.

Such representations were counterbalanced, however, by sizeable displays on working women in both the feudal period and the early modern era. Women from the feudal period were not only shown engaging in traditionally feminine labor such as embroidery and silk-weaving, but were portrayed as shrewd merchants, hardworking peasant farmers, and skilled printers and artisans. In coverage of industrialization during the Meiji Era (1868–1912), considerable space was devoted to "The Lives of Female Factory Workers," a display documenting the difficult conditions endured by female textile workers. That the display was paired with coverage of male ironworkers and steelworkers of the same period suggests to visitors that both women and men contributed to Japan's industrial revolution. And coverage of the "Revolution of Lifestyles" in the 1930s celebrated women's expanded educational and career opportunities, but also noted systematic wage discrimination and sexual harassment.

Thus coverage of women's lives in the NMJH went well beyond the female domestic role. Women were not merely portrayed as adjuncts of famous men, as chaste wives and daughters, or as pinup girls, but as active participants in national social life—private and public. At the same time, while relatively few named individuals appeared in the Museum's displays, the majority of those named were men, including military leaders, emperors, and scholars among others. Named men outnumbered their female counterparts by almost seven to one.

Where named women did appear, their contributions to national life were not always made explicit. The sizeable display on Heian courtly culture noted that the values and aesthetics of the Heian court are deeply ingrained in Japanese culture today. Interpretive signs explained that it was during this period that a uniquely Japanese writing system was developed and distinctively Japanese literary forms, such as *waka* poetry and diary literature, were born. Although women were listed among the authors of the period, conspicuously absent in the display was a discussion of the key role women played in reshaping the cultural landscape through their literary innovations.[25]

CROSS-NATIONAL COMPARISONS

In all four national museums examined here representations of men outnumber representations of women, sometimes by almost four to one (Table 11.2). And in qualitative terms, while there are exceptions like those at the NMJH, women tend to be confined to a narrower range of roles, and tend to be described in terms of their family roles, their relationship to famous men, or their emotions, despite their own accomplishments. Furthermore, women are often quite literally marginalized, placed in side galleries or other out-of-the-way and less visible places, and their contributions to national life are often not fully acknowledged. Such observations confirm Holcomb's assertion that, "... the heritage which gets conserved and interpreted in most contemporary societies is overwhelmingly 'male' in the sense that it was built by men, commemorates men's activities, celebrates male heroes and mourns male suffering and loss" (1998, 37).

Likewise, in all nations studied here, representations of majority populations vastly outnumber those of minority populations (Table 11.1). Even where the number of ethnoracial minorities included in a museum is roughly consistent with the proportion of minorities in the overall population of the host nation, ethnoracial Others tend to be relatively isolated from the flow of national history, either by being confined to one time period (Meiji Japan or post-1960 Britain) or in separate areas of the museum (the First Australians gallery or Separate Is Not Equal). Without exception the least visible people in these national museums are non-majority females, who are seldom seen and almost never named, quoted, or otherwise individuated. Where they do appear, their stories often simply serve the interests of dominant groups, as in the rescued Vietnamese girl in the US or the Aboriginal missionary in Australia.

I am not suggesting that the marginalization of women and ethnoracial minorities is due to some kind of a "museo-conspiracy" (Holcomb 1998, 49). In fact, it is clear that curators in each of these national museums have attempted to address imbalances of power by devoting space to historically disadvantaged groups and, on occasion, providing critical comment to challenge stereotypes and silences. Neither am I suggesting that curators should distort national histories by making it appear that women and ethnoracial minorities have long enjoyed equal power, influence, and opportunity compared with majority men. No one would be well served by such historical revisionism.

Nonetheless, even considering the more limited range of artefacts and records from historically subordinated groups that curators have at their disposal, we have seen here that it is possible for museums to provide visitors with both complex portrayals of these groups and opportunities for critical reflection. The fact remains, however, that museums are products of their respective national cultures. As long as widely circulating discourses of national identity position men and the ethnoracial majority as the natural creators, leaders, and rulers of the nation, museums will both reflect and help reproduce such notions.

GENDER, RACE, AND NATION IN LIVING HISTORY VENUES

As noted in the introduction of this chapter, living history sites differ from traditional museums in a variety of ways, one of the most prominent being the means by which historical information is presented. While traditional museums typically educate the public through detailed explanatory signs, living history venues tend to use signage sparingly so as not to intrude on the visitor's sense of stepping back through time. Instead, historical details are provided by a combination of hands-on experiences and costumed "interpreters." Also unlike national museums, living history venues are often located far from the centers of national power and prosperity, in regions facing increasing unemployment, depopulation, or other social and economic strains. Living history enterprises promise such regions not only jobs and revenue, but an opportunity to bolster regional pride by writing themselves back into narratives of nation. Such narratives differ, however, from those constructed in national museums.

Compared to national museums, representations in the static materials of the living history venues analyzed here were typically less ethnically and racially inclusive and less gender progressive.[27] In the venues' introductory galleries, representations were even more strongly dominated by majority males, and ethnoracial minorities were largely or entirely absent. This is explained, in part, by the location of these living history sites far from the intellectual, political, and cultural elites who generally lead initiatives for racial and gender equity. Moreover, because living history venues, as sites of pleasure, are less likely than national museums to be subjected to scholarly critique, there may be less incentive for site managers to carefully monitor issues of gender and ethnoracial balance.

But such representations are only part of the story at living history venues. In fact, at each of the venues analyzed, most visitors moved rapidly through the introductory galleries or even bypassed them altogether to reach what were clearly viewed as the real attractions, the hands-on historical learning activities led by costumed interpreters. These interpreters create particularly vivid and apparently politically innocent narratives not only about national history, but about national belonging and the national character.

Gendered Interpretations

In the living history venues of the UK, Australia, and Japan male and female costumed interpreters were employed in roughly equal numbers, and in the US at Lincoln's New Salem, female interpreters outnumbered male interpreters by two to one (Table 11.3).[28] Despite the strong presence of women interpreters, however, the gender roles enacted in all four venues reflected both historical and contemporary gender binaries and hierarchies in each nation, with women positioned largely in domestic and subordinate positions, and men serving as public and authority figures.

At Sovereign Hill in Australia, for instance, all interpreters portraying people in authority—constables, gold commissioners, soldiers—were men. All of those engaged in skilled productive labor—furniture makers, wheelwrights, ironsmiths, confectioners, boilermakers—were men. By contrast, most of those engaged in low-skill or traditionally unpaid labor—mucking out stables, serving food, or selling the goods produced by men—were women, and

Table 11.3 Percentage of Male and Female Interpreters by Race at Living History Venues

Living History Venue	Majority Male	Majority Female	Minority Male	Minority Female
Lincoln's New Salem (US)	33	67	—	—
Black Country Living Museum (UK)	50	50	—	—
Sovereign Hill (AUS)	48	47	2	2*
Edo Wonderland (JAPAN)	55	45	—	—
TOTAL (N=119)	49%	49%	>1%	>1%

*Less than 100% due to rounding.

only women were positioned in domestic settings. Likewise, at Lincoln's New Salem, all of the male interpreters were shown in public roles such as shop-keepers, while two-thirds of the women were positioned in domestic roles. And in Edo Wonderland in Japan, most women played prostitute/entertainer roles while most men played samurai, ninja, and merchant roles.

It is hardly surprising that in these recreations of nineteenth-century Australia and the US and Edo Era Japan, few or no women were shown in positions of authority or public influence. Such portrayals no doubt fairly accurately reflect the roles and statuses of most women in those historical contexts. Rather, the concern is that the implied continuity between past and present, and the lack of any critical perspective, subtly naturalizes contemporary gender hierarchies. Additionally, at the Black Country Living Museum in the UK, only male interpreters engaged in the ironworking and mining activities that gave the region its name, although historical evidence suggests that by 1860 women constituted roughly half of all metalworkers in the region (Morgan 2001, 99). This case highlights the degree to which women's paid productive labor may be obscured by the gendered assumptions of "heritage" interpretation.

Furthermore, while all of the living history sites included named and recognizable male historical figures, few women were named or otherwise individuated. The most prominent female characters in any of the four venues were two women of ill repute. At Sovereign Hill the focus was on Lola Montez, an Irish immigrant who took a Spanish stage name and performed erotic dances for the wealthy men of gold rush Victoria (Anderson 2001). In a scheduled "reenactment," Montez struck a prominent businessman who publicly accused her of being a "harlot" with "loose morals and even looser undergarments." The skit had a humorous tone and concluded with Montez smiling warmly and inviting gentleman visitors to attend one of her performances.

At Edo Wonderland, the focus was on an unnamed *Oiran*, a high-class courtesan. In a play featuring the elaborately costumed *Oiran* and her female apprentices, a male volunteer from the audience was courted by the women. As with the Lola Montez performance, the tone was light, humorous, and slightly risqué. At the play's conclusion, audience members were invited to come up to the stage to have their photos taken with the *Oiran*, an opportunity to possess this desirable woman, at least in the form of a tourist snapshot.

In an atmosphere of playful fun, it is not surprising that there was no discussion in either venue of the dire economic and social circumstances that led (and continue to lead) women to work as erotic performers and prostitutes. Instead, the more palatable message was that these women were liberated and empowered, reveling in their own sexual commodification. Furthermore, it is worth noting that these women were the only fully individuated female characters in any of the venues examined. As such, they served as the representatives of all women in these significant periods in their respective nations' histories. Selecting sex workers to represent all women not only obscures the contributions that women merchants, artists, activists, and others made to their nations, but in a sense reduces all women to the subordinate role of gratifying male desire.

Again we must remember that unlike national museums, these living history sites are primarily constructed as sites of recreation and pleasure. Presenting any serious social critique or challenging visitors to rethink commonly accepted versions of national history could easily disappoint and alienate visitors. Because most living history sites are at least partially dependent on ticket revenues, and because many residents of these marginal locations depend on the sites for their livelihoods, this is a risk that many venues cannot afford to take.

Racialized Interpretations

The most striking thing about representations of race and ethnicity at the four living history venues analyzed was the near total absence of any discussion of the issue. It is of course not surprising that no ethnoracial minority interpreters were employed at sites representing the industrializing Black Country or Edo Era Japan, since there was little ethnoracial diversity in those historical contexts. Likewise, although interpretive materials at Lincoln's New Salem noted that Lincoln fought in the Black Hawk War and played a crucial role in the abolition of slavery in the US, there is no reason to expect Native American or African American interpreters to feature in the New Salem site itself if these groups were not present in the community in the 1830s. However, Australia's Victorian gold rush, like other similar strikes around the world, was a multinational, multiracial affair with fortune seekers from Britain, the US, Europe, India, China, and elsewhere coming into contact with each other and with the local indigenous peoples. We might expect to see some hint of such diversity in a living history venue devoted to the period.

In fact, Sovereign Hill is the only one of the living history sites analyzed here to employ any ethnoracial minority interpreters, two Asian-Australian interpreters dressed as Chinese goldfields workers. During my visits, the pair stayed primarily in the Chinese Village section of the site, reflecting the historical segregation on the goldfields. However, in a special tour dedicated to "Chinese on the Goldfields" it was a white male guide who spoke for this marginalized group. While he addressed the issue of anti-Chinese discrimination, he also suggested in seemingly unscripted remarks that the Chinese had taken more than their fair share of the gold. And when asked about the number of Chinese on the goldfields, he informed visitors that they accounted for "less than 5 percent" of workers, while in reality they constituted roughly 20 percent of the goldfields workforce.[29] Certainly visitors with an interest in Chinese immigrants could have found additional and more accurate information in the introductory galleries of the site and in the reconstructed Chinese Protector's Office. However, with the small number of Asian interpreters, their relegation to the Chinese section of the site, and the presentation of Chinese immigrant history from the perspective of a white male who downplayed and subtly denigrated their participation in the gold rush, the Chinese were pushed to the margins of this construction of the nation's history.

Even more conspicuously absent from the Sovereign Hill site were indigenous Australians. The gold rush made the local Wurrung peoples exiles in their own land. Miners depleted scarce natural resources, and brought pollution, disease, and virulent racism to the district. While the site celebrates the significance of the gold rush to Australia's nationhood, it offers no hint of the ways that this quest for riches tragically and permanently transformed the lives of indigenous peoples. Such silences serve as a reminder that as much as living history venues and museums are sites of national remembrance, they are also sites of calculated amnesia.

Personal Identities and National Identities

Observing tourists and interpreters at living history sites further serves as a reminder that national identities and personal identities are often closely intertwined. To visit an historical site in one's own nation is, in a sense, to worship at the altar of collective identity.[30] Carefully preserved near-sacred artefacts—an admiral's sword, a statesman's desk, the bed where a monarch once rested—remind us of the knowledge, history, and culture that we share with our fellow citizens. Even if our own forebears did not found the nation, even if we ourselves are recent arrivals, the mere fact that we recognize the significance of the site and take the time to visit it suggests a commitment to the values and goals of the nation.

In addition, with their emphasis on experiencing history firsthand, living history sites in a sense invite visitors to actively write themselves into the nation's historical narrative. At each venue, visitors were observed commenting on artefacts that were "Just like Gran's" or detailing distant family connections to the site. Inspired by cues in the physical environment, they shared family lore and personal reminiscences, but also reflected on their luck at having been born into the relative ease of the modern era. Their own aspirations and ideals were also evidenced in the admiration they expressed for the fortitude, integrity, and other celebrated traits of historical role models. In these ways among others, living history venues provide tourists with an opportunity to reaffirm their personal connection to the nation's history and the national collective.

Likewise, living history sites present costumed interpreters with an opportunity to reflect on their own place in history and their own place in the nation. This was clearest at the Black Country Living Museum where interpreters frequently added their own experiences, family stories, and opinions to their historical narratives. One interpreter described himself, with evident pride, as a "proper Black Country man." He offered explanations of the Black Country dialect and expressed disdain for the "city people" of nearby Birmingham. Black Country culture, he suggested, was older and more authentic than anything in the city.

Another interpreter focused on the economic hardships faced by the inhabitants of one of the site's 1850s cottages. He explained that life has always been hard for Black Country working-class families, and added that as a child his own family could not even afford to buy him shoes. Two women interpreters told stories of their grandmothers and great-grandmothers working to support their families by making bricks and nails, enduring seventeen-hour shifts of backbreaking labor. "Black Country women are a very tough lot," one interpreter observed, adding that she herself was a single mother who had always struggled to provide for her family.

These interpreters may have been in marginal social locations, as working-class people in a rust-belt region commonly derided, or simply ignored, by the nation at large. But through their participation in this living history site, they could claim a place for themselves in the story of the nation. Their personal narratives become part of the larger narrative of nation, at least as it was locally articulated.

CONCLUSION: CREATING THE NATION
THROUGH DISCOURSE AND PRACTICE

All of the museums and living history venues described here construct stories about their respective nations and people. They all construct discourses of national identity. In both quantitative and qualitative terms, these discourses are gendered and racialized in ways that both reflect and reinforce long-standing inequalities in these nations. And this holds true for the Olympic opening ceremonies, television advertisements, letters to the editor, newspaper articles, and travel brochures examined in this volume.

In the clearest-cut cases, women and ethnoracial minorities are dramatically outnumbered by majority men, who seem to speak for, stand for, and rule the nation by virtue of their naturalized authority. Up to 79 percent of all individuals featured in the national museums studied were men. A stunning 95 percent of all people named in the letters to the editor examined here were men. In Australian television advertisements, up to 84 percent of characters were from the white majority; of the Japanese ads, 94 percent featured ethnoracial majority characters. Ethnoracial majority individuals were featured in between 93 and 100 percent of domestic travel brochures in the four nations, while few or no ethnoracial minorities were featured. And almost 100 percent of living history interpreters at the four venues analyzed were from the nation's dominant ethnoracial group.

Even where women and ethnoracial minorities have a strong showing numerically, they are often represented in ways that minimize and derogate their contributions to the nation or otherwise position them as inferior Others. In the Olympic opening ceremonies examined here, majority men typically represented national agency and modernity, while women and ethnoracial Others were largely represented as passive and archaic. Likewise, while the international travel brochures analyzed featured a significant proportion of ethnoracial Others, they were frequently positioned as exoticized, eroticized, and infantilized objects of the tourist gaze. In Japanese television advertisements, while women slightly outnumbered men as carriers of national identity, they were consistently relegated to subordinate positions. And while the newspaper coverage examined here afforded vastly more attention to Jessica Lynch than to any of her male or nonwhite colleagues, that coverage ultimately reinforced the notion that women are weak, vulnerable, and in need of male protection.

Perhaps most striking in terms of representations of the national Other were the letters to the editor examined here. In post-9/11 letters concerning terrorism, Muslims were consistently portrayed as violent, fanatical, inhumane, or evil, while authors from the US, the UK, and Australia represented their own (Judeo-Christian) nations as rational, civilized, free, just, and tolerant.

This is more than merely an academic exercise in deconstruction. The representations described here, these gendered and racialized discourses of national identity, *matter*.

They matter, in part, because of their sheer ubiquity. Despite frequent charges in the US, Australia, and elsewhere that political correctness and national self-criticism have gone so far that majority men are now pitiably denigrated and disadvantaged, systematic analysis of text after text, venue after venue reveals the continued dominance of ethnoracial majority males in narratives of nation. Any phenomenon so pervasive is worthy of critical interrogation.

Such discourses of national identity matter because they seem so innocent, so innocuous, and commonsensical that we tend to accept and repeat them without much critical reflection. Seldom do we challenge the national worship of Founding Fathers, fallen soldiers, and other real and mythic figures. As we teach our children these gendered and racialized stories, we reaffirm the naturalized hierarchies on which they are based.

Gendered and racialized discourses of national identity matter because they shape the way we see ourselves, both as individuals and as nations, and the way we see others. Narratives of nation that celebrate heroic masculinity and passive femininity encourage us to adhere to such conservative gender norms. Narratives of nation that privilege the ethnoracial majority encourage members of the majority to see themselves as naturally superior. Those same narratives may even work their way into the psyches of minority peoples, leading them to doubt their own contributions to the nation or accept their own marginalization.

This has consequences not only for the happiness and material well-being of individuals, but for relations between nations. Discourses of national identity that reinforce the idea that certain groups are naturally superior, naturally stronger, smarter, more godly, more civilized, can blind us in our dealings with other nations. How much easier it is to wage war on those considered fundamentally different and inferior. How much simpler to refuse to engage in dialog, to compromise, to work as equals with those we have come to see as essentialized Others.

Finally, gendered and racialized discourses of national identity matter because narratives of nation that are disproportionately focused on majority males serve to obscure and trivialize the contributions that women and ethnoracial minorities have made to their nations. This makes it all the more difficult to imagine women and ethnoracial minorities as equal participants in the life of the nation, as builders and leaders of the nation, and all the more difficult for these groups to achieve true material parity.

Notes

1. In most of the scholarly literature of recent decades, "race" refers to certain physical markers (such as skin color) that a given society considers significant enough to distinguish one group of people from another, while "ethnicity" refers to cultural markers (such as language and religion) that are used to distinguish one group from another. In everyday usage, however, "race" and "ethnicity" are frequently conflated. To acknowledge this widespread coalescence of the concepts, throughout this volume I adopt the terms "ethnoracial minority" and "ethnoracial Other" to refer to those groups that are constructed as different from the dominant racial or ethnic group. I retain the term "racialization" to refer to the process of attributing ethnoracial identity to a group.

2. 572 items with "national identity" as a keyword were published between 1985 and 2005, compared with only fifty-five in the period of 1965 to 1984.

3. Most individuals have a nationality. However, we cannot say that individuals *have* a national identity in the way they have a nationality, for national identity consists of collectively constructed and shared discourses of belonging; it does not, and *cannot*, belong to any one individual or institution.

4. Anthony Smith (1991) similarly views national identities as cultural (rather than simply political) productions. He suggests that symbols of nation-ness are found in a variety of cultural forms, from coins to buildings, from fairy tales to clothing. I do not draw extensively on Smith's work, however, because of his emphasis on relatively cohesive ethnic communities (what he calls *ethnie*) as the foundation of national identities. To my mind, attributing national identities to such primordial bonds ignores the fact that most modern nations are characterized by ethnic syncretism, and that ethnic diversity itself features prominently in many contemporary narratives of nation.

5. See, for instance, Banet-Weiser (1999), Blom, Hagemann, and Hall (2000), Caine and Sluga (2000), Hagemann and Schiller-Springorum (2002), Kapferer (1996), Lake (1986, 2000), McClintock (1993), Moghadam (1994), Radcliffe (1999), Radhakrishnan (1992), Ranchod-Nilsson and Tetreault (2000), Richardson and Hofkosh (1996), Roach Pierson and Chaudhuri (1998), Ryan (2002), Webster (1998), Willis (1993), Wilson (2003), Yuval-Davis (1997), and Yuval-Davis and Anthias (1989).

6. Also see Sui (2005) for a discussion of constructions of diasporic Chinese identity in Central American and Panamanian beauty pageants.

7. Also see Gilroy (1987) on representations of black Britons.

8. While globalization has been defined in myriad and often contradictory ways in popular and academic discourses, I draw on Waters (1995) to conceptualize

globalization as the increasing interconnectedness of individuals and social bodies worldwide in the realms of the economy, politics, and culture. See also Featherstone (1990), Giddens (1990), Harvey (1989), Robertson (1990, 1992, 1995), and Smith (1990) for a fuller discussion of the dynamics of globalization.

9. See Hogan (2004). Also see Curtice (2006), discussed in Chapter 4 of this volume.

10. I draw insights primarily from Saussure (1959) and Barthes (1972) in the field of semiotics, from Weedon (1996) and Rabinow (1984a, 1984b) on Foucauldian theory, from Fairclough and Wodak (1997) and Wodak et al. (1999) on CDA, and from Goffman's (1979) content analysis of gender in advertisements. While I adopt the guiding principles of CDA, I do not adopt its techniques as a whole. In CDA spoken and written texts are analyzed in minute detail for certain formal characteristics including discursive strategies, argumentation schemes, metonymy, synecdoche, and deixis. My analysis employs some of these tools, but with more emphasis on the gestalt meanings of the texts. I also examine visual as well as verbal data.

NOTES TO CHAPTER 2

1. By the time transportation was ended in 1868, roughly 162,000 convicts had been transported to the Australian colonies. As Alan Frost (2003) has argued, however, another motive for establishing a British stronghold in the Asia-Pacific region was to protect lucrative trade routes.

2. As late as 1841, for instance, in the more isolated "Squatting Districts" of the Australian colonies almost 84 percent of the white population was male (Ward 1958, 94).

3. While Australia experienced several gold rushes, the largest of these, and the one discussed here, was in Victoria.

4. See the following for a comprehensive discussion of the effects of the gold rush: Bate (1988), Blainey (1978), Clark (1995), and McCalman, Cook, and Reeves (2001).

5. See especially Davison (2001), McCalman, Cook, and Reeves (2001), and McKenzie and Cooper (2001).

6. See Anderson (2001), Bertola (2001), Curthoys (2001), Goodman (2001), McCalman, Cook, and Reeves (2001), McKenzie and Cooper (2001), and Pickering (2001).

7. By 1855 seventeen thousand Chinese had arrived in Victoria alone (Curthoys 2001, 105).

8. Ward views the gold rush differently. He writes that "In politics and economics the golden decade was a watershed, but in the development of the national *mystique* it was not. If anything, it had the over-all effect of delaying the emergence into full consciousness of the national legend" (1958, 140).

9. Artists including Tom Roberts, Arthur Streeton, Walter Withers, Fred McCubbin, Charles Condor, and Jane Sutherland abandoned the conventions of English landscape painting to develop a distinctively Australian style. They were dubbed the Heidelberg School after Heidelberg, Victoria, outside of Melbourne where many of them gathered.

10. For a fuller discussion of white masculinity (and femininity) in late nineteenth-century Australia see Crotty (2001), Dixson (1976), Summers (1975), and White (1981).

11. While a 1967 referendum removed a Constitutional clause (section 51 xxvi) that gave states authority over Aboriginal affairs, in practice state and local governments have continued to exercise substantial power over indigenous peoples.
12. Public opinion on the issue was divided. However one of Freeman's most vocal critics, Arthur Tunstall, was dismissed from his position as head of the Australian Commonwealth Games Association due in part to his comments on the Freeman matter.
13. While more than two thousand Australian women served as nurses in World War I, twenty-five of them dying, and seven receiving military medals for courage under fire, they seldom feature in discussions of Australia's role in the conflict. The Anzac soldier is now an Australian icon; the women who kept him alive are not.
14. The British, Indian, and French troops who participated in the campaign and the Turkish forces against whom they fought also suffered heavy casualties. An estimated 21,255 British soldiers, 9,798 French soldiers, 1,358 Indian soldiers, and 86,692 Turkish soldiers lost their lives in the campaign. 2,701 New Zealand Anzacs were lost (Australian Department of Veteran Affairs 2007).
15. With time even veterans of controversial wars have been incorporated into the "Anzac legend."
16. As White (1988) points out, however, it is important not to overstate the increases in women's workforce participation during the war. Furthermore, his analysis suggests that while women were certainly encouraged to leave paid work after the war, relatively few did so. Rather, most working women were shifted from the "men's jobs" they had temporarily filled to lower paid "women's jobs."
17. Speech by PM John Curtin in the British House of Commons, April 1944.
18. Rower Ned Trickett won Australia's first individual world title in 1876, and Australia defeated Britain in test cricket in 1877. Phar Lap remains a significant national icon, and his famously oversized heart now resides in the National Museum of Australia.
19. The Australian Post Office altered its Stamp Issue Policy in 1996 to allow for the portrayal of non-royal living persons on postage stamps. The only living persons allowed on stamps under the previous policy were members of the royal family.
20. See, for instance, Jupp (1966) and Martin (1972, 1978).
21. In a revised draft Preamble, the phrase was changed to ". . . honouring Aborigines and Torres Strait Islanders, the nation's first people, for their deep kinship with their lands and for their ancient and continuing cultures which enrich the life of our country," wording which still retains the us/them dichotomy.
22. The Australian Broadcasting Corporation, hereafter abbreviated ABC. The ABC is a state-owned but statutorily independent broadcaster. See ABC (1999a, 1999b, 1999c, 1999d, 1999e, 1999f, 1999g).
23. The image of a "sunburnt country," taken from Dorothea Mackeller's 1904 poem *My Country*, often features in contemporary discourses of national identity.
24. See, for instance, the Barton Lectures by Donald Horne (2001), Mary Kalantzis (2001), Lois Bryson (2001), and Elaine Thompson (2001), broadcast nationally on ABC Radio National.
25. Critics quickly pointed out haunting similarities with Hitler's "Final Solution," his plan to rid German territories of Jews through whatever means necessary.
26. The Australia Day Council reports to the Department of Prime Minister and Cabinet.

NOTES TO CHAPTER 3

1. Throughout this volume I use the revised Hepburn system for transliterating Japanese script. Long vowels are indicated by macrons (*ō*, *ū*) or doubling (*ii*). Japanese words that have entered the English language are written without long vowels indicated and without italics, as in "Tokyo" and "geisha." Consistent with Japanese cultural practice, Japanese surnames appear before personal names. Where an individual author or public figure has adopted Western name order or non-Hepburn spelling, their choices have been retained.

2. The Japanese historical eras are as follows:

Jomon Period	Circa 13,000 BC–300 BC
Yayoi Period	Circa 300 BC–AD 300
Kofun Period	Circa AD 300–AD 600
Asuka Period	Circa 600–710
Nara Period	710–784
Heian Period	794–1185
Kamakura Period	1185–1333
Period of North and South Courts	1336–1392
Muromachi Period	1392–1573
Warring States Period	1477–1573
Edo (Tokugawa) Period	1600–1867
Meiji Period	1868–1912
Taishō Period	1912–1926
Shōwa Period	1926–1989
Heisei Period	1989–present

3. The Yamato rulers established a complex system of laws and administrative procedures that came to be known as the *ritsyryō* state.

4. Influence from the West came first from the Portuguese in the sixteenth and seventeenth centuries (the so-called *Namban Kagaku* period), then from the Dutch in the eighteenth and nineteenth centuries (the *Rangaku* period), and then from the US and Western Europe in the Meiji Era when it became an urgent priority to learn from the West (*Yōgaku*) in order to resist Western imperialism.

5. It should be noted, however, that some scholars declared Yoshida Kenkō, a male author, to be the greatest writer of the genre (Chance 2000).

6. *Bushidō: The Soul of Japan* by Nitobe Inazō (1900) played an important role in popularizing this idea. Although the book, first published in English, was clearly addressed to a Western audience, it was also later published in Japanese and no doubt contributed to Japanese notions of national distinctiveness. See cogent critiques of the text by Hurst (1990) and Friday (1994).

7. The rule of "alternate attendance" (*sankin kōtai*) increased the power of the Shogun. It removed the regional lords from their lands for long periods of time, undermining their authority there, and forced them to spend large sums traveling to court and maintaining multiple households.

8. For a cogent critique of this view, see Dale's (1986) *The Myth of Japanese Uniqueness*.

9. The term Motoori used and contemporary commentators still claim as a unique Japanese trait, is *mono no aware*, the pathos of things, a profound appreciation for the natural world and for natural human experiences and emotions.

10. Perhaps most prominently, Watsuji Tetsurō, writing in the interwar period, asserted that all human societies are shaped by their natural environments: desert peoples are hostile and aggressive due to their inhospitable environment; grassland peoples, accustomed to regular seasons and moderate conditions, are rational and orderly; and the peoples of monsoon climates are

tolerant and easygoing. Japan, on the other hand, with its diverse topography and varied climates, has produced a people with a deep reverence for the natural world and flexible and empathetic human relations (Morris-Suzuki 1998, 56–59). See also Ohnuki-Tierney's (1993) discussion of such arguments.

11. Shinto is Japan's indigenous animistic religion. Shinto, Buddhism (which came via India, China, and Korea), and Confucianism (from China), coexist in Japan today. For a detailed discussion of Meiji imperial mythmaking, see Gluck (1985).

12. For a more detailed discussion of Japanese wedding practices past and present, see Edwards (1989) and Goldstein-Gidoni (1997).

13. For an overview of the *ie* family structure, see Hamabata (1990) and Ueno (1996).

14. Today, while the term *minzoku* (ethnicity) is usually used to refer to the Japanese, and the term *jinshu* (race) is more commonly applied to non-Japanese, there is considerable conceptual slippage between the two, as, in fact, there is between the English terms. *Minzoku* consists of the character for "people" or "nation" and the character meaning "family" or "tribe." *Jinshu* is comprised of the character for "person" and the character for "kind," "type," or "species." Both terms suggest that there are essential cultural and biological differences between the Japanese and their contextually defined Others. See Morris-Suzuki's discussion of these terms (1998, 87).

15. The Nara Era texts explain that the Sun Goddess sent her grandson to earth with the gift of rice, and he married the tree blossom deity (*Konohana-no-sakuya-hime*). Thus, both rice and cherry blossoms are strong symbols of nation (Ohnuki-Tierney 2002, 27–28).

16. Ohnuki-Tierney (2002) demonstrates that while the state cultivated the ideology of noble and beautiful self-sacrifice for the emperor, many military conscripts did not embrace these ideas.

17. Recent scholarship suggests that many Okinawans did not voluntarily take their own lives, but were coerced by the Japanese army into killing themselves and their family members. See Taira (1999, 39–49) and Field (1991, 67).

18. See, for instance, the 1995 film *Himeyuri no Tou* which valorizes the honorable suicides of a group of Okinawa school girls.

19. Although the exact numbers are difficult to calculate due to incomplete records and the long-term effects of radiation exposure, the number of deaths is usually estimated in excess of two hundred thousand.

20. See, for instance, Harvey's (1995) discussion of the popular television drama *Oshin*.

21. For a detailed discussion of wartime propaganda in Japan and the US, see Nornes and Fukushima (1994).

22. See Befu (1983), Hook and Weiner (1992), Itoh (1998), Kato (1992), and Mannari and Befu (1983).

23. Sugimoto (2003, 183–211) provides a succinct overview of these changes and continuing challenges faced by these groups. While the *Burakumin*, an outcaste group with origins in Japan's feudal system, are not racially distinct from majority Japanese, they are discriminated against on the basis of ancestry.

24. Among the many excellent volumes on Japanese gender relations are Allison (1994), Bernstein (1991), Brinton (1993), Buckley (1997), Fujimura-Fanselow and Kameda (1995), Imamura (1996), Iwao (1993), Kondo (1990), Martinez (1998), Morris-Suzuki (1998), Sievers (1983), and Skov and Moeran (1995).

25. There was a short-lived retreat from the *ryōsai kenbo* ideology in the Taishō Era when the "modern girl" (*moga*) was associated with progressiveness, but as noted earlier, she became a symbol of unpatriotic Western-style decadence in the conservative period leading up to and including World War II.

26. See Creighton (1992, 2001), Ivy (1995), and Robertson (1987).
27. One prominent example is Tsunoda Tadanabu's (1978) best seller *Nihonjin no nō* (*The Japanese Brain*), translated into English in 1985 as *The Japanese Brain: Uniqueness and Universality*.
28. The common term for this intuitive nonverbal communication is *haragei* (belly art). See Dale (1986, 101) for a discussion of the notion of Japanese "silent" communication.
29. See Iida's (2002, 244–258) perceptive discussion of historical revisionism in 1990s Japan.
30. The term commonly employed here is *tan'itsu minzoku*, a "monoracial people" (Hogan 2002).
31. Based on in-depth interviews conducted in rural Japan, 1997–1998. See Hogan (2002).
32. There are relevant discussions, however, in Chance (2000), Morris-Suzuki (1998, 110–139), Mostow (2000), and Suzuki (2000).

NOTES TO CHAPTER 4

1. The complex history of the national nomenclature makes it difficult to definitively state just when "Britain" was born. England annexed Wales between 1534 and 1542, and unified with Scotland in 1707 (creating the United Kingdom of Great Britain). With the unification of Great Britain and Ireland in 1801, the nation became the United Kingdom of Great Britain and Ireland. After the creation of the Irish Free State in 1921, the name was changed again to the United Kingdom of Great Britain and Northern Ireland (Colls 2002, 34). Technically, then, the term "British" does not include Northern Ireland. Both for this semantic reason and for more pressing historical and cultural reasons, I do not discuss Northern Ireland in any detail here.
2. The Romans considered northern England and Scotland (which they called Caledonia) and Ireland (which they called Hibernia) to be separate from Britannia.
3. Because John Bull is a specifically English archetype, rather than a symbol of Britain as a whole, I do not discuss him further here, but refer the reader to Hunt's (2003) *Defining John Bull*. See also MacDonald's (1987) discussion of Boadicea. Representations of this Celtic "warrior queen" overlap in places with representations of Britannia.
4. Arthur appears in the semifictional history *Historia Brittonum* (circa 829) and Robin Hood appears in *Piers Plowman* (with early versions circa 1362). Some scholars consider the earliest written appearance of Arthur to be the circa AD 600 Welsh poem, the *Gododdin*, while others suggest that references to Arthur were added at a later date. For an overview of the Arthur and Robin Hood legends over time, see Barczewski (2000). For additional overviews of the Robin Hood legend, see Blamires (1998) and Knight (1999).
5. For a detailed discussion of Arthur, see Barczewski's highly focused and carefully documented work *Myth and National Identity in Nineteenth-Century Britain: The Legends of King Arthur and Robin Hood* (2000).
6. In the twelfth century, the inventive historian Geoffrey of Monmouth even suggested that Arthur was of Norman descent (Barczewski 2000, 16–18).
7. At the same time, some critics of imperialism pointed out that Arthur's own forays abroad, his quest for the Holy Grail, left Camelot in ruins (Barczewski 2000, 28–31).
8. See especially Barczewski (2000, 11–12, 40–44, 73–80, 225–230).

9. See especially Barczewski (2000, 162–200). Of course, these representations vary considerably over time. Morgan, in particular, is more positively portrayed as a healer of fairy ("fay") origins in early tales and in recent feminist retellings. For a feminist reinterpretation of the Arthurian legend, see Marion Zimmer-Bradley's (1983) novel *The Mists of Avalon*.

10. According to early Roman writers, Boadicea was a Celtic leader who led a rebellion against the Romans in AD 60. Enraged by years of brutal Roman rule and the rape of her two daughters by Roman soldiers, this "warrior queen" is said to have led one hundred thousand Britons to victory over their occupiers.

11. Such representations resonate with the notion of the "Norman Yoke." In this interpretation of British history, before the Norman Conquest the English lived under a protodemocratic system which granted them significant liberties and protections; however when the Normans arrived these rights and institutions were lost.

12. Major conflicts between the two occurred 1689–1697, 1702–1713, 1743–1748, 1756–1763, 1778–1783, 1793–1802, and 1803–1815. Even when fighting ceased temporarily, the threat of war loomed large in the national consciousness (Colley 1992, 1).

13. As a measure of tensions between these peoples, a popular eighteenth-century children's game known as "English and Scotch" pitted teams against each other in a winner-takes-all tug-of-war (Colley 1992, 117).

14. See Colley (1992, 252) and Hunt (2003, 121–169). For a perceptive discussion of the use of gendered national imagery in wartime propaganda, see Nelson (2002).

15. This model is drawn from Friederich Engels' (1884) *The Origins of the Family, Private Property, and the State*.

16. For a brief overview of the complex international economics of slavery see Hobsbawm (1975, 178–189).

17. In the lead-up to the bicentenary of the 1807 Slave Trade Act, for instance, the British government allocated in excess of 16 million pounds to programs designed to promote an understanding of "the trans-Atlantic slave trade and its impact on national heritage" (Department for Culture, Media and Sport 2006).

18. While Kipling directed "The White Man's Burden" to Washington to urge the US to take on the responsibility of imperial rule, his model was clearly the British Empire.

19. Especially Gilbert and Sullivan's *The Mikado* (1885), Conan Doyle's *The Sign of Four* (1890), Conrad's *An Outpost of Progress* (1896) and *Heart of Darkness* (1899). See Wilson (2003) and Rutherford (1997) for a fuller discussion of race, gender, and the British Empire.

20. As Wilson (2003, 17) points out, it is ironic that the Irish and Scots, Britain's internal Others, migrated in such large numbers to the colonies, and thus served as global representatives of the British Empire and Britishness.

21. Harrison (1984, 356). See also Funck (2002) for a discussion of similar class dynamics in the Prusso-German officer corps.

22. See Rutherford's (1997) discussion of British masculinity and Kienitz's (2002) discussion of masculinity in Weimar Germany.

23. As Davis (1979, 31) has argued, such nostalgia is "deeply implicated in the sense of who we are, what we are about, and . . . whither we go. In short, nostalgia is one of the means . . . we employ in the never ending work of constructing, maintaining and reconstructing our identities."

24. Morton (1928: 163, 137, 98, 237).

25. For a discussion of the ways British women authors represented Englishness during this period, see Light (1991).
26. Thomas Dibdin referred to Britain as a "snug little island" in "Tight Little Island," a song from his 1797–1798 play, *The British Taft*.
27. Where historians differ in their estimates of the dead and wounded, I have used the more conservative estimates.
28. Likewise in 1588 when storms had helped the English navy defeat the Spanish Armada, Britons viewed this as evidence of divine sanction for their nation's Protestant mission. A commemorative English medal of the time proclaimed "God blew and they were scattered."
29. While the war helped reduce some internal differences, the Irish were still commonly discriminated against well into the postwar period.
30. Harrison (1984, 388) notes that the percentage of married women engaged in paid labor increased from 10 percent in 1931 to 22 percent in 1951. He stresses that increased workforce participation combined with easier access to reliable contraception and an easing of divorce law after the war improved the position of women.
31. For a detailed discussion of *Windrush*, see Phillips and Phillips (1998).
32. Cricket was pronounced the "national game" by *Badminton Magazine* in 1888, and was the first English sport to institute national rules, regulations, and governing bodies (Colls 2002, 122).
33. As a young man, Powell had been a passionate defender of the British Empire, as he took up positions in Australia, Northern Africa, and India. When India moved toward independence, a goal achieved in 1947, Powell entered British politics resolved to help save the Empire. But as Britain's imperial power waned, Powell redirected his energies to defending England and the English race from what he perceived as the corrosive effects of nonwhite immigration.
34. See Alibhai-Brown's incisive discussion of Thatcher and Thatcherism (2000).
35. From the *Sunday Telegraph*, 23 May 1982 and 27 June 1982, cited in Gilroy (1987, 51–52).
36. See especially Hewison (1987).
37. See also Johnson (1996) for the discussion of an exceptional case in which a private heritage site introduced social critique into their tours, eliciting mixed responses from tourists.
38. Patrick Jenkin, serving as Thatcher's Secretary of State for Social Services, suggested in 1979 that working women return to their unpaid domestic duties to free up jobs for unemployed men. Moreover, he implied that the government's position was divinely sanctioned when he stated, "Quite frankly I don't think that mothers have the same right to work as fathers do. If the Good Lord had intended us to have equal rights to go out to work, he wouldn't have created man and woman. These are biological facts" (quoted in Douglas 1990, 413). Although Thatcher's government promoted a highly conservative gender ideology, specific legislative acts often did have a positive impact on women's family and employment rights. See Douglas (1990) and Bashevkin (1994).
39. Opponents suggested that the Act was designed to prevent large numbers of Hong Kong–born ethnic Chinese from migrating to Britain before Hong Kong was turned over to the Chinese in 1997.
40. Although Labour won a record-setting 419 seats, it should be noted that the voter turnout was relatively low by British standards, at 71 percent.
41. Address to a joint session of Congress, 20 September 2001, United States Capitol, Washington, DC. Transcript available at www.whitehouse.gov/news/releases/2001/09/20010920-8.html.
42. The controversy over Britain's role in the invasion and occupation of Iraq was undoubtedly one of the factors that led to Blair's resignation in 2007.

43. In a 7 January 2003 address to British ambassadors in London, he noted, "The price of British influence is not, as some would have it, that we have obediently to do what the US asks. The price of influence is that we do not leave the US to face the tricky issues alone," quoted in Coates and Krieger (2004, 52).
44. Blair characterized the war on terror as a battle between the "civilized world and fanaticism" in a 2001 interview with CNN, quoted in Coates and Krieger (2004: 45).
45. Billig et al. (2006b) note the following Islamophobic headline from the 2005 campaign: "Muslim Loonies Hijack Election: Fundamentalists Won't Stop Until UK is an Islamic State," (the *Star*, 21 April 2005).

NOTES TO CHAPTER 5

1. According to Huntington, this Anglo-Protestant culture is characterized by "the English language; Christianity; religious commitment; English concepts of the rule of law, the responsibility of rulers, and the rights of individuals; and dissenting Protestant values of individualism, the work ethic, and the belief that humans have the ability and the duty to try to create a heaven on earth . . ." (2004, xvi).
2. For extensive consideration of the role of the frontier in the American national imaginary, see Frederick Jackson Turner's classic *The Frontier in American History*, along with critical extensions of this work by Potter (1954) and Slotkin (1973 and 1992).
3. Daniel Boone (1734–1820), Davy Crockett (1786–1836), General George Armstrong Custer (1839–1876), Jesse James (1847–1882), "Buffalo Bill" Cody (1846–1917), and John Wayne (1907–1979).
4. See, for instance, Faludi's (2007a, 255–262) brief but compelling dissection of the Daniel Boone story, and Slotkin's (1992) discussion of Crockett, Custer, James, and Cody.
5. From Roosevelt's *The Winning of the West*, quoted in Slotkin (1992, 49).
6. See Colley (2002, 137–238). Colley notes, however, that prior to the Revolutionary period, most settlers still identified more strongly as Britons than Americans.
7. Writing in more general terms, Peterson (1996, 7) has observed that because nations are ordered by patriarchy, "The land's fecundity, upon which the people depend, must be protected by defending the body/nation's boundaries against invasion and violation by foreign males. . . . The rape of the body/nation not only violates frontiers but disrupts—by planting alien seed or destroying reproductive viability—the maintenance of the community through time."
8. See especially Slotkin (1992) and Colley (2002).
9. Bellesiles (2000) argued that America's so-called "gun culture" did not develop out of the frontier experience, but rather emerged only after the Civil War when American-made firearms were mass marketed. His book provoked great controversy, and was criticized for its methodology. Leaving aside the issue of the accuracy of its claims, the heated debate over the book demonstrated how central notions of judicious violence are to discourses of American national identity.
10. While there are earlier representations of Uncle Sam, James Montgomery Flagg's rendering has become the most recognizable incarnation of the icon. The image first appeared on a magazine cover in 1916, and was widely circulated as a poster in 1917–1918. (Available http://www.loc.gov/exhibits/treasures/trm015.html. Accessed 14 January 2008.)

11. For a full discussion of the theme of "plenty" in American national discourses, see Potter (1954).
12. From "America the Beautiful" by Katharine Lee Bates (1911).
13. According to Weber's "Protestant Ethic" thesis, American economic success is explained in part by the Protestant emphasis on hard work and moderation which encouraged Protestant Americans first to produce surplus, and then, rather than spend the surplus on luxuries, to reinvest it in the means of production.
14. For instance, in his two Presidential campaigns, George W. Bush, adopted a folksy Southern persona while downplaying his Connecticut birth and elite East Coast education.
15. For a cogent discussion of the ways media constructions of the "American dream" are implicated in continuing racial inequality, see Jhally and Lewis (1992).
16. For a fuller discussion of the significance of the car in American popular culture, see Dettelbach (1976).
17. Thomas Jefferson referred to such a "wall of separation" in a letter to the Danbury Baptist Association in 1802. See Jacoby's (2004) meticulously documented work on secularism in America.
18. Israel Zangwill, *The Melting Pot*, act I, scene 33.
19. As Zangwill's musings on French*men*, English*men*, and so on suggest, the generic immigrant was implicitly male.
20. The struggles and contributions of gays and lesbians have not, for the most part, been acknowledged yet.
21. See also Faludi (1991).
22. While the term "nanny state" originated in the UK, in the US it has been widely used by those critical of state programs perceived as coddling and overly protective. See Sawer (1996).
23. See Faludi's (2007a, 46–64) discussion of what she calls "The Return of Superman."
24. Specifically, "French fries" became "freedom fries" and "French toast" was transformed into "freedom toast."
25. See especially the numerous vitriolic criticisms of antiwar protester Cindy Sheehan by Rush Limbaugh and Ann Coulter; the boycott against The Dixie Chicks for anti-Bush remarks; the dismissal of Professor Ward Churchill from the University of Colorado after he suggested that many of those who died in the World Trade Center were complicit in US policies that created violence and inequality elsewhere in the world; and David Horowitz's (2006) polemic *The Professors: The 101 Most Dangerous Academics in America*.
26. See especially the web sites of recent anti-immigration and vigilante border control groups including The Minuteman Project, Wake up America, Unite to Fight, and Operation Sovereignty. The inflammatory language quoted here was taken from www.minutemanproject.com and http://stopspp.com/stopspp.
27. From *The New Colossus*, the 1883 poem by Emma Lazarus, excerpted on the Statue of Liberty.

NOTES TO CHAPTER 6

1. An earlier version of this chapter appeared in the *Journal of Sport and Social Issues* 27, no. 2: 100–123. Used here with permission.
2. See especially Brohm (1978), Bryson (1987), Hargreaves (1982), and Tomlinson and Whannel (1984).

3. All dollar amounts are in US$, calculated at an exchange rate of .57 US$ to the Australian dollar. Sources: Toohey and Veal (2000) and http://www.olympics. org/uk/organisation/facts/report/index_uk.asp (accessed 2 June 2004).

4. www.olympics.org/uk/organisation/facts/revenue/broadcast_uk.asp (accessed 2 June 2004).

5. Perhaps because the IOC is drawing on the rhetoric of human rights, this is one of the few places in the Charter where gender-inclusive language is used. In its introduction to the Charter the IOC states, "In the Olympic Charter, the masculine gender used in relation to any physical person . . . shall, unless there is a specific provision to the contrary, be understood as including the feminine gender" (IOC 2001, 7).

6. See discussion in Chapter 3 of this volume.

7. See Chapter 2 of this volume.

8. Throughout this volume, the Bush administration's term "war on terror" is used because of its currency in national discourses. However, this is a contentious and in many ways unsatisfactory term for the diverse range of policies and practices advocated by the administration.

9. See discussion in Chapter 3 of this volume.

10. Of Japan's 128 million people, the largest ethnic minority groups include roughly 1.6 million ethnic Okinawans (the *Ryūkyū*), more than one million ethnic Koreans, over 200,000 ethnic Chinese, more than 24,000 *Ainu* and an estimated three million *Burakumin*; in addition, approximately 700,000 migrant workers mostly from East and Southeast Asia, the Middle East, and South America reside in Japan today.

11. See Hogan (2002), Sodei (1995), the Japanese Ministry of Education (2001), and The *Buraku* Liberation and Human Rights Research Institute (2001).

12. See discussion in Chapter 2 of this volume.

13. There are many fine works on Ned Kelly and the Kelly gang. Peter Carey's (2000) treatment of the topic in the form of an historical novel provides a compelling introduction to this important Australian archetype.

14. There was at least one female officer visible as the World Trade Center flag was paraded around the stadium; and the police officer who sang *God Bless America* was of Hispanic descent.

15. See Chapters 8 and 9 in this volume.

NOTES TO CHAPTER 7

1. Parts of this chapter previously appeared as Hogan, "Gender, Ethnicity and National Identity in Australian and Japanese Television Advertisements," *National Identities* 7, no. 2 (January 2005): 193–211. Reprinted by permission of Taylor & Francis Ltd., http://www.tandf.co.uk/journals.

2. See, for instance, Ewen (1976), Marchand (1985), McClintock (1995), and Williamson (1978).

3. See Kilbourne (1999).

4. With the spread of cable and satellite television, this is changing. However, this sample of advertisements was taken only from free-to-air stations.

5. These were WIN TV (8:00 AM to midnight on 1 October 1996) and Southern Cross Television (8:00 AM to midnight on 23 January 1997) in Australia; and HBC (8:00 AM to midnight on 20 April 1995) and STV (8:00 AM to midnight on 13 July 1995) in Japan.

6. For the purpose of this analysis, "foregrounded" characters are characters which feature prominently. Therefore, advertisements showing only crowd scenes with no prominent characters were excluded.

7. Names of the communities and individuals involved in the study have been changed to protect the anonymity of research participants. To be consistent with both cultural practice and my fieldwork practice, I refer to Australian participants by first names and Japanese participants by surnames. All Japanese men are given the title Mr. and all women the title Ms. regardless of social or marital status, a practice which most closely resembles the Japanese use of *san*.

8. Sources: *Asahi Shimbun* (1996); Australian Bureau of Statistics, hereafter abbreviated ABS (2000a, 2000b, 2000c, 1999a); and Japanese Statistics Bureau (1998, 2001).

9. Sources: ABS (2000b, 1998) and town council publications from the communities studied. In order to protect the anonymity of participants, I do not provide a list of these community documents.

10. Plainsview figures have been aggregated for comparison with Hirogawa aggregate categories.

11. The Australian sample includes several migrants from the United Kingdom and New Zealand, one migrant from Southern Europe, and several Australian-born descendants of European migrants. All Japanese participants were ethnically Japanese.

12. Appeals to National Identity in Australian and Japanese Advertisements

	Images of the Environment	Images of Leisure Activities	Images of Material and Symbolic Culture	Images of Social Relations and Social Ethics	Total
Representations of Australian national identity (n=148)*	18%	34%	22%	26%	100%
Representations of Japanese national identity (n=215)	6%	19%	35%	40%	100%

*Advertisements frequently use more than one kind of appeal to national identity. Advertisements were first coded for the kinds of appeals they utilized. Then all instances of each coding category (environment, leisure, and so on) were tallied. Out of 185 Japanese advertisements, there were 215 appeals to national identity. Out of 114 Australian advertisements, there were 148 appeals to national identity.

13. See discussion in Chapter 2 of this volume, and in Bennett et al. (1992), Kapferer (1996), Summers (1975), Turner (1994), White (1981), and Willis (1993).

14. See discussion in Chapter 3 of this volume, and in Befu (1983), Dale (1986), Denoon et al. (1996), Mouer and Sugimoto (1983, 1986), Weiner (1995, 1997a, 1997b), and Yoshino (1992).

15. The "carrier" is defined as the main locus of discourses of national identity in the advertisement: for instance, the person situated in an iconic geographical setting; the person involved in distinctive leisure activities; the historical figure; the person practicing traditional arts or occupations; the person wearing a distinctive national costume or using distinctive linguistic forms; the person associated with selected artefacts, such as the national flag; or the person who engages in particular social relations or enacts certain social ethics.

Gender of Carriers of National Identity in Australian and Japanese
Advertisements

	Male Only	*Female Only*	*Both Male and Female*	*Total*
Carrier of Australianness (n=114)	38%	19%	43%	100%
Carrier of Japaneseness (n=185)	33%	38%	29%	100%

There is also a conspicuous difference between the Australian and Japanese
data in the number of advertisements in which national identity is carried
by both male and female characters. The much smaller number of Japanese
advertisements in which both men and women are carriers of national identity
is consistent with the more highly differentiated (homosocial) realms of males
and females in Japan.

16. See Dixson (1976), Magarey, Rowley, and Sheridan (1993), Pettman (1988),
Summers (1975), and Willis (1993).

17. See Chapters 2 and 3 in this volume, as well as Befu (1983), Dale (1986),
Denoon et al. (1996), Hage (1998), Mouer and Sugimoto (1983, 1986), Weiner
(1995, 1997a, 1997b), and Yoshino (1992).

18. Representations of Ethnoracial Others in Australian and Japanese
Advertisements

	Everyday Work, Domestic, or Leisure Settings	*Celebrities or Entertainers*	*Professional Athletes*	*Low-Status Providers of Goods and Services*	*Ethnic Others in Foreign Settings*	*Recipients of Charity*	*Other*	*Total*
Australian advertisements with ethnic Others (n=48)	17%	27%	21%	15%	2%	8%	10%	100%
Japanese advertisements with ethnic Others (n=79)	18%	24%	10%	9%	24%	—	15%	100%

In the Australian advertisements, most ethnoracial Others are Asian or aboriginal characters. In the Japanese advertisements, most ethnoracial Others are
white; however, black, South American, and non-Japanese Asian characters
also appear in some advertisements.

19. The Australian focus groups were held in Tasmania between March and June
of 1998, and the Japanese focus groups were held in Hokkaido between
December of 1997 and February of 1998.

20. Ad Types Screened in Focus Groups

Nostalgic-serious	Advertisements with predominantly traditional and sentimental imagery used to evoke the cherished ways of life in days gone by.
Nostalgic-humorous	Advertisements with traditional or historical images used for humorous effect.

Humorous mixture of old and new	Advertisements which combine traditional and contemporary images for humorous effect.
Changing social roles	Advertisements in which characters step outside the customary social roles for individuals of their gender, age, ethnicity, or occupational status.
Contemporary leisure	Advertisements in which characters are engaged in contemporary leisure pursuits.
Multiculturalism or internationalization	Advertisements which feature ethnoracial Others and/or evoke the contemporary ethics of Australian multiculturalism or Japanese internationalization.
Neutral	Advertisements which do not contain any discernible images of Australianness or Japaneseness.

21. I make no claims regarding the statistical significance of the differences between the scores. Rather, the numbers are presented here as a rough ranking of the Australianness and Japaneseness of the advertisements as perceived by participants.
22. Perceptions of the Australianness and Japaneseness of the advertisements varied little with the age, sex, and occupation of the participants. The table here illustrates the similarity of perceptions of Australianness and Japaneseness for top-ranked and bottom-ranked advertisements among participants of different ages, sexes, and occupations. These similarities are consistent across all the advertisements in the sample.

	Mean Score of Least Australian Advertisement	*Mean Score of Most Australian Advertisement*	*Mean Score of Least Japanese Advertisement*	*Mean Score of Most Japanese Advertisement*
All participants	1.55	4.57	2.14	4.63
14–55 years	1.39	4.47	2.13	4.63
55+ years	2.15	4.78	2.18	4.61
Female	1.83	4.57	2.27	4.68
Male	1.20	4.60	2.07	4.60
Student	1.55	4.55	2.12	4.88
Teacher*	—	—	2.00	4.54
Public Servant	1.22	4.56	1.90	4.75
Private Sector Employee	1.20	4.40	2.56	4.66
Business Owner	1.00	4.63	2.09	4.45
Farmer	1.65	4.59	2.26	4.42
Retiree	1.58	4.70	2.33	4.66

*Data for Australian teachers are unavailable because, due to scheduling complications, in-depth interviews rather than focus groups were conducted with Australian teachers.

23. "Ocker" is a term for an unsophisticated, boorish, usually working-class Australian. The term is more often applied to men. A "singlet" is a sleeveless undershirt.

24. As a measure of Tasmania's marginality within the nation, there are widely circulating jokes about two-headed Tasmanians, people so insular, backward, and inbred that they have genetically mutated. The cliché has been embraced by the makers of tourist souvenirs who market a full range of products featuring images of two-headed mutant humans.

25. This acknowledgement of the negative side of the presumed national character itself reflects a cultural emphasis on modesty.

26. *Oshin* was a 1983 NHK minidrama series that set records for viewership in Japan. The title character was a poor farm girl who was sold into servitude and endured a life of hardship and cruelty; however, she persevered and eventually became a successful business owner. The minidrama (with daily fifteen-minute episodes) was eventually telecast to more than fifty countries worldwide. See Harvey (1995) for a discussion of the *Oshin* phenomenon.

NOTES TO CHAPTER 8

1. Parts of this chapter previously appeared in *Mass Communication & Society* 9, no. 1: 63–83. Used here with permission.

2. Throughout this chapter, the Bush administration's term "war on terror" is used due to its prominence in public discourses. However, it should be noted that the term "war" does not strictly refer to military actions, and the term "terror" is highly contested and politicized.

3. See the Runnymede Trust (1997) and Karim (1997).

4. *The New York Times*, for example, prints only about 3 percent of the letters it receives (Page 1996, 20).

5. Hill (1981, 391) has argued that letters addressing pivotal social issues (the Equal Rights Amendment in his research) more accurately represent actual patterns of public opinion than letters on less prominent issues, because pivotal issues elicit a larger number of letters, making it necessary for editors to engage in "representative sampling of opinions." For a more extensive discussion of the nature of letters to the editor, see Brown (1976), Ghadessy (1983), Hogan (2006), Morrison and Love (1996), Page (1996), Richardson (2001), and Sotillo and Starace-Nastasi (1999).

6. In the letters to the editor examined here, as in much public discourse in these three nations, the terms Muslim, Arab, and Middle Eastern are often used more or less interchangeably. While I acknowledge significant differences between these categories, I adopt the categories used by the letter writers themselves. Thus, I generally employ the term Muslim/Arab to refer to all those judged by letter writers to be Muslim or of Arab or Middle Eastern descent.

7. *The New York Times* is a New York Times Company Daily, while *The Times* of London and *The Australian* are both News Corporation (Rupert Murdoch) dailies. Previous analysis of this content (Hogan 2006) found the greatest differences between the two News Corporation broadsheets, indicating that the inclusion of two Murdoch papers has not introduced a sampling bias.

8. Such groups, he asserted, had separated the nation from God, leading to the withdrawal of a divine "veil of protection." Falwell made his comments on the 13 September 2001 telecast of the Christian Broadcasting Network's *The 700 Club*.

9. See Said (1978, 1981, 1993). Historian Linda Colley (2002, 99–134) argues, however, that British Islamophobia was not always racialized, and that prior to the 1750s Britons often expressed admiration for the Muslim science and civilization.

10. See discussion of Said's work in Chapter 1 of this volume.

11. The gender of the letter writer cannot be determined in this case.
12. See also and Bernard Lewis' (2002) *What Went Wrong? Western Impact and Middle Eastern Response*, and Said's (2002) critique of such arguments.
13. Wedeen (2003) argues, for instance, that radical Islamicist movements grew out of globalizing cultural, economic, and political changes from the 1970s onward. As globalization has intensified, many visible markers of cultural identity (clothing, food, popular culture) have become Westernized, leading in some areas to a backlash against the West and a call for more "traditional" ways of life. At the same time, as less industrialized nations have been integrated into the global economy, they have been increasingly encouraged to reform their domestic economies by privatizing resources and reducing subsidies and social services, even as elites are enjoying unprecedented affluence. In this climate, radical Islamicists have capitalized on resentment (both of the West and of domestic elites), have offered a robust vision of cultural identity, and have provided at least some material support to those who may feel abandoned by the state.
14. McVeigh was convicted of the 19 April 1995 bombing of the Alfred P. Murrah Federal Building in Oklahoma City, in which 168 people were killed.
15. See, for example, Broinowski (1992), Kondo (1997), Lewis (1996, 2004).
16. For a discussion of representations of Arabs in the Western media, see Said (1997), Lind and Danowski (1998), Shaheen (2001), and Gavrilos (2002).
17. *Sydney Morning Herald* (2005); Davies and Peatling (2005).
18. See Merskin's (2004) analysis of the ways Bush's speeches constructed Arabs and enemies.
19. See discussions in Broinowski (2003) and Coates and Krieger (2004).

NOTES TO CHAPTER 9

1. See, for instance, Holland (2006), Kumar (2004), Prividera and Howard (2006), and Takacs (2005).
2. For a perceptive discussion of gendering warfare, see Cooke and Woollacott (1993).
3. Significant at the .05 level (chisq=5.85, df 1, p < .05).
4. See recent discussions of media slant and bias by Barrett and Barrington (2005), Hoffman and Wallach (2007), and Kahn and Kenney (2002).
5. *USA Today*, *The Independent*, and the *Sydney Morning Herald* were classified as popular/populist. The remaining newspapers were classified as serious/elitist. Degree of significance (chisq = 3.11, df 1, p < .10).
6. *The Times* of London and *The Australian* are both News Corporation (Rupert Murdoch) dailies, a fact that no doubt contributed to similarities between the two in style and content.
7. Kumar (2004) argues that the BBC report had little impact on US media coverage of Lynch. I would argue that while the immediate impact was not dramatic, the British report did contribute to a shift in representations of Lynch over time. After the exposé, media outlets more openly questioned the veracity of official accounts of Lynch's experiences, although it is true, as Kumar points out, that the US media often seemed to characterize any inaccuracies as a consequence of the "fog of war" rather than as propaganda.
8. See, for instance, Hoagland (2003).
9. See Brison (2002), Drew (2004), Faludi (2007a, 2007b), Hogan (2003b), Radstone (2002), and Young (2003).
10. Although we do not know, and likely will never know, what actually happened onboard that hijacked airliner, media accounts have suggested that a small

group of men attempted to overpower the hijackers, an effort that prevented the plane from being flown into a high-profile target. Faludi (2007a) points out, however, that stories of women's heroism on that day have been largely ignored by the media.

11. See discussion in Broinowski (2003) and Coates and Krieger (2004).

NOTES TO CHAPTER 10

1. See perceptive discussions of tourist photography in Crawshaw and Urry (1997), Crang (1997), O'Barr (1994), and Taylor (1994).
2. The number of brochures for each nation is as follows:

Nation	Domestic Brochures	International Brochures	Total Brochures
US	43	42	85
UK	19	91	110
Australia	40	61	101
Japan	48	85	133
TOTAL	150	279	429

3. No assumptions have been made about the actual ethnoracial background or national origin of the models featured in the brochures. Instead, I coded for the character "type" or "role" portrayed. See my discussion of this issue in Chapter 7.
4. Depending on the nation, between 91 to 98 percent of all characters represented were judged to be in their fifties or younger. No brochures in any nation featured characters constructed as homosexual or disabled.
5. Australian ethnic diversity, current and projected, based on 1999 Census data, analyzed in Price (1999):

Ethnic Origin	1999	2025 (Projected)
Anglo-Celtic	70%	62%
European	18%	16%
West Asian/African	3%	5%
Other Asian/Pacific Islander	7%	15%
Aboriginal	2%	2%
Other	2%	>1%

6. Although it is commonly reported that 99.8 percent of Japan's 128 million people are Japanese, this figure does not differentiate adequately between majority Japanese and marginalized groups including an estimated 1.6 million ethnic Okinawans (the *Ryūkyū*), more than one million ethnic Koreans, over two hundred thousand ethnic Chinese, more than twenty-four thousand *Ainu*, and an estimated three million *Burakumin*, a stigmatized caste-like group (Hogan 2002). And it is highly unlikely that Japan's increasing illegal migrant population is accurately represented in census data.
7. See Chapter 3 of this volume.
8. For a discussion of cultural tourism and the feminization of the tourist gaze see Craik (1997).

9. Likewise, Okinawa is managed in part by the national-level Okinawa Development Agency. In this way, both prefectures are constructed as "developing" areas, significantly different than the rest of Japan and still not mature enough to manage their own affairs. In the travel brochures, Okinawa is likewise positioned as an almost-foreign destination.

10. Although Hokkaido is in one sense defined here by its "whiteness," it has also long been symbolically associated with the *Ainu* who are commonly represented as "hairy," dark subalterns.

11. Such a position is typical of what Gilroy and others have dubbed Britain's "new racism."

12. In the census, the category "white" includes both British and Irish whites and "other" whites. "Asians" include mainly South and Southeast Asians, especially Indians, Pakistanis, and Bangladeshis. And British Chinese are placed in a separate category. In vernacular use, "black" is still sometimes used to refer to any person or group perceived to be nonwhite.

13. 50 percent of the domestic brochures feature the familiar icons of "high culture," including castles, palaces, and formal gardens.

14. Other perceptive discussions of class, gender, and race in heritage tourism include Bennett (1988), Johnson (1996), Magelssen (2002), and West (1988).

15. Based on 2003 figures from the Office of Travel and Tourism Industries, US Department of Commerce.

16. See MacCannell (1992) and Ritzer and Liska (1997).

17. Of course men and boys also work in the sex industry, but most sex workers are women and girls.

18. See the more extensive discussion of "heritage" tourism in Chapter 11.

19. See Creighton (1997, 2001), Ivy (1995), and Robertson (1987) on nostalgic tourism in Japan. At the same time, the emergence of a small ethnic tourism market in Japan, focused mainly on the indigenous *Ainu* of Hokkaido, highlights the extent to which constructions of the internal Others through domestic tourism help to define the national self. See Cheung (2005).

NOTES TO CHAPTER 11

1. Rosenzweig and Thelen (1998). Such perceptions did not vary significantly by the gender, ethnicity, or class of the visitors.

2. On museums and collective identity, also see Appadurai and Breckenridge (1992), Crane (2000), Fladmark (2000), Kaplan (1994), and Sherman and Rogoff (1994).

3. While "heritage" is a vague term, it is generally used to refer to the cultural and natural resources that a given group has inherited over time. Professional historians often criticize "heritage" discourses and productions for distorting history. On heritage tourism, see especially Hewison (1987), Kirshenblatt-Gimblett (1998), Lowenthal (1998), Timothy and Boyd (2003), and Uzzell and Ballantyne (1998). Thought-provoking case studies of the place of history and identity in heritage and cultural tourism include Bruner (2005), Creighton (2001), Dickinson, Ott, and Aoki (2005), Frost (2005), Johnson (1996), and Magelssen (2002).

4. See Kirshenblatt-Gimblett (1998), Magelssen (2002), and Markwell, Stevenson, and Rowe (2004).

5. There are three other Edo Wonderland living history parks in Japan at Ise, Nikko, and Kaga. Noboribetsu was chosen because it is the furthest away from what are generally considered the main cultural and historical sites of the nation.

6. The figure here provides percentages of men and women by ethnoracial group featured in the exhibits of the SNMAH. Children and individuals whose gender, race, or ethnicity could not be determined were excluded from the analysis. This is the case for all of the quantitative data presented in this chapter.

Exhibit	Majority Men	Majority Women	Minority Men	Minority Women
Communities in a Changing Nation (N=175)	31	13	35	21
The Price of Freedom (N=832)	64	17	16	3
Separate Is Not Equal (N=329)	37	3	49	10
TOTAL PERCENTAGES (N=1336)	53	13	27	7

7. I spoke and corresponded on several occasions with public relations officers at the SNMAH and with the former curator of the exhibit, inquiring about the decision to include this story. Although I was told that they would respond after consulting their records, I have yet to receive a response.
8. See Cathcart (1995), Hudson (1995), Marsden (1995).
9. The electronic database contained data on 63,626 works of the Gallery's more than 330,000 works at the time of analysis (July 2005). I analyzed a systematic random sample of 10,142 portraits, excluding fifty-seven with subjects whose gender could not be determined. Additional analysis of the Gallery's collections reveals that 86 percent of the artists whose works are held by the museum are male and 93 percent of the artworks were created by male artists.
10. The Gallery is arranged chronologically. Because the range and number of representations of women and ethnoracial Others were so limited in the earliest periods, I chose to give more detailed attention to the late eighteenth century onwards. The figure here presents counts for subjects featured in eleven of the Gallery's rooms by gender and ethnoracial background. The majority here includes whites and those of European descent. The minority category includes nonwhites and those of non-European descent.

Room in the National Portrait Gallery	Majority Men	Majority Women	Minority Men	Minority Women
The Arts in the Later 18th Century	26	8	0	0
The Regency	21	5	0	0
Art, Invention and Thought: The Romantics	24	3	0	0
The Victorians	31	2	0	0
Early Victorian Arts	54	13	0	0
Turn of the Century	16	1	0	0
Early 20th Century (1914–1918)	14	3	0	0
A National Portrait, Britain 1919–1959	101	45	0	0
Britain from 1960–1990	70	14	3	1

Room in the National Portrait Gallery	Majority Men	Majority Women	Minority Men	Minority Women
Britain Since 1990	73	38	16	7
The Royal Family	2	6	0	0
TOTALS (N=597)	432	138	19	8
PERCENTAGES*	72%	23%	3%	1%

*Less than 100% due to rounding.

11. The text also avoids any mention of the scandalous love triangle that threatened the careers and reputations of Lords Nelson and Hamilton and eventually left a widowed and penniless Lady Hamilton to raise a child reputed to be Nelson's.
12. In addition to Austen, the other three women were Amelia Opie, Mary Wollstonecraft, and Mary Wollstonecraft Shelley.
13. Based on analysis of the exhibition catalog, 51 percent of the 1,466 featured people were men and 49 percent women. Children were excluded from the analysis, as were large crowd scenes and individuals whose gender could not be determined.
14. Of people engaged in sport, 81 percent were men, while all of the soldiers were male and all of those shown under the categories of fashion and hair were female. Of prizewinners, 85 percent were male, and 57 percent of readers were female.
15. From Kipling (1899) *The White Man's Burden*. See discussion in Chapter 4.
16. While the 1975 *Report of the Committee of Inquiry on Museums and National Collections* called for such a museum and the National Museum of Australia Act of 1980 made the museum a national priority, construction did not begin on the project until 1997.
17. Ashton Raggatt McDougall and Robert Peck von Hartel Trethowan, architects.
18. See NMA (2003) and Stead (2004) for examples of these contrasting perspectives.
19. Individuals featured in the major exhibits of the National Museum of Australia by gender and ethnoracial background.

Exhibit	Majority Men	Majority Women	Minority Men	Minority Women
Tangled Destinies	18	6	4	0
Living with the Land	69	7	6	0
Eternity	34	20	3	2
Horizons: The People of Australia Since 1788	100	33	11	3
First Australians: Gallery of Aboriginal and Torres Strait Islander Peoples	28	2	110	61
Nation: Symbols of Australia	135	30	11	0
Snapshots of Glory: Rugby World Cup Images	81	0	0	0
Totals (N=774)	465	98	145	66
Percentages	60%	13%	19%	9%

20. See Chapter 2 of this volume, for a discussion of the Anzac "digger" in discourses of national identity.
21. For an overview of the history and aims of the museum, see Hashimoto (1998).
22. Representations of featured individuals in the National Museum of Japanese History by race and gender.

Representations	Japanese Men	Japanese Women	Non-Japanese Men	Non-Japanese Women
Named individuals	32	5	10	1
Pictures and figures	372	244	21	8
Totals (N=693)	404	249	31	9
Percentages by Gender and Race*	58%	36%	4%	1%

*Total is less than 100% due to rounding.

23. See Larson, Johnson, and Murphy (2007) for a discussion of recent *Ainu* rights initiatives.
24. Japanese citizenship is conferred according to the rule of *jus sanguinis*, blood-descent. Therefore descendants of Korean immigrants to Japan will be considered citizens of Korea, even if their families have lived in Japan for generations and they themselves were born in Japan, only speak Japanese, and have never set foot in Korea. While it is theoretically possible for such people to become naturalized Japanese citizens, for most it is an impractical proposition. Therefore, they remain foreigners in the eyes of the Japanese government and are not entitled to full civic participation.
25. See the discussion of women's diary literature in Chapter 3 of this volume.
26. Estimates of the percentage of minorities in the general national population vary greatly depending on definitions of minority and majority. I have based my estimates here on the most recent census data available for each nation, and have defined "minority" as those not of the dominant ethnoracial group of each nation. The low range of the figure for Japan is based on the number of foreigners in Japan; the higher figure includes minority groups such as the *Ainu, Ryūkyū*, and *Burakumin*, not identified in government population statistics.
27. All of the living history venues included introductory galleries that provided visitors with an overview of the relevant historical period. These galleries were structured like traditional museum exhibits. The table here summarizes gender and racial representations in these static displays versus those in national museums. Individuals whose gender or race could not be determined were excluded from analysis.

	Venue	Majority Men	Majority Women	Minority Men	Minority Women
US	Lincoln's New Salem	81%	19%	—	—
	SNMAH	53%	13%	27%	7%
UK	Black Country Living Museum	67%	27%	2%	4%
	NPG	72%	23%	3%	1%

Venue		Majority Men	Majority Women	Minority Men	Minority Women
Australia	Sovereign Hill*	87%	9%	5%	—
	NMA	60%	13%	19%	9%
Japan	Edo Wonderland	76%	24%	—	—
	NMJH	58%	36%	4%	1%
TOTALS	All Living History Venues	79%	18%	2%	1%
	All National Museums	61%	21%	13%	5%

*Based on analysis of the galleries of the adjoining Gold Museum.

28. The dearth of male interpreters at Lincoln's New Salem is undoubtedly due to the fact that most interpreters are unpaid volunteers. At the other three sites studied here, interpreters are paid.
29. Based on 1857 Census data presented in the introductory galleries of the site.
30. In fact, Lowenthal describes heritage tourism as a "secular religion" that gives us faith in "who we are, where we came from, and to what we belong" (1998, xvii).

Bibliography

ACLU. 2004. "Sanctioned Bias: Racial Profiling Since 9/11." http://www.aclu.org/
SafeandFree/SafeandFree.cfm?ID=15102&c=207 (accessed 14 June 2004).

Adams, P., ed. 1997. *The Retreat From Tolerance: A Snapshot of Australian Society*.
Sydney: ABC Books.

Alibhai-Brown, Y. 2000. *Who Do We Think We Are? Imagining the New Britain*.
London: Penguin.

Allison, A. 1994. *Night Work: Sexuality, Pleasure, and Corporate Masculinity in a
Tokyo Hostess Club*. Chicago: University of Chicago Press.

Amino, Y. 1996. "Emperor, Rice and Commoners." In *Multicultural Japan, Palaeolithic to Postmodern*, trans. G. McCormack, ed. D. Denoon, M. Hudson, G.
McCormack, and T. Morris-Suzuki. Cambridge: Cambridge University Press, pp.
235–244.

Anderson, B. 1983. *Imagined Communities*. London and New York: Verso.

Anderson, M. 2001. "Mrs. Charles Clacy, Lola Montez and Poll the Grogseller:
Glimpses of Women on the Early Victorian Goldfields." In *Gold: Forgotten Histories and Lost Objects of Australia*, ed. I. McCalman, A. Cook, and A. Reeves,
225–250. Cambridge: Cambridge University Press.

Appadurai, A., and C. Breckenridge. 1992. "Museums are Good to Think: Heritage
on View in India." In *Museums and Communities: The Politics of Public Culture*,
ed. I. Karp, C. Kreamer, and S. Lavine, 34–55. Washington, DC: Smithsonian
Institution Press.

Asahi Shimbun. 1996. Japan Almanac 1996. Tokyo: Asahi Shimbun Publishing.

Asahi Shimbun. 2006. "Tokyo Trials Poll." 2 May.

Australian Broadcasting Corporation. 1999a. "Opposition Keeps Up Preamble Attack." http://abc.net.au/local/news/1999/03/item199903241743081.htm (accessed 15 January 2000).

———. 1999b. "Democrats Offer Hope of Compromise on Preamble." http://abc.
net.au/am/s37234.htm (accessed 15 January 2000).

———. 1999c. "New Preamble Generous to Indigenous People: Howard." http://abc.
net.au/news/1999/08/item199908111407201.htm (accessed 15 January 2000).

———. 1999d. "Mateship." http://abc.net.au/m/arts/ling/stories/s25262.htm (accessed 15 January 2000).

———. 1999e. "New Constitution Preamble." http://abc.net.au/7.30/stories/s43232/
htm (accessed 15 January 2000).

———. 1999f. "Democrats Discuss Their Cutting Deal on Howard's Preamble."
http://abc.net.au/worldtoday/s43051.htm (accessed 15 January 2000).

———. 1999g. "Howard Defends 'Mateship' in Preamble." http://abc.net.au/
news/1999/03/item199903231700141.htm (accessed 15 January 2000).

————. 2005. "Budget Set to Deliver Some Serious Cuts." http://www.abc.net. au/7.30/content/2005/s1353975.htm (accessed 30 October 2007).

Australian Bureau of Statistics. 1998. *1996 Census of Population and Housing, Selected Family and Labour Force Characteristics for Statistical Local Areas, Tasmania (2017.6).* Canberra: Commonwealth of Australia.

————. 1999a. *Tasmanian Yearbook 2000 (1301.6).* Canberra: Commonwealth of Australia.

————. 1999b. *The Health and Welfare of Australia's Aboriginal and Torres Strait Islander Peoples 1999 (4704.0).* Canberra: Commonwealth of Australia.

————. 1999c. *Labour Force Australia (6203.0).* Canberra: Commonwealth of Australia.

————. 2000a. *Australia Now: A Statistical Profile.* http://www.abs.gov.au (accessed 13 January, 2002).

————. 2000b. *Tasmanian Statistical Indicators (1303.6).* Canberra: Commonwealth of Australia.

————. 2000c. *Year Book Australia 2000 (1301.0).* Canberra: Commonwealth of Australia.

————. 2002. *Yearbook Australia 2002 (1301.0).* Canberra: Commonwealth of Australia.

Australian Department of Veteran Affairs. 2007. *The Gallipoli Campaign.* http:// www.dva.gov.au/commem/commac/studies/anzacsk/aday4.htm#gall (accessed 20 September 2007).

Australian Election Commission. 1999. *Ballot Paper: Referendum on Proposed Constitution Alteration.* Canberra: Australian Election Commission.

Banet-Weiser, S. 1999. *The Most Beautiful Girl in the World: Beauty Pageants and National Identity.* Berkeley: University of California Press.

Barclay, K. 2006. "Between Modernity and Primitivity: Okinawan Identity in Relation to Japan and the South Pacific." *Nations and Nationalism* 12 (1): 117–137.

Barczewski, S.L. 2000. *Myth and National Identity in Nineteenth-Century Britain: The Legends of King Arthur and Robin Hood.* Oxford: Oxford University Press.

Barrett, A.W., and L.W. Barrington. 2005. "Bias in Newspaper Photograph Selection." *Political Research Quarterly* 58 (4): 609–618.

Barthes, R. 1972. *Mythologies.* Trans. A. Lavers. New York: Farrar, Straus and Giroux.

Bashevkin, S. 1994. "Confronting Neo-Conservatism: Anglo-American Women's Movements Under Thatcher, Reagan and Mulroney." *International Political Science Review/Revue Internationale de Science Politique* 15 (3): 275–296.

Bate, W. 1988. *Victorian Gold Rushes.* Ballarat, VIC: Sovereign Hill Museums Association.

Baudrillard, J. 1995. *The Gulf War Did Not Take Place.* Trans. Paul Patton. Bloomington: Indiana University Press.

BBC Correspondent. 2003. "War Spin." Broadcast on BBC Two, 18 May 2003 at 1915 BST.

BBC News. 2007. "Anti-Terror Chief Misled Public." http://news.bbc.co.uk/1/hi/ uk/6927140.stm (accessed 20 August 2007).

Beasley, W.G. 1999. *The Japanese Experience: A Short History of Japan.* Berkeley: University of California Press.

Beaton, L. 1982. "The Importance of Women's Paid Labour: Women at Work in World War II." In *Worth Her Salt: Women at Work in Australia,* ed. M. Bevege, M. James, and C. Shute, 87–91. Sydney: Hale & Iremonger.

Befu, H. 1983. "Internationalization of Japan and *Nihon Bunkaron*" In *The Challenge of Japan's Internationalization: Organization and Culture,* ed. H. Mannari and H. Befu, 232–265. Tokyo: Kodansha International.

Bell, P., and R. Bell, eds. 1999. *Americanization and Australia*. Sydney: University of New South Wales Press.

Bellesiles, M.A. 2000. *Arming America: The Origins of a National Gun Culture*. New York: Alfred P. Knopf.

Bennett, T. 1988. "Museums and 'The People.'" In *The Museum Time-Machine*, ed. R. Lumley, 63–85. London: Routledge.

Bennett, T., P. Buckridge, D. Carter, and C. Mercer, eds. 1992. *Celebrating the Nation: A Critical Study of Australia's Bicentenary*. St. Leonard, NSW: Allen and Unwin.

Berger, J. 1972. *Ways of Seeing*. London: BBC/Penguin.

Bernstein, G., ed. 1991. *Recreating Japanese Women, 1600–1945*. Berkeley: University of California Press.

Bertola, P. 2001. "Undesirable Persons: Race and West Australian Mining Legislation." In *Gold: Forgotten Histories and Lost Objects of Australia*, ed. I. McCalman, A. Cook, and A. Reeves, 124–140. Cambridge: Cambridge University Press.

Bhabha, H. 1990. *Nation and Narration*. New York: Routledge.

Billig, M. 1995. *Banal Nationalism*. London: Sage.

Billig, M., J. Downey, J. Richardson, D. Deacon, and P. Golding, P. 2006a. *'Britishness' in the Last Three General Elections: From Ethnic Nationalism to Civic Nationalism, Report for the Commission for Racial Equality*. Loughborough: Loughborough Centre for Communication Research, Loughborough University.

———. 2006b. "Chilly Britannia?" *Catalyst*, 17 May 2006.

Blainey, G. 1978. *The Rush That Never Ended*. Melbourne: Melbourne University Press.

———. 1984. *All for Australia*. North Ryde, NSW: Methuen Haynes.

Blamires, D. 1998. *Robin Hood: A Hero for All Times*. Exhibition guide to "Robin Hood: A Hero for All Times" at The John Rylands Library, 30 January–26 June 1998. Manchester: The John Rylands Library.

Blom, I., K. Hagemann, and C. Hall, eds. 2000. *Gendered Nations: Nationalisms and Gender Order in the Long Nineteenth Century*. Oxford: Berg.

Booth, W. 1998. "One Nation Indivisible: Is it History?" *The Washington Post*, 22 February.

Bowler, J.M., H. Johnson, J.M. Olley, J.R. Prescott, R.G. Roberts, W. Shawcross, and N.A. Spooner. 2003. "New Ages for Human Occupation and Climatic Change at Lake Mungo, Australia." *Nature* 421 (February): 837–840.

Brinton, M.C. 1993. *Women and the Economic Miracle: Gender and Work in Postwar Japan*. Berkeley: University of California Press.

Brison, S. 2002. "Gender, Terrorism, and War." *Signs* 28 (1): 435–437.

Brohm, J.M. 1978. *Sport, A Prison of Measured Time*. London: Ink Links.

Broinowski, A. 1992. *The Yellow Lady: Australian Impressions of Asia*. Melbourne: Oxford University Press.

———. 2003. *Howard's War*. Melbourne: Scribe Publications.

Broome, R. 1988. "The Struggle for Australia: Aboriginal-European Warfare, 1770–1930." In *Australia: Two Centuries of War and Peace*, ed. M. McKernan and M. Browne, 92–120. Canberra: Australian War Memorial.

Brown, R.U. 1976. "Letters to the Editor." *Editor and Publisher* 109 (September): 68.

Bruner, E.M. 2005. *Culture on Tour: Ethnographies of Travel*. Chicago: University of Chicago Press.

Bryson, L. 1987. "Sport and the Maintenance of Masculine Hegemony." *Women's Studies International Forum* 10 (4): 349–360.

———. 2001. *The New Differences Between Women*. Barton lecture, part 8, broadcast on ABC Radio National, 1 April.

Buckley, S. 1997. *Broken Silence, Voices of Japanese Feminism*. Berkeley: University of California Press.

Buraku Liberation and Human Rights Research Institute. 2001. "About the *Buraku* Liberation and Human Rights Research Institute." www.blhrri.org/index_e.htm (accessed 1 October 2001).

Bush, G.W. 2001. "Address to a Joint Session of Congress and the American People, September 20, 2001, Washington, DC." http://www.whitehouse.gov/news/releases/2001/09/20010920-8.html (accessed 1 June 2007).

Caine, B., and G. Sluga. 2000. *Gendering European History*. London: Leicester University Press.

Carey, P. 2000. *True History of the Kelly Gang*. New York: Random House.

Cathcart, B. 1995. "Museum of the Future—No Glass Cases." *The Independent*, 2 April.

Cavendish, J.C., and I. Disha. 2007. "Reporting of Hate Crimes Against Arabs and Muslims after September 11, 2001: Assessing the Importance of Group Threat and Political Mediation Theories." Paper delivered at the Midwest Sociological Society annual conference, Chicago, IL, April.

Chance, L. 2000. "*Zuihitsu* and Gender: *Tsurezuregusa* and *The Pillow Book*." In *Inventing the Classics: Modernity, National Identity, and Japanese Literature*, ed. H. Shirane and T. Suzuki, 120–147. Stanford: Stanford University Press.

Cheung, S.C.H. 2005. "Rethinking *Ainu* Heritage: A Case Study of an *Ainu* Settlement in Hokkaido, Japan." *International Journal of Heritage Studies* 11 (3): 197–210.

Clark, M. 1995. *A Short History of Australia*. 4th ed. Camberwell, VIC: Penguin Books.

Clinton, H.R. 2003. *Living History*. New York: Simon & Schuster.

Coates, D., and J. Krieger. 2004. *Blair's War*. Cambridge: Polity Press.

Colley, L. 1992. *Britons: Forging the Nation 1707–1837*. New Haven and London: Yale University Press.

———. 2002. *Captives: Britain, Empire and the World, 1600–1850*. New York: Anchor Books.

Colls, R. 2002. *Identity of England*. Oxford: Oxford University Press.

Committee on the Elimination of Racial Discrimination. 2000. "Concluding Observations by the Committee on the Elimination of Racial Discrimination: Australia 19/04/00." http://www.unhchr.ch/tbs/doc.nsf/ (accessed 14 May 2002).

Commonwealth of Australia. 2000. *The Parliament of the Commonwealth of Australia and Indigenous Peoples 1901–1967, Research Paper 10 2000–2001*. Canberra: Department of the Parliamentary Library.

Cooke, M., and A. Woollacott. 1993. "Introduction." In *Gendering War Talk*, ed. M. Cooke and A. Woollacott, ix–xii. Princeton: Princeton University Press.

Craik, J. 1997. "The Culture of Tourism." In *Touring Cultures: Transformations of Travel and Theory*, ed. C. Rojek and J. Urry, 113–136. London & New York: Routledge.

Crane, S.A., ed. 2000. *Museums and Memory*. Stanford: Stanford University Press.

Crang, M. 1997. "Picturing Practices: Research Through the Tourist Gaze." *Progress in Human Geography* 21 (3): 359–373.

Crawshaw, C., and J. Urry. 1997. "Tourism and the Photographic Eye." In *Touring Cultures: Transformations of Travel and Theory*, ed. C. Rojek and J. Urry, 177–195. London: Routledge.

Creighton, M. 1992. "The *Depaato*: Merchandising the West While Selling Japaneseness." In *Re-Made in Japan: Everyday Life and Consumer Taste in a Changing Society*, ed. J.J. Tobin. New Haven: Yale University Press.

———. 1997. "Consuming Rural Japan: The Marketing of Tradition and Nostalgia in the Japanese Travel Industry." *Ethnology* 36 (3): 239–254.

———. 2001. "Spinning Silk, Weaving Selves: Nostalgia, Gender, and Identity in Japanese Craft Vacations." *Japanese Studies* 21 (1): 5–29.

Crotty, M. 2001. *Making the Australian Male, Middle-Class Masculinity 1870–1920.* Carlton South, VIC: Melbourne University Press.

Curtice, J. 2006. "A Stronger or Weaker Union? Public Reactions to Asymmetric Devolution in the United Kingdom." *Publius: The Journal of Federalism* 36 (1): 95–113.

Curthoys, A. 2001. "'Men of all Nations, Except Chinamen': Europeans and Chinese on the Goldfields of New South Wales." In *Gold: Forgotten Histories and Lost Objects of Australia*, ed. I. McCalman, A. Cook, and A. Reeves, 103–123. Cambridge: Cambridge University Press.

Dale, P.N. 1986. *The Myth of Japanese Uniqueness.* London: Routledge.

Danielsen, F., M.K. Sorensen, M.F. Olwig, V. Selvam, F. Parish, N.D. Burgess, T. Hiraishi, V. Karunagaran, M.S. Rasmussen, L.B. Hansen, A. Quarto, and N. Suryadiputra. 2005. "The Asian Tsunami: A Protective Role for Coastal Vegetation." *Science* 310 (5748): 643.

Davies, A., and S. Peatling. 2005. "Australians Racist? No Way Says Howard." *Sydney Morning Herald*, 15 December.

Davis, F. 1979. *Yearning for Yesterday: A Sociology of Nostalgia.* New York: The Free Press.

Davison, G. 2001. "Gold Rush Melbourne." In *Gold: Forgotten Histories and Lost Objects of Australia*, ed. I. McCalman, A. Cook, and A. Reeves, 52–66. Cambridge: Cambridge University Press.

Deflem, M., and F.C. Pampel. 1996. "The Myth of Postnational Identity: Popular Support for European Unification." *Social Forces* 75 (1): 119–143.

De Groot, J. 1993. "The Dialectics of Gender: Women, Men, and Political Discourses in Iran c. 1890–1930." *Gender and History* 5 (2): 256–268.

Denoon, D., M. Hudson, G. McCormack, and T. Morris-Suzuki, eds. 1996. *Multicultural Japan, Palaeolithic to Postmodern.* Cambridge: Cambridge University Press.

Department for Culture, Media and Sport. 2006. "2007 Bicentenary of the Abolition of the Slave Trade Honouring the Past and Looking to the Future." http://www.culture.gov.uk/global/press_notices/archive_2006/dcms006_07.htm. (accessed 12 June 2006).

Dettelbach, C.G. 1976. *In the Driver's Seat: The Automobile in American Literature and Popular Culture.* Westport, CT: Greenwood.

Dickinson, G., B.L. Ott, and E. Aoki. 2005. "Memory and Myth at the Buffalo Bill Museum." *Western Journal of Communication* 69 (2): 85–108.

Dittmer, J. 2005. "Captain America's Empire: Reflections on Identity, Popular Culture, and Post-9/11 Geopolitics." *Annals of the Association of American Geographers* 95 (3): 626–643.

Dixon, T. 1905. *The Clansman: An Historical Romance of the Ku Klux Klan.* New York: Doubleday.

Dixson, M. 1976. *The Real Matilda: Women and Identity in Australia, 1788 to 1975.* Hammondsworth, England: Penguin.

Douglas, G. 1990. "Family Law Under the Thatcher Government." *Journal of Law and Society* 17 (4): 411–426.

Drew, J. 2004. "Identity Crisis: Gender, Public Discourse, and 9/11." *Women and Language* 27 (2): 71–77.

Edensor, T. 2002. *National Identity, Popular Culture and Everyday Life.* Oxford: Berg.

Edwards, W. 1989. *Modern Japan Through Its Weddings: Gender, Person and Society in Ritual Portrayal.* Stanford: Stanford University Press.

Ehrenberg, M. 1989. *Women in Prehistory.* Norman and London: University of Oklahoma Press.

Ehrenreich, B. 1997. *Blood Rites, Origins, and History of the Passions of War.* New York: Henry Holt and Company.

Elder, C. 2007. *Being Australian: Narratives of National Identity.* Crows Nest, NSW: Allen and Unwin.

Engels, F. 1884/1972. *The Origin of the Family, Private Property, and the State.* New York: Pathfinder Press.

Ewen, S. 1976. *Captains of Consciousness: Advertising and the Social Roots of the Consumer Culture.* New York: McGraw-Hill Book Company.

Fairclough, N., and R. Wodak. 1997. "Critical Discourse Analysis." In *Discourse as Social Interaction,* ed. T.A. van Dijk, 258–284. London: Sage.

Faludi, S. 1991. *Backlash: The Undeclared War Against American Women.* New York: Doubleday.

———. 2007a. *The Terror Dream: Fear and Fantasy in Post-9/11 America.* New York: Metropolitan Books.

———. 2007b. "America's Guardian Myths." *The New York Times,* 7 September.

Featherstone, M., ed. 1990. *Global Culture: Nationalism, Globalization and Modernity.* London: Sage.

Fendrich, H. 2000. "NBC Puts More Ads With Olympic Telecasts." http://archive.sport server.com/olympics/00sydney/funfacts/story/0,4822,500260280-50040155 (accessed 1 June 2002).

Field, N. 1991. *In the Realm of a Dying Emperor.* New York: Pantheon.

Fish, S. 1997. "Boutique Multiculturalism, or Why Liberals are Incapable of Thinking About Hate Speech." *Critical Inquiry,* no. 23:378–395.

Fladmark, J.M., ed. 2000. *Heritage and Museums: Shaping National Identity.* Aberdeen: The Robert Gordon University.

Friday, K.F. 1994. "*Bushidō* or Bull? A Medieval Historian's Perspective on the Imperial Army and the Japanese Warrior Tradition." *The History Teacher* 27 (3): 339–349.

Frost, A. 2003. *The Global Reach of Empire: Britain's Maritime Expansion in the Indian and Pacific Oceans, 1764–1815.* Melbourne: Melbourne University Publishing.

Frost, W. 2005. "Making an Edgier Interpretation of the Gold Rushes: Contrasting Perspectives from Australia and New Zealand." *International Journal of Heritage Studies* 11 (3): 235–250.

Fujimura-Fanselow, K., and A. Kameda, eds. 1995. *Japanese Women, New Feminist Perspectives of the Past, Present and Future.* New York: The Feminist Press at the City University of New York.

Funck, M. 2002. "Ready for War? Conceptions of Military Manliness in the Prusso-German Officer Corps Before the First World War." In *Home/Front: The Military, War and Gender in Twentieth-Century Germany,* ed. K. Hagemann and S. Schüler-Springorum, 43–67. Oxford and New York: Berg.

Gavrilos, D. 2002. "Arab Americans in a Nation's Imagined Community: How News Constructed Arab American Reactions to the Gulf War." *Journal of Communication Inquiry* 26:426–445.

Gellner, E. 1983. *Nations and Nationalism.* Ithaca, NY: Cornell University Press.

Ghadessy, M. 1983. "Information Structure in Letters to the Editor." *IRAL XXX/I:* 46–56.

Giddens, A. 1990. *The Consequences of Modernity.* Stanford: Stanford University Press.

Gilroy, P. 1987. *"There Ain't No Black in the Union Jack": The Cultural Politics of Race and Nation.* Chicago: University of Chicago Press.

Giroux, H.A. 1994. "Consuming Social Change: The 'United Colors of Benetton.'" *Cultural Critique,* no. 26:5–32.

Gluck, C. 1985. *Japan's Modern Myths: Ideology in the Late Meiji Period*. Princeton: Princeton University Press.

Goffman, E. 1979. *Gender Advertisements*. London: Macmillan.

Goldstein-Gidoni, O. 1997. *Packaged Japaneseness: Weddings, Business, and Brides*. Honolulu: University of Hawaii Press.

Goodman, D. 2001. "Making an Edgier History of Gold." In *Gold: Forgotten Histories and Lost Objects of Australia*, ed. I. McCalman, A. Cook, and A. Reeves, 23–36. Cambridge: Cambridge University Press.

Grosvenor, I. 1997. *Assimilating Identities: Racism and Educational Policy in Post 1945 Britain*. London: Lawrence and Wishart.

Gruneau, R. 1984. "Commercialism and the Modern Olympics." In *Five-Ring Circus: Money, Power and Politics at the Olympic Games*, ed. A. Tomlinson and G. Whannel, 1–15. London and Sydney: Pluto Press.

Hage, G. 1998. *White Nation: Fantasies of White Supremacy in a Multicultural Society*. Annandale, NSW: Pluto Press.

Hagemann, K., and S. Schüler-Springorum, eds. 2002. *Home/Front: The Military, War and Gender in Twentieth-Century Germany*. Oxford: Berg.

Hall, S. 1992. "The Question of Cultural Identity." In *Modernity and its Futures*, ed. S. Hall, D. Held, and T. McGrew, 273–326. Cambridge: Polity Press.

Hall, S., C. Chricter, T. Jefferson, J. Clark, and B. Roberts. 1978. *Policing the Crisis: Mugging, the State and Law and Order*. London: Macmillan.

Hamabata, M.M. 1990. *Crested Kimono: Power and Love in the Japanese Business Family*. Ithaca and London: Cornell University Press.

Hargreaves, J., ed. 1982. *Sport, Culture, and Ideology*. London, Boston, Melbourne, and Henley: Routledge and Kegan Paul.

Harrison, J.F.C. 1984. *The Common People: A History from the Norman Conquest to the Present*. London: Fontana Press.

Harvey, D. 1989. *The Condition of Postmodernity*. Oxford: Basil Blackwell.

Harvey, P.A.S. 1995. "Interpreting *Oshin*—War, History, and Women in Modern Japan." In *Women, Media, and Consumption in Japan*, ed. L. Skov and B. Moeran: 75–110. Honolulu: University of Hawaii Press.

Hashimoto, H. 1998. "Exhibiting Japanese History and Culture." *Curator* 41 (3): 200–211.

Hermes, J. 1995. *Reading Women's Magazines: An Analysis of Everyday Media Use*. Cambridge, UK: Polity Press.

Hewison, R. 1987. *The Heritage Industry: Britain in a Climate of Decline*. London: Methuen.

Hill, D.B. 1981. "Letter Opinion on ERA: A Test of the Newspaper Bias Hypothesis." *Public Opinion Quarterly* 45:384–392.

Hoagland, J. 2003. "Clarity: The Best Weapon." *The Washington Post*, 1 June.

Hobsbawm, E.J. 1975. *The Age of Capital 1848–1875*. New York: Charles Scribner's Sons.

———. 1990. *Nations and Nationalism Since 1780*. Cambridge: Cambridge University Press.

Hobsbawm, E.J., and T. Ranger, eds. 1983. *The Invention of Tradition*. Cambridge and New York: Cambridge University Press.

Hoffman, A.J., and J. Wallach, J. 2007. "The Effects of Media Bias." *Journal of Applied Social Psychology* 37 (3): 616–630.

Hofstede, G. 1998. "A Case for Comparing Apples with Oranges: International Differences in Values." *International Journal of Comparative Sociology* 39 (1): 16–31.

Hogan, J. 2002. "Gendered and Ethnicised Discourses of National Identity in Australia and Japan." PhD diss., University of Tasmania.

————. 2003a. "Staging the Nation: Gendered and Ethnicized Discourses of National Identity in Olympic Opening Ceremonies." *Journal of Sport and Social Issues* 27 (2): 100–123.

————. 2003b. "The Return to Imperialism: Restoring American Manhood." *Clio's Psyche*, December.

————. 2004. "Constructing the Global in Two Rural Communities in Australia and Japan." *Journal of Sociology* 40 (1): 21–40.

————. 2005. "Gender, Ethnicity, and National Identity in Australian and Japanese Television Advertisements." *National Identities* 7 (2): 193–211.

————. 2006. "Letters to the Editor in the 'War on Terror': A Cross-National Study." *Mass Communication & Society* 9 (1): 63–83.

Holcomb, B. 1998. "Gender and Heritage Interpretation." In *Contemporary Issues in Heritage and Environmental Interpretation: Problems and Prospects*, ed. D. Uzzell and R. Ballantyne, 37–55. London: The Stationery Office.

Holland, S.L. 2006. "The Dangers of Playing Dress-Up: Popular Representations of Jessica Lynch and the Controversy Regarding Women in Combat." *Quarterly Journal of Speech* 92 (1): 27–51.

Home Office. 2007. "Terrorism and the Law." http://www.homeoffice.gov.uk/ security/terrorism-and-the-law/ (accessed 4 June 2007).

Hook, G., and M. Weiner. 1992. *The Internationalisation of Japan*. London: Routledge.

Horne, D. 2001. *What Holds Australians Together Despite Their Diversity?* Barton lecture, part 1, broadcast on ABC Radio National, 11 February.

Horowitz, D. 2006. *The Professors: The 101 Most Dangerous Academics in America*. Washington, DC: Regnery Publishing.

Howard, J. 1996. *The Liberal Tradition: The Beliefs and values Which Guide the Federal Government*. Sir Robert Menzies lecture, Melbourne, 18 November 1996. Canberra: National Library of Australia.

————. 2001a. "Address at Centennial Ceremony, Sydney, 1 January 2001." http:// www.pm.gov.au (accessed 30 May 2006).

————. 2001b. "Prime Minister the Honorable John Howard MP Joint Press Conference with the Deputy Prime Minister and the Minister for Foreign Affairs, Parliament House, 14 September 2001." http://www.pm.gov.au (accessed 30 May 2006).

Hudson, K. 1995. "A House for History?" *The Times*, 26 April.

Human Rights and Equal Opportunity Commission. 1997. "Bringing Them Home: Report of the Inquiry into the Separation of Aboriginal and Torres Strait Islander Children from Their Families." http://www.humanrights.gov.au/social_justice/bth _report/report/index.html (accessed 7 February 2008).

————. 2004. "IsmaListen: National Consultations on Eliminating Prejudice Against Arab and Muslim Australians." http://www.humanrights.gov.au/racial% 5Fdiscrimination/isma/index.html (accessed 1 November 2007).

Human Rights Watch. 2002. "US Officials Should Have Been Better Prepared for Hate Crime Wave: Anti-Muslim Bias Crimes Rose 1700 Percent After September 11." http://www.hrw.org/press/2002/11/usahate.htm (accessed 7 February 2008).

Hunt, T. 2003. *Defining John Bull: Political Caricature and National Identity in Late Georgian England*. Hampshire, England: Ashgate Publishing.

Huntington, S. 1996. *The Clash of Civilizations and the Remaking of the World Order*. New York: Simon and Schuster.

————. 2004. *Who Are We? The Challenges to America's National Identity*. New York: Simon and Schuster.

Hurst, G.C. 1990. "Death, Honor, Loyalty: The *Bushidō* Ideal." *Philosophy East and West* 40 (4): 511–527.

Iida, Y. 2002. *Rethinking Identity in Modern Japan: Nationalism as Aesthetics*. London and New York: Routledge.

Imamura, A., ed. 1996. *Re-imagining Japanese Women*. Berkeley: University of California Press.

Institute of Race Relations. 2004. "New Study Highlights Discrimination in Use of Anti-Terror Laws." http://www.irr.org.uk/2004/september/ak000004.html (accessed 17 June 2006).

International Olympic Committee. 2001. *Olympic Charter*. Lausanne, Switzerland: International Olympic Committee.

Itoh, M. 1998. *Globalization of Japan, Japanese Sakoku Mentality and U.S. Efforts to Open Japan*. New York: St. Martin's Press.

Ivy, M. 1995. *Discourses of the Vanishing: Modernity, Phantasm, Japan*. Chicago: University of Chicago Press.

Iwao, S. 1993. *Japanese Women, Traditional Image and Changing Reality*. Cambridge, MA: Harvard University Press.

Jacoby, S. 2004. *Freethinkers: A History of American Secularism*. New York: Metropolitan Books.

Jansson, D. 2004. "American National identity and the Progress of the New South in *National Geographic Magazine*." *The Geographical Review* 93 (3): 350–369.

———. 2005. "'A Geography of Racism': Internal Orientalism and the Construction of American National Identity in the film *Mississippi Burning*." *National Identities* 7 (3): 265–285.

Japanese Ministry of Education. 2001. Ministry of Education, Culture, Science, Sports, and Technology Homepage. http://gojapan.about.com/gi/dynamic/offsite.htm?site=http%3A%2F%2Fwww.mext.go.jp%2Fenglish%2Findex.htm (accessed 9 March 2001).

Japanese Statistics Bureau. 1998. *Dai 45 Kai Nihon Tokukei Nen, Heisei 10 Nen* [Japan Statistical Yearbook 1998]. Tokyo: Management and Cooperation Agency, Government of Japan.

———. 2001. "Population by Labour Force Status—Regions." http://www.stat.go.jp/english/154b.htm (accessed 10 August, 2002).

Jeffords, S. 1989. *The Remasculinization of America: Gender and the Vietnam War*. Bloomington: Indiana University Press.

Jhally, S., and J. Lewis. 1992. *Enlightened Racism: The Cosby Show, Audiences, and the Myth of the American Dream*, Boulder: Westview Press.

Johnson, N. 1996. "Where Geography and History Meet: Heritage Tourism and the Big House in Ireland." *Annals of the Association of American Geographers* 86 (3): 551–566.

Jones, T. 2003. "In Palestine, West Virginia, All is Joyful; Word of Rescue Races Across Town." *The Washington Post*, 4 April.

Jupp, J. 1966. *Arrivals and Departures*. Melbourne: Cheshire-Lansdowne.

Kahn, K.F., and P.J. Kenney. 2002. "The Slant of the News: How Editorial Endorsements Influence Campaign Coverage and Citizens' Views of Candidates." *American Political Science Review* 96:432–446.

Kalantzis, M. 2001. *Recognizing Diversity*. Barton lecture, part 3, broadcast on ABC Radio National, 25 February.

Kalantzis, M., and B. Cope. 1997. "An Opportunity to Change the Culture." In *The Retreat From Tolerance: A Snapshot of Australian Society*, ed. P. Adams, 57–85. Sydney: ABC Books.

Kapferer, J. 1996. *Being All Equal: Identity, Difference and Australian Cultural Practice*. Oxford: Berg.

Kaplan, F.E.S., ed. 1994. *Museums and the Making of 'Ourselves': The Role of Objects in National Identity*. London and New York: Leicester University Press.

Karim, K.H. 1997. "The Historical Resilience of Primary Stereotypes: Core Images of the Muslim Other." In *Language and the Politics of Exclusion: Others in Discourse*, ed. S.H. Riggins, 153–182. London: Sage.

Kato, S. 1992. "The Internationalization of Japan." In *The Internationalization of Japan*, ed. G.D. Hook and M.A. Weiner, 269–283. London and New York: Routledge.

Kaushal, N., R. Kaestner, and C. Reimers. 2007. "Labor Market Effects of September 11th on Arab and Muslim Residents of the United States." *Journal of Human Resources* 42 (2): 275–309.

Kelsky, K. 2001. *Women on the Verge: Japanese Women, Western Dreams*. Durham and London: Duke University Press.

Kienitz, S. 2002. "Body Damage: War Disability and Constructions of Masculinity in Weimar Germany." In *Home/Front: The Military, War, and Gender in Twentieth-Century Germany*, ed. K. Hagemann and S. Schüler-Springorum, 181–203. Oxford and New York: Berg.

Kilbourne, J. 1999. *Can't Buy My Love: How Advertising Changes the Way We Think and Feel*. New York: Touchstone.

Kipling, R. 1899. "The White Man's Burden," published in *The Times* of London and *McClure's Magazine* (US), 12 February, 1899.

Kirshenblatt-Gimblett, B. 1998. *Destination Culture: Tourism, Museums, and Heritage*. Berkeley: University of California Press.

Knight, S.T., ed. 1999. *Robin Hood: An Anthology of Scholarship and Criticism*. Woodbridge, Suffolk: D.S. Brewer.

Kondo, D. 1990. *Crafting Selves: Power, Gender, and Discourses of Identity in a Japanese Workplace*. Chicago: University of Chicago Press.

———. 1997. *About Face, Performing Race in Fashion and Theatre*. New York and London: Routledge.

Kōnoshi, T. 2000. "Constructing Imperial Mythology: *Kojiki* and *Nihon Shoki*." In *Inventing the Classics: Modernity, National Identity, and Japanese Literature*, ed. H. Shirane and T. Suzuki, 51–67. Stanford: Stanford University Press.

Kumar, D. 2004. "War Propaganda and the (ab)Uses of Women: Media Constructions of the Jessica Lynch Story." *Feminist Media Studies* 4 (2): 297–313.

Lack, J., and J. Templeton. 1995. *Bold Experiment: Documentary History of Australian Immigration since 1945*. Melbourne: Oxford University Press.

Lake, M. 1986. "The Politics of Respectability: Identifying the Masculinist Context." *Historical Studies* 86:116–131.

———. 2000. "The Ambiguities for Feminists of National Belonging: Race and Gender in the Imagined Australian Community." In *Gendered Nations: Nationalisms and the Gender Order in the Long Nineteenth Century*, ed. I. Blom, K. Hagemann, and C. Hall, 159–176. Oxford and New York: Berg.

Larson, E., Z. Johnson, and M. Murphy. 2007. "Emerging Global Norms and Indigenous Governance: Institutional Influences on *Ainu* Rights in Japan." Paper delivered at the Midwest Sociological Society conference, Chicago, IL, April 6.

Lawson, M. 1993. "The inter-Continental address: an analysis," *The Independent*, 27 April, 1993: 20.

Levin, A.K., ed. 2007. *Defining Memory: Local Museums and the Construction of History in America's Changing Communities*. Lanham, MD: AltaMira Press.

Lewis, B. 2002. *What Went Wrong? Western Impact and Middle Eastern Response*. New York: Oxford University Press.

Lewis, R. 1996. *Gendering Orientalism: Race, Femininity and Representation*, London: Routledge.

———. 2004. *Rethinking Orientalism: Women, Travel, and the Ottoman Harem*. New York: Tauris & Co.

Lie, J. 2001. *Multiethnic Japan*. Cambridge, MA: Harvard University Press.

Light, A. 1991. *Forever England: Femininity, Literature and Conservatism Between the Wars*. London: Routledge.

Lind, R.A., and J.A. Danowski. 1998. "The Representation of Arabs in US Electronic Media." In *Cultural Diversity and the US Media*, ed. Y.R. Kamalipour and T. Carilli, 156–167. New York: State University of New York Press.

Lindstrom, L. 1995. "Cargoism and Occidentalism." In *Occidentalism: Images of the West*, ed. J.G. Carrier, 33–60. Oxford: Clarendon Press.

Lowenthal, D. 1998. *The Heritage Crusade and the Spoils of History*. Cambridge: Cambridge University Press.

MacCannell, D. 1992. *Empty Meeting Grounds: The Tourist Papers*. London and New York: Routledge.

Macdonald, S. 1987. "Boadicea: Warrior, Mother, and Myth." In *Images of Women in Peace and War: Cross-Cultural and Historical Perspectives*, ed. S. Macdonald, P. Holden, and S. Ardener, 40–61. Madison: University of Wisconsin Press.

Macintyre, S. 2003. *The History Wars*. Carlton: Melbourne University Press.

Magarey, S., S. Rowley, and S. Sheridan, eds. 1993. *Debutante Nation: Feminism Contests the 1890s*. St. Leonards, NSW: Allen and Unwin.

Magelssen, S. 2002. "Remapping American-ness: Heritage Production and the Staging of the Native American and the African American as Other in 'Historyland.'" *National Identities* 4 (2): 161–178.

Mannari, H., and H. Befu, eds. 1983. *The Challenge of Japan's Internationalization: Organization and Culture*. Tokyo: Kodansha International.

Marchand, R. 1985. *Advertising, the American Dream: Making Way for Modernity 1920–1940*. Berkeley: University of California Press.

Markwell, K., D. Stevenson, and D. Rowe. 2004. "Footsteps and Memories: Interpreting an Australian Urban Landscape Through Thematic Walking Tours." *International Journal of Heritage Studies* 10 (5): 457–473.

Marsden, G. 1995. "Best and Worst of British." *New Statesman & Society* 8, no. 354 (May): 22.

Martin, J. 1972. *Community and Identity: Refugee Groups in Adelaide*. Canberra: Australian National University Press.

———. 1978. *The Migrant Presence, Australian Responses, 1947–1977: Research Report for the National Population Inquiry*. Sydney: Allen and Unwin.

Martinez, D.P., ed. 1998. *The Worlds of Japanese Popular Culture, Gender, Shifting Boundaries and Global Cultures*. Cambridge: Cambridge University Press.

McCalman, I., A. Cook, and A. Reeves. 2001. "Introduction." In *Gold: Forgotten Histories and Lost Objects of Australia*, ed. I. McCalman, A. Cook, and A. Reeves, 1–20. Cambridge: Cambridge University Press.

McClintock, A. 1993. "Family Feuds: Gender, Nationalism, and the Family." *Feminist Review* 44:61–80.

———. 1995. *Imperial Leather: Race, Gender, and Sexuality in the Colonial Contest*. London and New York: Routledge.

McGowan, B. 2001. "Mullock Heaps and Tailing Mounds: Environmental Effects of Alluvial Goldmining." In *Gold: Forgotten Histories and Lost Objects of Australia*, ed. I. McCalman, A. Cook, and A. Reeves, 85–100. Cambridge: Cambridge University Press.

McKenzie, K., and C. Cooper. 2001. "Eyewitness?: Drawings by Oscar of Cooktown." In *Gold: Forgotten Histories and Lost Objects of Australia* ed. I. McCalman, A. Cook, and A. Reeves, 157–163. Cambridge: Cambridge University Press.

Menzies, J., ed. 1998. *Modern Boy Modern Girl: Modernity in Japanese Art 1910–1935*. Sydney: Art Gallery of New South Wales.

Merskin, D. 2004. "The Construction of Arabs as Enemies: Post-September 11 Discourse of George W. Bush." *Mass Communication & Society* 7 (2): 157–175.

Moghadam, V.M., ed. 1994. *Gender and National Identity: Women and Politics in Muslim Societies*. London: Zed Books.

Monaghan, E. 2003. "Jessica Enters the Realms of Bonnie and Clyde—Iraq War—America." *The Times*, 4 April.

Morgan, C.E. 2001. *Women Workers and Gender Identities, 1835–1913: The Cotton and Metal Industries in England*. London: Routledge.

Morrison, A., and A. Love. 1996. "A Discourse of Disillusionment: Letters to the Editor in Two Zimbabwean Magazines 10 Years After Independence." *Discourse and Society* 7 (1): 39–75.

Morris-Suzuki, T. 1996. "A Descent Into the Past: The Frontier in the Construction of Japanese Identity." In *Multicultural Japan, Palaeolithic to Postmodern*, ed. D. Denoon, M. Hudson, G. McCormack, and T. Morris-Suzuki, 81–94.Cambridge: Cambridge University Press.

———. 1998. *Re-inventing Japan: Time Space Nation*. New York and London: ME Sharpe.

Morton, H.V. 1928. *In Search of England*. New York: Robert M. McBride and Company.

Mostow, J.S. 2000. "Modern Constructions of *Tales of Ise*: Gender and Courtliness." In *Inventing the Classics: Modernity, National Identity, and Japanese Literature*, ed. H. Shirane and T. Suzuki, 96–119. Stanford: Stanford University Press.

Mouer, R.E., and Y. Sugimoto. 1983. "Internationalization as a Japanese Ideology." In *The Challenge of Japan's Internationalization: Organization and Culture*, ed. H. Mannari and H. Befu, 267–297. Tokyo: Kodansha International.

———. 1986. *Images of Japanese Society: A Study in the Structure of Social Reality*. London: Kegan Paul.

National Archives of Australia. 2006. *Fact Sheet 198: Cowra Outbreak, 1944*. http://www.naa.gov.au/Publications/fact_sheets/fs198.html (accessed 24 May 2006).

National Museum of Australia. 2001. *Yesterday Tomorrow: The National Museum of Australia*. Canberra: National Museum of Australia.

———. 2003. *National Museum of Australia Exhibitions and Programs: A Report to the Council of the National Museum of Australia*. Canberra: Commonwealth of Australia.

National Museum of Japanese History. 2002. *National Museum of Japanese History: A Visitor's Guide*. Sakura-shi, Chiba: Foundation for Museums of Japanese History.

National Portrait Gallery. 2001. *National Portrait Gallery: A Visitor's Guide*. London: National Portrait Gallery Publications.

———. 2008. "History of the National Portrait Gallery." http://www.npg.org.uk/live/history.asp (accessed 9 January 2008).

Nelson, R.L. 2002. "German Comrades, Slavic Whores: Gender Images in the German Soldier Newspapers of the First World War." In *Home/Front: The Military, War and Gender in Twentieth-Century Germany*, ed. K. Hagemann and S. Schüler-Springorum, 69–85. Oxford and New York: Berg.

Nitobe, I. 1900/1969. *Bushidō: The Soul of Japan*. Rutland, VT: Charles E. Tuttle Company.

Nornes, A.M., and Y. Fukushima, eds. 1994. *The Japan/America Film Wars: WWII Propaganda and Its Cultural Contexts*. Chur, Switzerland: Harwood Publishers.

Nornes, A.M., H. Komatsuzawa, and S. Yamane. 1994a. "Manufacturing the Enemy." In *The Japan/America Film Wars: WWII Propaganda and Its Cultural Contexts*, ed. A.M. Nornes and Y. Fukushima, 189–195. Chur, Switzerland: Harwood Publishers.

———. 1994b. "Pearl Harbor." In *The Japan/America Film Wars: WWII Propaganda and Its Cultural Contexts*, ed. A.M. Nornes and Y. Fukushima, 221–241. Chur, Switzerland: Harwood Publishers.

O'Barr, W.M. 1994. *Culture and the Ad: Exploring Otherness in the World of Advertising*. Boulder: Westview Press.

Ohnuki-Tierney, E. 1993. *Rice as Self, Japanese Identities Through Time*. Princeton, NJ: Princeton University Press.

———. 2002. *Kamikaze, Cherry Blossoms, and Nationalisms: The Militarization of Aesthetics in Japanese History*. Chicago: University of Chicago Press.

Orr, D. 2003. "Even in Battle, Blondes Get All the Attention." *The Independent*, 4 April.

Orr, T.B. 2003. *Ronald Reagan: Portrait of An American Hero*. New York: Publications International.

Page, B. 1996. *Who Deliberates? Mass Media in Modern Democracy*. Chicago: University of Chicago Press.

Papastergiadis, N. 2004. "The Invasion Complex in Australian Political Culture." *Thesis Eleven*, no. 78:8–27.

Parliament of Australia. 2002. "Select Committee for an Inquiry into a Certain Maritime Incident." http://www.aph.gov.au/senate/committee/maritime_ incident_ctte/index.htm (accessed 25 September 2007).

Pearson, W. 2007. "Forward." In *The Australians: Insiders and Outsiders on the National Character Since 1770*, ed. J. Hirst, vi–viii. Melbourne: Black Inc.

Peterson, V.S. 1996. "The Politics of Identification in the Context of Globalization." *Women's Studies International Forum* 19 (½): 5–15.

Pettman, J.J. 1988. *Whose Country is it Anyway? Cultural Politics, Racism and the Construction of Being Australian*. Canberra: Peace Research Centre, Research School of Pacific Studies, Australian National University.

Phillips, M., and T. Phillips. 1998. *Windrush: The Irresistible Rise of Multi-Racial Britain*. London: HarperCollins.

Phillips, T. 2004. *We Are the People: Postcards from the Collection of Tom Phillips*. London: National Portrait Gallery Publications.

Pickering, P.A. 2001. "'The Finger of God': Gold's Impact on New South Wales." In *Gold: Forgotten Histories and Lost Objects of Australia*, ed. I. McCalman, A. Cook, and A. Reeves, 37–51. Cambridge: Cambridge University Press.

Potter, D. 1954. *People of Plenty: Economic Abundance and the American Character*. Chicago: University of Chicago Press.

Poynting, S., and V. Mason. 2006. "The Resistible Rise of Islamophobia: Anti-Muslim Racism in the UK and Australia Before September 11." *Journal of Sociology* 43 (1): 61–86.

Preuss, H. 1998. "Problematizing Arguments of the Opponents of Olympic Games." In *Global and Cultural Critique: Problematizing the Olympic Games*, ed. R. K. Barney, K. B. Wamsley, S. G. Martyne, and G. H. MacDonald, 197–218. London, Ontario: International Centre for Olympic Studies, University of Western Ontario.

Price, C. 1999. "Australian Population: Ethnic Origins." *People and Place* 7 (4): 12–16.

Prividera, L.C., and J.W. Howard. 2006. "Whiteness, and the Warrior Hero: Perpetuating the Strategic Rhetoric of US Nationalism and the Marginalization of Women." *Women and Language* 29 (2): 29–38.

Rabinow, P., ed. 1984a. "What is an Author?" In *The Foucault Reader*, 101–119. New York: Pantheon Books.

———. 1984b. "Complete and Austere Institutions." In *The Foucault Reader*, 214–225. New York: Pantheon Books.

Radcliffe, S. 1999. "Embodying National Identities: Mestizo Men and White Women in Ecuadorian Racial-National Imaginaries." *Transactions of the Institute of British Geographers* vol. 24, no. 2, 213–225.

Radhakrishnan, R. 1992. "Nationalism, Gender, and the Narrative of Identity." In *Nationalisms and Sexualities,* ed. A. Parker, M. Russo, D. Sommer, and P. Yaeger, 77–95. New York: Routledge.

Radstone, S. 2002. "The War of the Fathers: Trauma, Fantasy, and September 11." *Signs* 28 (1): 457–459.

Ranchod-Nilsson, S., and M.A. Tetreault, eds. 2000. *Women, States, and Nationalism: At Home in the Nation?* London: Routledge.

Richardson, J.E. 2001. "'Now is the Time to Put an End to All This': Argumentative Discourse Theory and 'Letters to the Editor.'" *Discourse and Society* 12 (2): 143–168.

Richardson, A., and S. Hofkosh, eds. 1996. *Romanticism, Race, and Imperial Culture, 1780–1834.* Bloomington: Indiana University Press.

Ritzer, G., and A. Liska. 1997. "'McDisneyization' and 'Post-Tourism': Contemporary Perspectives on Contemporary Tourism." In *Touring Cultures: Transformations of Travel and Theory,* ed. C. Rojek and J. Urry, 96–109. London and New York: Routledge.

Roach Pierson, R., and N. Chaudhuri, eds. 1998. *Nation, Empire, Colony.* Bloomington: Indiana University Press.

Robertson, J. 1987. "A Dialectic of Native and Newcomer: The Kodaira Citizens' Festival in Suburban Tokyo." *Anthropological Quarterly* 60 (3): 124–136.

Robertson, J.O. 1980. *American Myth, American Reality.* New York: Hill & Wang.

Robertson, R. 1990. "Mapping the Global Condition: Globalization as the Central Concept." In *Global Culture: Nationalism, Globalization and Modernity,* ed. M. Featherstone, 15–30. London: Sage.

———. 1992. *Globalization: Social Theory and Global Culture.* London: Sage.

———. 1995. "Glocalization: Time-Space and Homogeneity-Heterogeneity." In *Global Modernities,* ed. M. Featherstone, S. Lash, and R. Robertson, 25–44. London: Sage.

Rose, S.O. 2003. *Which People's War? National Identity and Citizenship in Britain 1939–1945.* Oxford: Oxford University Press.

Rosenzweig, R., and D. Thelen. 1998. *The Presence of the Past: Popular Uses of History in American Life.* New York: Columbia University Press.

Runnymede Trust. 1997. *Islamophobia: A Challenge for Us All.* London: Runnymede Trust.

Rutherford, J. 1997. *Forever England: Reflections on Masculinity and Empire.* London: Lawrence & Wishart, Ltd.

Ryan, L. 2002. *Gender Identity and the Irish Press, 1922–1937: Embodying the Nation.* Lewiston: Edwin Mellen Press.

Said, E. 1978. *Orientalism.* London: Routledge and Kegan Paul.

———. 1993. *Culture and Imperialism.* New York: Vintage Books.

———. 1997. *Covering Islam: How the Media and the Experts Determine How We See the Rest of the World.* New York: Vintage Books.

———. 2002. "Impossible Histories: Why the Many Islams Cannot Be Simplified." *Harpers Magazine,* July, 69–74.

Saussure, F. 1959. *A Course in General Linguistics.* New York: Philosophical Library.

Sawer, M. 1996. "Gender, Metaphor, and the State." *Feminist Review* 52:118–134.

Schmidt, A. 1990. *The Loss of Australia's Aboriginal Language Heritage.* Canberra: Aboriginal Studies Press.

Schmidt, S., and V. Loeb. 2003. "She Was Fighting to the Death." *The Washington Post,* 3 April.

Schudson, M. 1984. *Advertising, the Uneasy Persuasion: Its Dubious Impact on American Society*. New York: Basic Books.

Seidel, G. 1987. "The White Discursive Order: The British New Right's Discourse on Cultural Racism With Particular Reference to the Salisbury Review." In *Approaches to Discourse, Poetics and Psychiatry*, ed. I. Zavala, T. van Dijk, and M. Diaz-Diocaretz, 39–66. Amsterdam: John Benjamins.

Sen, S. 1993. "Motherhood and Mothercraft: Gender and Nationalism in Bengal." *Gender and History* 5 (2): 231–243.

Shaheen, J.G. 2001. *Reel Bad Arabs: How Hollywood Vilifies a People*. Northampton, MA: Olive Branch Press.

Sherman D.J., and I. Rogoff. 1994. *Museum Culture: Histories, Discourses, and Spectacles*. Minneapolis: University of Minnesota Press.

Sievers, S.L. 1983. *Flowers in the Salt: The Beginnings of Feminist Consciousness in Modern Japan*. Stanford: Stanford University Press.

Singh, J.P., and S.A. Hart. 2007. "Sex Workers and Cultural Policy: Mapping the Issues and Actors in Thailand." *Review of Policy Research* 24 (2): 155–173.

Sivanandan, A. 2006. "Race, Terror, and Civil Society." *Race & Class* 47 (3): 385–396.

Skov, L., and B. Moeran, eds. 1995. *Women, Media, and Consumption in Japan*. Honolulu: University of Hawaii Press.

Slotkin, R. 1973. *Regeneration Through Violence: The Mythology of the American Frontier, 1600–1860*. Middletown, CT: Wesleyan University Press.

———. 1992. *Gunfighter Nation: The Myth of the Frontier in Twentieth-Century America*. New York: Atheneum.

Smith, A. 1990. "Towards a Global Culture?" In *Global Culture: Nationalism, Globalization and Modernity*, ed. M. Featherstone, 171–206. London: Sage.

———. 1991. *National Identity*. Reno, NV: University of Nevada Press.

Sodei, T. 1995. "Care of the Elderly: A Women's Issue." In *Japanese Women, New Feminist Perspectives on the Past, Present, and Future*, ed. K. Fujimura-Fanselow and A. Kameda, 213–228. New York: The Feminist Press.

Sotillo, S.M., and D. Starace-Nastasi. 1999. "Political Discourse of a Working-Class Town." *Discourse and Society* 10:411–438.

Stead, N. 2004. "The Semblance of Populism: National Museum of Australia." *The Journal of Architecture* 9:385–396.

Stiehm, J. 1982. "The Protected, The Protector, The Defender." *Women's Studies International Forum* 5 (3/4): 367–376.

Sugimoto, Y. 2003. *An Introduction to Japanese Society*. Cambridge: Cambridge University Press.

Sui, L. 2005. "Queen of the Chinese Colony: Gender, Nation, and Belonging in Diaspora." *Anthropological Quarterly* 78 (2): 511–542.

Summers, A. 1975. *Damned Whores and God's Police*. Ringwood, VIC: Penguin.

Suzuki, T. 2000. "Gender and Genre: Modern Literary Histories and Women's Diary Literature." In *Inventing the Classics: Modernity, National Identity, and Japanese Literature*, ed. H. Shirane and T. Suzuki, 71–95. Stanford: Stanford University Press.

Sydney Morning Herald. 2005. "Don't Over-Complicate Riots: PM." 15 December.

Taira, K. 1999. "The Battle of Okinawa in Japanese History Books." In *Okinawa: Cold War Island*, ed. C. Johnson, 39–49. Cardiff, CA: Japan Policy Research Institute.

Takacs, S. 2005. "Jessica Lynch and the Regeneration of American Identity and Power Post 9/11." *Feminist Media Studies* 5 (3): 297–311.

Taylor, J. 1994. *A Dream of England: Landscape, Photography and the Tourist's Imagination*. Manchester: Manchester University Press.

The Australian. 2003. "Jessica's Bloody Firefight—War on Iraq." 4 April.

Thompson, E. 2001. "Challenges to Egalitarianism: Diversity or Sameness." Barton lecture, part 9, broadcast on ABC Radio National, 8 April.

Tickner, J.A. 2002. "Feminist Perspectives on 9/11." *International Studies Perspectives* 3 (4): 333–350.

Timothy, D.J., and S.W. Boyd. 2003. *Heritage Tourism*. Harlow: Prentice Hall.

Tobin, J.J. 1992. *Re-made in Japan: Everyday Life and Consumer Taste in a Changing Society*. New Haven and London: Yale University Press.

Tomlinson, A. 1996. "Olympic Spectacle: Opening Ceremonies and Some Paradoxes of Globalization." *Media, Culture, and Society* 18:583–602.

Tomlinson, A., and G. Whannel, eds. 1984. *Five-Ring Circus: Money, Power and Politics at the Olympic Games*. London and Sydney: Pluto Press.

Toohey, K., and A.J. Veal. 2000. *The Olympic Games, A Social Science Perspective*. New York and Oxon, UK: CABI Publishing.

Tsunoda, T. 1985. *The Japanese Brain: Uniqueness and Universality*. Trans. Y. Oiwa. Tokyo: Taishukan Publishing.

Turner, F.J. 1962. *The Frontier in American History*. New York: Holt, Reinhart and Winston.

Turner, G. 1994. *Making it National: Nationalism and Australian Popular Culture*. St. Leonards, NSW: Allen and Unwin.

Ueno, C. 1996. "Modern Patriarchy and the Formation of the Japanese Nation State." In *Multicultural Japan, Palaeolithic to Postmodern*, ed. D. Denoon, M. Hudson, G. McCormack, and T. Morris-Suzuki, 213–223. Cambridge: Cambridge University Press.

Urry, J. 1990. *The Tourist Gaze*. London: Sage.

Uzzell, D., and R. Ballantyne, eds. 1998. *Contemporary Issues in Heritage and Environmental Interpretation: Problems and Prospects*. London: The Stationery Office.

Vogel, E. 1979. *Japan as Number One: Lessons for America*. Cambridge, MA: Harvard University Press.

Wallsten, P. 2006. "Falwell Says Faithful Fear Clinton More than Devil." *Los Angeles Times*, 24 September 24.

Ward, R. 1958. *The Australian Legend*. Melbourne, VIC: Oxford University Press.

Waters, M. 1995. *Globalization*. New York and London: Routledge.

Weber, M. 1930. *The Protestant Ethnic and the Spirit of Capitalism*. London and Boston: Hyman and Unwin.

Webster, W. 1998. *Imagining Home: Gender, 'Race' and National Identity, 1945–64*. London: University College London Press.

Wedeen, L. 2003. "Beyond the Crusades: Why Huntington, and Bin Laden, Are Wrong." *Middle East Policy* 10 (2): 54–61.

Weedon, C. 1996. *Feminist Practice and Poststructuralist Theory*. Oxford: Blackwell.

Weiner, M. 1995. "Discourses of Race, Nation, and Empire in Pre-1945 Japan." *Ethnic and Racial Studies* 18 (3): 433–456.

———, ed. 1997a. *Japan's Minorities: The Illusion of Homogeneity*. London: Routledge.

———. 1997b. "The Invention of Identity: Race and Nation in Pre-War Japan." In *The Construction of Racial Identities in China and Japan*, ed. F. Dikotter, 96–117. Honolulu: University of Hawaii Press.

Weisenfeld, G. 1998. "Imaging Calamity: Artists in the Capital after the Great Kantō Earthquake." In *Modern Boy Modern Girl: Modernity in Japanese Art 1910–1935*, ed. J. Menzies, 125–129. Sydney: Art Gallery of New South Wales.

West, B. 1988. "The Making of the English Working Past: A Critical View of the Ironbridge Gorge Museum." In *The Museum Time-Machine*, ed. R. Lumley, 36–62. London: Routledge.

White, R. 1981. *Inventing Australia*. St. Leonards, NSW: Allen & Unwin.

————. 1988. "War and Australian Society." In *Australia: Two Centuries of War and Peace*, ed. M. McKernan and M. Browne, 390–423. Canberra: Australian War Memorial.

Williamson, J. 1978. *Decoding Advertisements: Ideology and Meaning in Advertising*. London: Marion Boyars.

Willis, A.M. 1993. *Illusions of Identity: The Art of Nation*. Sydney: Hale and Iremonger.

Wilson, K. 2003. *The Island Race: Englishness, Empire and Gender in the Eighteenth Century*. London: Routledge.

Wodak, R., R. de Cillia, M. Reisigl, and K. Liebhart. 1999. *The Discursive Construction of National Identity*. Trans. A. Hirsch and R. Mitten. Edinburgh: Edinburgh University Press.

Wright, T., and A. Gamble. 2000. "The End of Britain?" *Political Quarterly* 71 (1): 1–3.

Yeatman, A. 1990. *Bureaucrats, Technocrats, Femocrats, Essays on the Contemporary Australian State*. Sydney: Allen and Unwin.

Yoshino, K. 1992. *Cultural Nationalism in Contemporary Japan*. London: Routledge.

Young, I.M. 2003. "The Logic of Masculinist Protection: Reflections on the Current Security State." *Signs* 29 (1): 1–25.

Yuval-Davis, N. 1997. *Gender and Nation*. London: Sage.

Yuval-Davis, N., and F. Anthias, eds. 1989. *Women-Nation-State*. London: Macmillan.

Zangwill, I. 1909. *The Melting Pot Drama in Four Acts*. New York: Macmillan.

Zeppel, H. 1998. "Selling the Dreamtime: Aboriginal Culture in Australian Tourism." In *Tourism, Leisure, Sport: Critical Perspectives*, ed. D. Rowe and G. Lawrence, 23–38. Rydalmere, NSW: Hodder Education.

Zimmer-Bradley, M. 1983. *The Mists of Avalon*. New York: Knopf.

Index

Printed in the USA/Agawam, MA
April 20, 2012

565432.092